SAFEGUARDING
HISTORY

Publications by Kenneth W. Rendell

With Weapons and Wits: Propaganda and Psychological Warfare in World War II, Overlord Press, 1992.

Forging History: The Detection of Fake Letters and Documents, University of Oklahoma Press, 1994.

History Comes to Life: Collecting Historical Letters and Documents, University of Oklahoma Press, 1995.

The Western Pursuit of the American Dream: Selections From the Collection of Kenneth W. Rendell, University of Oklahoma Press, 2004.

World War II: Saving the Reality, Whitman Publishing, 2009. Foreword by Doris Kearns Goodwin.

The Great American West: Pursuing the American Dream, Whitman Publishing, 2013. Foreword by Senator Alan Simpson.

Politics, War, and Personality: 50 Iconic Documents of World War II, Whitman Publishing, 2013. Foreword by John Eisenhower.

The Power of Anti-Semitism: The March to the Holocaust, 1919–1939, Boston, 2016. Foreword by Louise Mirrer.

Safeguarding History: Trailblazing Adventures Inside the Worlds of Collecting and Forging History, Whitman Publishing, 2023. Foreword by Doris Kearns Goodwin.

As coauthor/editor:

Autographs and Manuscripts: A Collector's Manual, Charles Scribners' Sons, 1978.

Manuscripts: The First Twenty Years, Greenwood Press, 1984.

As foreword writer and collaborator:

Ronald Reagan: An American Legend—Golden Anniversary Collector's Vault, by Q. David Bowers, Whitman Publishing, 2011.

The Secret History of World War II: Spies, Code Breakers, and Covert Operations, National Geographic Books, 2016. Based entirely on artifacts in Rendell's Museum of World War II.

Atlas of World War II: History's Greatest Conflict Revealed Through Rare Wartime Maps and New Cartography, National Geographic Books, 2018. Based on original maps in Rendell's collection.

Safeguarding History

Whitman Publishing is a leading publisher of antiques/collectibles reference books, supplies, and storage and display products that help you build, appreciate, and share great collections. To browse our complete catalog, visit Whitman Publishing online at www.Whitman.com.

WHITMAN®

SAFEGUARDING
HISTORY

Trailblazing Adventures Inside the
Worlds of Collecting and Forging History

By Kenneth W. Rendell
Foreword by Doris Kearns Goodwin

Whitman
Publishing, LLC
PUBLISHING SINCE 1934
Whitman.com

Praise for the Work
of Kenneth W. Rendell

"Kenneth Rendell's Museum of World War II simply has no equal. I am—despite my several decades as curator at the Imperial War Museum—still breathless in admiration for its rich content and diversity." — **Phil Reed OBE, Director (ret.), Churchill Museum and Cabinet War Rooms**

"*World War II: Saving the Reality* is a notable book in every way. . . . Ken Rendell has produced a book as magnificent and important as his museum." — **Dan C. Pinck,** The OSS Society Journal

"I have never seen anything quite like [*World War II: Saving the Reality*] before. When Cardinal Cajetan unwrapped his new Gutenberg Bible in 1456, he can hardly have been more amazed. . . . Your text jumps from history to personal collecting and back again, with a stature and an assurance which probably no-one but you in the world could achieve, without loss of academic credibility. It is superb. The objects described are so magnificent." — **Dr. Christopher de Hamel, Fellow Librarian, Corpus Christi College, Cambridge University, England**

"Ken Rendell's *The Great American West: Pursuing the American Dream* illustrates the daily life of those who have defined America. It puts their letters in the reader's hands, their lives in the reader's mind, and their dreams in the reader's heart." — **Senator Alan Simpson of Wyoming**

"Ken Rendell—master collector, literary sleuth, and historian—has given us a book, *Politics, War, and Personality*, that I will long treasure and restudy. Thousands of others will do the same." — **John S.D. Eisenhower, retired ambassador, U.S. Army Brigadier General, son of Dwight D. Eisenhower**

Dedications

To my father, who instilled in me a sense of confidence in myself, a belief in my ideas, and the importance of understanding people. I have always regretted he didn't live to see his belief in me was justified.

To my mother, who brought stability to our family and, in the crisis after my father's death, saved us. Despite our Catholic atmosphere, a foundation of women's equality was normal in our family and benefited me, especially in my generation, in appreciating life. She did live to see how it all turned out.

To my wife Shirley, who dramatically changed and enhanced my life when we met at forty years old. I never thought my world could be better, but she didn't just enhance my life, she had a multiplier effect onto mountaintops I never thought of. Words cannot express my appreciation.

To my son Jeffrey who endured and survived with me a disastrous first marriage. We have never grown apart and our relationship, and more importantly our friendship, has grown as we have. His ability to turn his imagination into words and action on screen amazes me.

To my daughter Julia who I have had a special connection with from the moment I first looked into her eyes. Her combination of creative ideas and the practical ability to fulfill them is as unique as she is. We both constantly learn from our different generational perspectives. I appreciate her undiminished warmth and wisdom.

To the memory of our son Jason, with whom I shared a love of mountaineering, until the inherent male teenage inability to assess risk caused his early death at eighteen.

And, to the America I grew up in, a culture based on merit, innovation, knowledge, and hard work.

Contents

Foreword

This eloquent, captivating, and moving memoir takes the reader on the journey of an eleven-year-old boy, Kenneth Rendell, growing up in a poor neighborhood, who, with the sale of a single 1806 coin, experiences the magic of collecting and goes on to become the world's most notable collector, dealer, and appraiser in historical letters, documents, and artifacts.

And what a journey it is! We share his excitement when, at the age of sixteen, he meets a dealer in presidential documents and trades his entire British coin collection for a group of presidential letters. While old coins were great historical artifacts, he fell in love with handwritten letters that provide a window into the hopes and dreams—the very soul—of figures who have shaped the destiny of our country. Collecting became an emotional pursuit as well as an intellectual one.

In an essay on the nature of collectors, the philosopher Walter Benjamin argues that collecting allows children a small corner where they can order a disordered world. For the teenage boy whose father fell into bankruptcy and committed suicide, collecting provided a sanctuary where he could be on his own, free from the pandemonium of his household.

He had found his vocation, the arena in which he felt he was most vitally alive, when, as the philosopher William James suggested, a voice inside speaks and says, "This is the real me!" And how lucky we are to share in his passion, to savor the moments he comes upon breathtaking documents and letters—manuscript pages written by Henry David Thoreau, a George Washington letter discovered in a New Hampshire auction, a Thomas Jefferson letter about the future of slavery. (This letter, which Rendell bought in the early 1970s for $20,000, a princely sum when still in his twenties, and then immediately sold to Malcolm Forbes for $25,000, was eventually sold again in the 1990s after Forbes died for $700,000.)

Over the decades, as Rendell's collecting interests expand from modern to ancient times, from North America to every continent in the world, we meet a cast of intriguing characters and are privy to an inside look at the complex world of collecting—a world filled with adventures, mysteries, sensational hoaxes, thefts, and even murders.

Self-taught in foreign languages, culture, and history, Rendell becomes an expert in authenticating handwritten materials and documents and is called upon as a special consultant in a number of high-profile cases that read like fast-moving detective stories.

A master storyteller, with keen insight into the motivations of people, Rendell brings the reader into the drama of uncovering the biggest hoaxes in modern literary times—the discovery of sixty volumes of a purported Hitler diary; the dramatic unearthing of a diary by Jack the Ripper, promising to reveal the mind of one of the most notorious serial killers; the sensational Mormon White Salamander letter and the related murders.

We follow Rendell's painstaking work that revealed the forgeries—his examination of the individual characteristics of handwriting and the known habits of the writer. A uniformity in the writing and the ink used would suggest a diary written in a short period rather than over a number of years. He knew how to date the ink, the paper, the bindings, the use of words not yet in use in colloquial language. In Jack the Ripper's supposed 1880s diary, the use of the phrase "one off," which was not in common use until 1925, was a clear warning signal.

Rendell's role in debunking these multi-million-dollar hoaxes landed him in the front pages of newspapers and magazines. In print and on television, he was dubbed the Indiana Jones of the collecting world.

In each case, other independent experts had authenticated the material, and a great deal of time and money had been spent in publicity and publishing rights. Rendell concluded that publishers had seen only what they wanted to see—beating the competition, fame and fortune.

There are additional compelling stories behind Rendell's creation of a 10,000-book library for Bill and Melinda Gates, and the building of the most comprehensive World War II collection that follows the war from beginning to end through tens of thousands of documents and artifacts, including Hitler's writings, Nazi party banners, anti-Semitic broadsides, Resistance newspapers, Churchill's propaganda posters and manuscripts, a first edition of Anne Frank's diary, and the surrender documents.

In the end, however, this compelling memoir is the story of a boy who rises above adversity with ambition, a curiosity that allows him to keep learning his entire life, a powerful work ethic, an ability to think outside the box, and, most importantly, a recognition that reputation and character are the true driving forces of success.

Doris Kearns Goodwin
Boston, Massachusetts

Doris Kearns Goodwin is a presidential historian, international keynote speaker, and *New York Times* #1 best-selling author. Her book *No Ordinary Time: Franklin and Eleanor Roosevelt: The Home Front in World War II* earned the Pulitzer Prize in history. She is a consultant to PBS and the History Channel, and executive producer of Pastime Productions.

Preface

Over the years many publishers have wanted me to write memoirs of my adventures in business, and in life. They saw me as an adventurer who looked at challenges with new ways of thinking and unconventional approaches to solving problems.

My role in debunking the Hitler diaries for *Newsweek* magazine, the Mormon forgeries and murders, proving Jack the Ripper's diary was a hoax for Warner Books, appraising Richard Nixon's White House papers and Watergate tapes, and building extraordinary libraries for billionaires were all situations where I brought unconventional thinking and approaches resulting in successful achievements. The fact that, at the same time, I was a successful ski racer, helicopter extreme skier, and Hawaiian windsurfer added to the adventurer image.

Some years ago CBS even wanted to base a television detective series on me, and I did everything to kill it. I was very uncomfortable with the image people had of me personally. The successes over these decades were more complex than just their outcomes, and yet I was not yet ready to delve into the person whose unconventional thinking had made so many things turn out the way they did.

I finally decided to write these memoirs, in part, because for me, there is more to my adventures I have become known for than just the notoriety of the events themselves. They were more complex than anyone ever knew and required psychological analysis and techniques I had developed as well as the ability to control my reactions to changing and challenging situations. They were more demanding of my private self and called on my life experiences, and lessons learned through painful early years.

I have always felt that I was very lucky to have a brain and personality wired for ambition and accomplishment, and I was especially fortunate in meeting my wife, when we were both 40 years old, and having a marriage where we both thrived beyond how life would have been without each other.

The turning point in my decision to write these memoirs has been my meetings with students at Somerville High School in the Massachusetts community I grew up in during the 1940s and 1950s. These students were chosen by the school for summer college scholarships in a program I founded and funded, the Spark Foundation, for those with excellent academic performance who are otherwise boxed in by their economic and social situations. In my first meeting with the initial dozen students, I was emotionally floored by the similarities of their hopes and perceived limitations to how I had felt 60 years earlier. I left that meeting knowing that I wanted to finally understand and share how I've pioneered and accomplished so much in my life.

Reviewing a life like mine, with multiple tragedies (my father dying, a disastrous first marriage, our son dying suddenly at 18), is very painful and something I have always put behind me as I looked forward, not backward, in life. Yet there have been many rewarding reminders of the good things in my early life: My father believed I could become anything I could dream of. I felt support in taking on challenges at 10 and 12 years old. I didn't believe there was anything I could not do. I had a sense of self-esteem that seems not understandable given my family situation. While my family life was chaos and fear of "what's next," it was also strangely supportive of my pursuits, of being in business at 12 years old and speed skating in the North American championships at the same time. My chaotic family atmosphere was at the same time critically supportive and important to my pursuing life outside of it.

I have been told that the story of my life will be an adventure saga in many different venues: life, collecting, sports, and business. I hope it is an adventure story in exploring yourself and in understanding the importance of looking at situations in unconventional ways, the importance of creativity in everything, and most of all the importance of people. My father liked people, but without any business sense, that wonderful quality led to our family's bankruptcy and his death. It took me a decade of psychotherapy to free myself from the fear that liking and caring about people would be my downfall as well.

Introduction

Thinking Out of the Box and Other Ideas

P inball machines were very popular in the 1940s and 1950s, and I felt like a pinball, ricocheting from person to person when I was very young. My maternal grandparents lived upstairs—they owned the house—while my father's mother lived with us, another family lived in the spare bedroom upstairs, and another in the attic (the house was designed for two families). The clash of personalities was intense, and the neighborhood was also an intense social scene, with people crowded into multiple-family houses with barely any space between them. I realize now that what I saw at the time as a suffocating environment caused me to instinctively see these people individually, with their personal traits both good and bad, and to cope with the stresses this mix of personalities created.

Seeing everyone as individual human beings, with normal concerns about their lives, families, beliefs, hopes, worries, and perceptions of events, formed the basis of my fundamental approach to everything in my life. It has also caused me to have an understanding of myself that has been critical in business but, more importantly, personally. The greatest adventure is in exploring yourself, discovering who you really are, learning what is important to you, and finding out what you really want and enjoy in life and—equally important—what you don't want.

This personal understanding has been crucial when I have been involved in complicated business situations. Understanding what you want to believe in a situation, what you are predisposed to believe, warns you that this is where your thinking is the most vulnerable. It was a startling reality to see otherwise very competent business executives so overwhelmingly focused on what they wanted to see that they ignored what, to me, were obvious indications something was a fraud. This was most notable with journalistic frauds, such as the Hitler diaries and Jack the Ripper, where beating the competition for publication rights was the focus, not authenticity. They wanted the documents to be genuine, and they did not critically look at the authentication reports. Instead they focused on the numbers of magazines and books that would be sold.

Knowing what you don't know is also a very important factor in a professional life as complicated as mine. It is all too common for successful people and experts in one area to think the success automatically applies to other areas they know little about. When I was a teenage rare-coin dealer, an older dealer who was my idol offered me a junior partnership and the chance to take over his business when he retired. I wanted my independence, and he retired a few years later to Florida. He bought a restaurant, a bar, and an office building and discovered, to his detriment, that while he was a brilliant dealer in rare coins, he knew nothing about, nor did he have the temperament for, these businesses he automatically thought he would be successful in as well. He wasn't.

In the field of expert opinions, I have been startled at how common it is for so-called experts to venture outside their area of expertise and pontificate in fields where they aren't authorities. Pressure from the media all too frequently leads to experts giving uninformed opinions when they should have simply said they didn't know the answer, that it was outside of their area of expertise. The media compounds a natural inclination of too many experts to think they know everything, when they should have said they don't know.

The major journalistic frauds I will discuss in this book were all authenticated by historians who gave their positive opinion of handwriting authentication (not one knew anything about the subject) and "questioned document examiners" who specialized in modern forged check cases. Nearly everyone was giving important opinions outside their areas of expertise, and they were all proved wrong. Just because someone asks you a question does not mean you have to answer it.

"The box" is one of the most limiting factors in people's lives. People have always described me as thinking outside of the box, and that is a good description. I could never have lived in "the box" I was born into. My mind had to be outside of that physical and mental constraint and everything I have gotten involved with in my life has been heavily influenced by thinking outside of the box. However, I do consider what "the box" is, because there can be some factors you can't change, so you have to think around, if not outside of, it. The trick is to recognize limitations or factors that are unchangeable, but otherwise look at everything as an open field where you can try anything, be anybody, and challenge the limitations others have set.

It is a challenge to understand why others don't have the curiosity to think out of the box or the interest in trying new things. I was once seated next to the winemaker Bob Mondavi at lunch and had no idea what I could talk to him about. I asked him why he was so successful, and he responded that the question was why other winemakers didn't try new grapes and new locations for vineyards, didn't take risks to improve what they were doing. He said some of his ideas didn't succeed, but many did. How, he asked, could other winemakers be content and not try new ventures and ideas? Seeing the world as a great open plain, with endless opportunities limited only by one's imagination and hopes, is the basis for progress in everything. Alan Turing, the father of computers, said that "those who can imagine can do the impossible."

Throughout all the ventures in this book I have had my "linebacker" mentality. Football is one of the few sports I have never tried, but all my life I have thought of myself as a linebacker, well prepared with every possible response to how situations develop. Thinking out what could happen, what issues could arise, and researching the possible answers and correct responses makes you prepared for whatever develops in every aspect of your life. Flexible thinking is necessary for innovative outcomes; rigid thinking keeps you in the box you can't escape. "Be Prepared" was the Boy Scouts motto when I was growing up, and I think my generation heard it so often it became a hackneyed joke, but they were right—being prepared for every situation is one of the keys to success in life.

My collecting and business life has had a constant counterbalance with my relationship with and in nature. It is more than just the importance of nature in our family's cabin in the woods when I was young, though that escape from the city was critical to my mental health. Being in nature has always given me a sense of wellbeing, of connection with the basics of life itself. Nature has always been there and has been an integral part of my athletic and sports life as well.

Nature has not been a vacation for me—it is a major part of my everyday life. My home for the past 40 years has been in a woodland setting, on a river in a magical wildlife setting. Everywhere I have traveled throughout my business career, I have tried to find hotels next to a park where I could organize my thinking and jog. In some university towns a golf course had to suffice.

All the major projects that I write about here were thought out in advance while in nature. When I agreed to take on the tax appraisal of 12 million uncataloged documents in the archives of the Northern Pacific Railroad, I had no idea how I could ever organize it. After nearly two weeks of walking in a forest every day, I had my plan. During the Hitler diaries forgery case, I spent part of every day in Central Park in New York City to maintain my mental balance in this fast-moving and very complex situation.

My sports all involve a close relationship with nature: sailing the wind and riding the waves windsurfing, skiing and snowboarding the contours of the mountains, gliding over the ice, climbing and hiking the mountains.

The American West continues to be a magical place for me, combining nature and the ghosts of the explorers and settlers who went west for a better life.

I could never have done all that I am writing about without this always-present, deep-seated, almost-mystical relationship with nature.

Chapter 1

The Drugstore

The first 10 years of my life were seemingly normal. I was the older of two boys in a stable family in a neighborhood of blue- and white-collar middle-class households. My father, Harry, had been a pharmacist, but he worked for most of his adult life as a pharmaceutical salesman to physicians. My mother, Pauline, who had gone to art school, was a stay-at-home mom. She organized Cub Scout meetings and birthday parties and all the other family activities that mothers did. Every summer, we moved to our cabin north of Boston. Even though there was no running water nor electricity nor a toilet, our cabin was comfortable, and the woods around it were an adventurous wonderland. Every good memory I have of these boyhood years is about this summer refuge.

In contrast, our multi-family house in Somerville, Massachusetts, was very confining. Somerville was then described as the most densely populated urban area in the country. Living there felt like being trapped in a box. We lived in a small two-family house that accommodated three and a half families plus my grandmother. My mind always escaped to the outdoors and summer adventures. I played with the neighborhood boys on the railroad tracks about 100 yards behind our house. The trains headed north to Montréal, but at the time, I didn't know where they went. I knew only that they were leaving my socially suffocating Irish Catholic neighborhood. To this day, the sound of a train whistle brings back childhood memories of escape.

In 1953, when I was ten years old, my father was transferred to the headquarters of Schering Pharmaceuticals in Newark, New Jersey. My mother didn't want to leave her parents, who lived on the second floor of our house. My father assumed that being a pharmacist qualified him to run a drugstore—a mistake he soon realized. Meanwhile, my mother's parents wanted to invest their savings in something that would provide them income in their later years. My grandparents helped my parents buy a drugstore in Boston, each putting up $7,500.

The day they took me to see the drugstore is an unfortunately unforgettable memory. O'Connell Pharmacy was a half-century-old drugstore in a decrepit building in Allston, a poor section of Boston. Even at age ten, with my latent interest in history, I thought the drugstore looked ancient and dingy, nothing like the two drugstores up the street from our home in Somerville.

I felt my parents' new drugstore was walking into a time machine to the last century. The wood-planked floor was almost black and heavily worn, and the one showcase, prescription counter, and soda fountain were best described as worn out, in need of being cleaned up and hopefully replaced. The only good thing was the lighting—it was so dim you couldn't clearly see just how worn out and out of date the interior looked.

The time warp of entering O'Connell Pharmacy paled in comparison to the sense that my family had passed from what we considered a normal life into a science fiction–like other world we didn't know anything about. Just walking around the neighborhood was a shock. The houses were poorly kept up, if at all, some blocks were true slums, and there seemed to be no zoning. There were gas stations, a lot of car-repair shops, a trucking terminal, and small stores with houses mixed in. Zoning didn't seem to exist.

Jim and Rebba O'Connell, the couple who sold the drugstore to my parents, stayed for several weeks to show them how everything operated. Rebba, who was tall with a big frame and a blustery personality to match, seemed to be the one in charge. Her priority was pinching pennies, usually by shorting customers. To save money, the O'Connells cleverly made ice-cream cones with hidden hollow centers. They never put more than two-thirds of the standard portion of milk into a milkshake. These practices seemed absurdly cheap to us. When it came to filling drug prescriptions, the O'Connells' methods were downright dangerous. Jim O'Connell always held back some of the prescribed pills, and he made less of the compounds than a doctor's prescription called for. The O'Connells were unlikable people, and my parents had no intention of following any of their policies and practices.

My father, tall and thin and typically well dressed in his white shirt and bow tie, had a big smile for everyone. My mother dressed equally well and was warm and always smiling. My parents could not have been more out of place in this antique, cave-like drugstore. But this drugstore was only the setting for their incomprehensible passage into life in a poor neighborhood, where indigent customers couldn't pay. My father always ordered medicines for people's prescriptions, whether or not they could pay him. The City of Boston Old Age Assistance paid a minimal reimbursement a year and a half to two years after he had to pay the wholesaler. With those not on old-age assistance, he never got paid.

My parents in our family's drugstore.

My father in the antique interior of the drugstore.

My family quickly realized that the O'Connells' dishonesty was in keeping with everything in the neighborhood. I remember the day when the local cop came for his cash payoff. My father had no idea what the policeman was talking about. The cop bluntly explained to him "the way things work": If my father didn't pay, a health inspector would find something wrong with the soda fountain and close it down. Part of the weekly bribe was also to ensure that the police would take care of any real troublemakers who might be threats to my parents. (This was done in the basement of the police station with a rubber hose.)

Across the street from the drugstore was one of Boston's biggest playgrounds, where baseball games and soccer matches could go on simultaneously. The playground was also the site of a lot of gambling, fights, and troublemaking by the teenagers who hung out there. This brought a lot of business to the soda fountain. On summer nights, sports turned to sex, bringing business to the drugstore for condoms, which could not be openly sold because of opposition from the Catholic Church.

I played ball with neighborhood kids and soon got to know the prison sentences for just about every crime. Everyone's father seemed to be in prison, had just gotten out of prison, or was awaiting trial. The kids I knew all aspired to do better than their fathers—they weren't going to get caught as often.

Later in life, I realized that I had learned an important lesson. My normal, stable family had no understanding or experience with such dishonest thinking and a criminal culture. As they crossed over from their normal culture to one of crime and deceit, they were completely vulnerable. My parents never anticipated that the O'Connells were cheating everyone—including them—with how they operated the drugstore. It was outside of their comprehension that an entire neighborhood operated as a criminal enterprise.

Still later in life, I realized that people in the history and art world are frequently vulnerable to conmen and thieves for the same reason—it would never occur to them that such people would come into their erudite world. Crime existed in other parts of society, not in the arts, which is why so many sophisticated con artists have found easy prey, just as my parents were early in my life.

Chapter 2

Rare Coins (1950s)

At the same time that my parents were dealing with the shock of what they had gotten into, one seemingly small incident became the unlikely spark in my life. Paying for a purchase in the drugstore, a customer gave my mother a half dollar. She immediately felt that it was a bit bigger than a normal half dollar, and then she saw the date: 1806. She gave the coin to me as a curiosity. That coin ignited in me a wonder about the world 147 years earlier. I suddenly possessed a window into that world.

I had just seen Thomas Paine's pamphlet "Common Sense," which inspired the American Revolution, illustrated in my fourth-grade history book. The photograph showed a water stain on the cover of the pamphlet and said that it was probably dropped in the muddy streets of Boston during demonstrations. This was an incredibly romantic idea, and now I held in my hand a coin used by people only 30 years later.

I learned that there were people in Boston who were dealers in old coins. I had never imagined people making a business out of old coins. Two dealers had street-level stores, which really impressed me. The larger of these two shops had hundreds of coins for sale in flat showcases. I was mesmerized . . . and ignored by the shopkeeper, until I pulled out my half dollar and asked what he would pay for it. The guy took a quick look and offered me $2. He turned away as quickly as he had arrived at his offer, displaying no need to show any courtesy. I was excited because $2 represented a profit of four times what the half dollar had cost my mother.

I then went into the smaller store next door. There, the man offered $1.75. The phone book listed one other dealer on Bromfield Street. This dealer had a third-floor office at number 45, with a sign on the door reading "B.A. Barstow." Mr. Barstow was a tall, lanky man who greeted me with a smile. This already was a great improvement. I showed Mr. Barstow my coin, and he offered me $3.50. I readily and gladly accepted. All the way home on the bus, I thought, "Wow, this is the way to make a lot of money."

I was ten years old, and for the first time, I felt excited about something outside of the world I knew.

After school, I worked on the soda fountain in the drugstore. As soon as I arrived at the store, I went to the cash register to check the coins they had received so far that day. Lightning did not strike twice.

With 25¢ from my $3.50 windfall, I bought a book about coin values. As a business, buying and selling pennies made the most sense: If you could get 10¢ for a penny, you were making ten times your cost. Getting 50¢ for a quarter was only double. I asked the guy who filled the drugstore's gumball machine if I could give him dollar bills for pennies from the machine. He obliged, and I quickly started finding scarce dates.

My mother at the fateful cash register where the 1806 half dollar was found.

When I had a full bag of coins to sell, I went back to 45 Bromfield Street, but Mr. Barstow wasn't interested in small-value coins. He recommended another dealer, Malcolm O.E. Chell-Frost at 120 Tremont Street. Mr. Chell-Frost's name matched his middle-age decorum. He wore conservative three-piece suits. He was a gentleman. He had pictures on the walls—no showcases to display his coins for sale. His office was not the sort of setting where you would think you could sell a penny for 10¢, and another for 12¢. Maybe Mr.

The 1806 half dollar
that started it all.

Chell-Frost was buying my pennies just to encourage me, but I was starting to make good money. My parents were very supportive of my enterprise. My mother put a sign in the drugstore window that I would pay money for old coins. My weekly trips into Boston now occasionally included a visit to Burt Barstow's shop, where I peered into the showcase and could see my 1806 half dollar, now priced at $5. When my total capital reached $10, I told Mr. Barstow that I wanted to buy the half dollar back. He offered to sell it to me for $4.50, and relative to my total assets, it was the most extravagant purchase that I ever made in my life—and the most satisfying.

That half dollar has sat on my desk ever since that day in 1954.

In Somerville the local bank was a five-minute ride by bicycle. I expanded by getting rolls of pennies from the bank every day, going through the coins, and rerolling the ones I didn't want. Ads in the Somerville newspaper for old coins presented opportunities, and I biked or took the bus to see potential sources. Back in the 1950s coin collecting was in its infancy, and it was a novel idea to sell coins for more than their face value. I enjoyed meeting new people and soon was spending more time going to see people than rummaging through hundreds of coins.

The following winter, when I was 11, my coin career almost ended. I had started ice skating down the street from the drugstore and went there almost every night. I never had to pay. The man who ran the skate shop was a drugstore customer and would unlock the back door for me. Speed skating seemed naturally appealing, and I got involved in races. I wore dungarees—not jeans—while everyone else had speed-skating suits, and I felt—and was—very out of place. In a weak moment, I decided to sell my coin inventory for the price of a speed-skating suit: $13. I remember being at the bus stop in painful detail. It was snowing, and I had my coins in a bag when my mother got off the bus and asked me where I was going. I told her and she broke down, desperately crying that they would come up with the $13. Things in the drugstore were so bad that this was a huge amount of money for my parents, but she came up with it. Giving me the 1806 half dollar and not expecting any of the proceeds from its sale, and then coming up with the $13 were major events in the founding of my coin business. (My mother lived long enough to see what I made out of all of the support they gave me at this critical time for them and for me.)

Speed skating had an unexpected impact on my view of the future. Many races were in Worcester, west of Boston, and we would drive from Allston through a wealthy neighborhood to get there. For the first time I saw mansions, where there was space between houses and there were no fences. I knew where I wanted my future to be.

Just as I turned 12 in 1955, in a feature article in the *Somerville Journal* newspaper headlined "12-Year-Old Lad Becomes Coin Dealer," I was quoted as saying I no longer wanted to sell coins wholesale to dealers but wanted to develop a business selling to collectors, so I could make more money. My father drove me to coin shows, where I started to see the different areas of coins that people collected. My mother took me to several meetings of the Boston Numismatic Society, where we felt distinctly out of place. The Numismatic Society people were "old Brahmins" from the "right" neighborhood, and they treated me as a curiosity because of my age.

My first important business concept, shortly after I turned 12 years old, was realizing I couldn't build a business on people being amused by my age and I had to figure out what I could add to some aspect of coin collecting to become a real dealer. I had to focus on what I could do, what advantages I had, and not what I couldn't do. When I look back at myself at 12 years old, I realize that I had begun what became a lifelong process of always looking at what value I could add to a business situation. What would make me successful, how did I improve a process, how could I offer more service, why should I be successful? If I wasn't adding something there was no point in my going into it. I needed coin dealing to be financially successful; it wasn't a hobby, it wasn't a pastime. I wanted to contribute to my family's welfare and I had a serious business attitude, but I needed the idea of how to do that.

I knew that capital was important: Once you move away from pennies, rare coins cost real money, and it takes a lot of capital to be a dealer. Virtually every dealer in every show focused on United States coinage after 1792, by date and by where a coin was minted (Philadelphia, Denver, or San Francisco). I had nothing to add to what these people were already doing. Fortunately, I was fascinated by coins issued by Britain's American colonies before the national

BUSINESSBOY: 12-year-old Kenneth Rendell, 62a Bristol rd., displays his sets of Indian head and Lincoln pennies, part of the stock in his brisk rare coin exchange. With business acumen, he paid $40 for the Indian heads now worth from $65-$70. (Photo by Berman)

12-year-old Lad Becomes Coin Dealer through Chance Finding Of 1806 Liberty Half Dollar

Look over those coins in your pocket before you spend them. They may be worth a lot more than face value!

That's the lesson Mr. and Mrs. Harry H. Rendell of 62a Bristol rd. learned from their 12-year-old son, Kenneth.

It was barely two years ago that Mrs. Rendell, at her husband's Allston drug store, took in the 1806 Liberty half dollar that launched the pre-teen Kenney on a full-scale business venture.

She almost gave it out in change again, but her son asked for it as a curiosity, and then figured —

It to a Boston coin dealer for $3.50.

But the four-bit piece convinced its enchantment for him, and every time he visited the coin store to buy other coins, Kenney would press his luck to the clerk —

and catalogues wholesale from Boston dealers and re-sells them at a price slightly lower than the prevailing scale.

He talks like a business administration graduate, explaining that "I try to sell the coins and albums for a little less so that I'll get more customers and make more money."

At first, Kenny admits, he succumbed to temptation and overcharged some youngsters in Allston, but he soon saw the error of his ways and prefers to build up a steady clientel that he can help build a worthwhile collection.

The businessboy has no interest in foreign coins, but prefers to specialize in post-revolutionary American money, collecting them in "sets." A set of a certain coin — Lincoln pennies or Roosevelt dimes — includes one from every year it was issued and is worth a higher cash value than their total individually, explains Kenny.

He is now working on his third complete set of Lincoln pennies, since he sold two sets to buy a $70 pair of speed skates during the winter.

Financing all his dealings with his own money, Kenny bought 100 rolls of pennies from a bank recently ($50 worth in two lots). The "loot" from the bank included a 1909 San Francisco mint one-cent piece with the letters "VDB", the initials of the designer, on the back worth approximately $10. From the 100 roll he made up about 1-3 of a Lincoln penny set, none worth less than 25 cents, and sold a number of "junk" coins worth 7 or 8 cents each to get some "working capital."

Kenny regularly looks over the change in his father's cash register. The officials at St. Clement's school, where he is a sixth grade honor student, save all the office change for him to inspect.

Got any money you think you were "gypped" on in change, because the picture is cracked or the letters on the date broken? Don't spend it until you've checked, advises Kenny.

His most —

These come shiny and new from the bank and have none of their markings rubbed off. The more nearly perfect the coin, the greater the value.

If you're going to go in for that collection of Roosevelt dimes, try to save the ones that still have a tiny spot sticking up in the middle of the "tail" side.

In its present state of partial completion Kenny's set of Indian heads, for which he paid an approximate total of $40, is worth $65-$70. His stock also includes 1857 and 1829 "half" dimes, worth 65 cents; an 1864 two-cent piece, worth 30 cents; 1865 and 1851 three-cent coins, worth 35 cents; and some paper currency, issued during a Civil War metal shortage, for 50, three, and 10 cents, now worth $5, 75 and 50 cents, respectively.

In checking and following up coins, Kenny incidentally acquires a vast knowledge of American history and the people who get their faces on our money.

His one secret yearning is to get his hands on an 1804 half dollar, a very rare coin that was recalled because its silver content was worth more than its face value. One sold at a numismatic auction last year for $12,500.

Kenny's business is brisk. It includes youngsters who respond to the sign on his porch, others who reply to his newspaper advertisements, and even a mail order business with several adults.

Despite this fact, he himself can't participate in a numismatic auction or join such societies until he is 18. His father joins them for him so Kenny can attend the meetings and Kenny hopes his father will get him into an auction in a few years. An adult friend displayed Kenny's Indian heads at an auction in Connecticut last year.

Sometimes even before replacing stock or buying those coveted "proof" coins, Kenny spends his profits on speed skating. He's a member of the Boston and Bay State Skating Club and the ... ssociation.

... Kenny ... this year ... the New ... Skating ... Hamp-

... Rendell ... own up?

KENNY RENDELL, SILVER SKATES ENTRANT Shows his coin-currency collection used in his mail-order business. (Photo by Lee Tierney)

My coin business was heralded by the local papers.

government was formed. The colonies used some European coinage and silver Spanish coins, and they also minted various copper coins. These were generally hard to categorize, required research to know what they were, and lacked dealers who specialized in them. If I specialized in this area, I might be able to do well.

The value I would be adding was the cataloging and expertise, and also making these colonial coins available from a single person, rather than the happenstance of possibly being able to find one or two at a coin show. I would do the canvassing of dealers and issue price lists. And, most importantly, I was passionately interested in the coins myself. (I still have a collection of colonial coins, long after I stopped being a coin dealer.)

I found my niche as a young coin dealer in early American colonial coins like these. (Left) The first coin minted in America, a 1652 New England shilling. (Middle and right) A Massachusetts Pine Tree shilling.

The dealers in regular federal coinage were happy to put these earlier coins aside and sell them to me for almost nothing. At 13 years old I made my first trip to New York City by myself on the bus. A large number of the coin dealers in New York were Jewish refugees from Europe, and they were wonderful to me. Several had become coin dealers by initially taking jobs in the subway, making change for tokens and watching for scarce dates. These New York dealers had boxes marked "Ken Rendell," and they filled them with all the coins they couldn't easily identify. They encouraged me and respected my enthusiasm and initiative.

Researching, cataloging, and exhibiting my colonial coins at shows, I built a good clientele of collectors who bought from my monthly mimeographed price lists. In 1955 I was sending out 500 copies of my two-page price list each month. Everything was moving so fast, especially my determination, that I don't think I appreciated how unusual it was for someone my age to be doing this alongside actual adults.

At coin shows I was looking for my specialty, colonial coins, but I was also noticing other areas that didn't fit into the standard types, such as tokens issued by merchants during periods when coins weren't available, and political campaign medals. Nothing had been written about these fascinating artifacts of presidential elections. In 1956, when I was 13 years old, I worked on a book to catalog all the different ones I could find. Years later I turned over my research to the pioneer collector in this field, Doyle DeWitt, who was president of the Travelers Insurance Company. He had the resources to publish the book himself: *A Century of Campaign Buttons, 1789–1889*. I was proud of the contribution that I made to what still is a standard reference book.

At an auction in Boston that year, a friendly and eccentric fellow showed me that a silver dollar minted in 1795 had not been cataloged properly and was worth far more than the estimate. He urged me to buy the coin and gave me the name of a collector who would pay a significant price. I bought the silver dollar and sold it at the price he indicated. This was my introduction to Walter Breen, the most erudite coin researcher and author of his generation. Walter was a complex genius who let everyone know he had completed a four-year program at Johns Hopkins University in ten months. He wore his Phi Beta Kappa key with the most dingy, worn-out, homeless-looking clothes. Walter was the preeminent numismatic authority in my specialty of colonial coinage. He was enormously helpful, introducing me to collectors and advising me on national dealers I might buy from, and he was my bridge from the Boston market to collectors and dealers in the Eastern and Midwestern states.

I was, seemingly with lightning speed, moving upward and outward. With Walter Breen's help, I expanded my world beyond shows in New England. In August 1957, at age 14, I attended the biggest coin show, the annual convention of the American Numismatic Association, in Philadelphia. I also delivered a prepared talk on political campaign medals to a new coin-collecting group. Today, with the hindsight of more than 60 years, my talk holds up well.

Exhibiting coins for sale, around 14 years old.

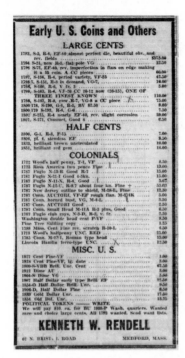

As I built my business, I began making price lists of the coins I had for sale, which I mailed out to clients.

By this time my world was far from Allston and my parents' drugstore, which was struggling badly. The economic burden and long hours were taking a terrible toll on my mother and father physically, mentally, and psychologically. Yet while their world was falling apart, my parents were instrumental in allowing me to expand my world as I wanted to. My father had an unlimited imagination and was excitedly supportive of every dream I had and everything I wanted to do.

My mother, though, was concerned about my education. I was attending the local parochial school and had A+ grades in everything, but I spent little time on schoolwork. A customer who stopped regularly in the drugstore happened to come in when my mother was showing off an article in the Boston newspaper about my success in speed skating. He was active in the alumni of one of the best exam schools in the greater Boston area, Malden Catholic, and offered to get me a full scholarship to play hockey. In 1957 I was so bored with my school that I was happy to please my mother.

I went from star student to struggling. I had to be tutored every night in Latin. And, while I could skate faster than anyone, I had to learn how to play hockey. The two experiences were good for character building! As I began to succeed in school, I realized I couldn't run my business, do decently in school, and go to hockey practice at 5 every morning.

In my second year I was financially able to pay my own tuition and drop out of hockey. The teachers began to appreciate my different observations about history and also what I was doing with my business. They were very accommodating in rescheduling tests from Fridays to Mondays to accommodate my weekly travelling to coin shows, and we both kept careful records of my school attendance for the legal minimum of days. The transition from superstar to struggling in school taught me the lesson that I had to study hard, and my whole life since has been about studying everything I am involved in.

I was in my mid-teens when I built a relationship with a Pennsylvania collector named Don Miller. I shared his interest in "Hard Times" tokens issued by merchants during the Panic of 1837, when people were hoarding coins for their intrinsic metal value. Don, a trial attorney by day, called me every night to talk about our mutual fascination. I met him in New York City, and he gave me his duplicate tokens on consignment and paid to print a catalog that I produced. This catalog turned out to be a sensation among the limited number of collectors and gave me instant credibility and the important experience of dealing with wealthy collectors. The price for the entire collection was $8,000. I had never before had anything for sale at such a high price.

A consultant to one of the wealthy collectors wanted to meet with me. My father drove me to New Britain, Connecticut, and patiently waited for hours while I answered questions. This led to a more important meeting in New Jersey with the collector himself, Herbert Oechsner. Mr. Oechsner told me he was considering purchasing half of the collection. (My list of prices of individual pieces totaled more than $10,000.) He wanted to go over each piece in the collection and discuss whether or not I thought he should buy it. For

A Descriptive List of an Outstanding

Collection of

Hard Times Tokens

Presenting a unique opportunity for the discriminating collector to acquire an unusual and outstanding collection — unsurpassed in condition — rich in coins of such excessive rarity that they are familiar to only a very few dealers or collectors today.

FOR SALE BY

KENNETH W. RENDELL

62a BRISTOL ROAD   MEDFORD, MASS.

**One of my early catalogs,
featuring Hard Times tokens.**

several hours I told him what I thought the most important pieces were, explaining each of my opinions. In many cases I said that if he bought one specific piece, it represented, as a type, three or four others that he wouldn't need to acquire. He was very surprised I didn't encourage him to buy the whole collection, and I replied that I was giving him honest answers to his questions, which were based on his not being able to afford the whole collection. He said that he was impressed with my analysis and trusted my overall judgment. To my astonishment, Mr. Oechsner took out his checkbook, wrote a check for $4,000, and said he would pay the balance of the $8,000 within the week.

This was the biggest deal I could ever imagine pulling off. I had no expectation that my straightforward, critical, and honest opinions would create a trust that would result in the sale of the entire collection. (When the Oechsner collection was sold years later, I bought back some of the key Hard Times tokens for my own collection.)

I was attending more and more coin shows on weekends and became friendly with a relatively new dealer named Dave Bowers. Dave had an appreciation for all the areas that I was specializing in, but he had the financial backing to deal in all general areas as well. When I was 15, he and I attended the annual convention of the American Numismatic Association in Los Angeles, and we then traveled together to Mexico and up through California's national parks to San Francisco. Until then, I had been west of the Mississippi River only in my imagination. Dave, four years older than I, drove the entire way because I didn't yet have a driver's license. (More than six decades later, Dave is not only a dear friend but also the patriarch of the rare-coin business—its most prolific author and the recipient of every numismatic award possible.)

Around this time I ventured into a consumer area of coin collecting. I had the idea of producing a rectangular bag, opening at the top with two overlapping flaps, to carry coin boxes. I went to a luggage manufacturer north of Boston to make the bags. Dave Bowers advised me to create a separate business entity to sell the bags because everyone who knew me would expect to get one for free. I followed Dave's advice. The bags

Dave Bowers as a young coin enthusiast and dealer.

sold extremely well—and then I was shocked to see a New York department store ad (in the *New York Times*) promoting an identical bag. The store was selling it as a salesman's bag to carry products or catalogs. I couldn't compete at their lower price and my nascent luggage business faded. Since then, I have never ventured again into a market outside of my areas of expertise.

In 1959, at 16 years old, I was greatly honored to be invited to be on the committee of 35 leading rare-coin dealers who set the values published in the *Guide Book of United States Coins*, the principal reference book in numismatics. At about this time a group of us formed the Rittenhouse Society of serious numismatists. That same year, Mr. and Mrs. Henry Norweb, to whom I regularly sold colonial coins, invited me to visit them in Cleveland, Ohio, and see their collection. I knew the Norwebs' reputation for having an extraordinary collection, but I wasn't prepared for the experience of going to 9511 Lakeshore Boulevard, which was more like a public park than a residential setting.

The Norwebs were as impressive as their residence. Mr. Norweb had been ambassador to several different countries, and he had the movie-star looks of Cary Grant: very distinguished, exceptionally gracious, and friendly. Mrs. Norweb was the powerhouse. She was descended from the founder of the *Cleveland Plain Dealer* newspaper and appeared to be the more enthusiastic and knowledgeable collector. During my first night at dinner, the Norwebs told me that the dining-room table had been brought to Mexico by Hernán Cortés, and they acquired it while Mr. Norweb was the U.S. ambassador to Mexico. The next day Mr. Norweb took me into Cleveland, where we visited his bank. It was indeed "his" bank. Inside the vault he showed me many of the most valuable coins in their collection.

Eager to build my own business, I looked around for other areas of numismatics that were undervalued and underrepresented in the American marketplace. British coins seemed to fit both criteria. They weren't offered by any dealers at the mainstream coin shows. The designs were quite beautiful, and I thought that they could be a successful venture if they were made available in America. A friend of mine in New York City, who shared my appreciation of underrepresented numismatics, and I decided to go to London during my Christmas break from high school.

The first thing we learned was how unprepared we were outside of our knowledge about British coins. We thought we would simply find a hotel when we arrived. At the airport, a uniformed person from the Savoy Hotel told us that they had vacancies and offered us a ride into London. The Savoy lobby was grand and impressive. We checked in and somehow missed the part about what it would cost. When we walked into our room's bathroom and saw that there was a telephone beside the bathtub, I called downstairs and found out what the daily rate was.

We had naïvely checked into one of the most expensive hotels in London! We checked out and moved across the street to a hotel where many of the rooms didn't have toilets or bathrooms. I came to understand what the phrase "a room and a path" meant. We felt foolish, but our new hotel, while stripped down to bare necessities and offering appallingly bad British food, was a very good value. And we were there to buy rare coins, not for a tourist experience.

There were basically three rare-coin dealers in London. All were old firms, one founded in the late 1700s and the other two in the late 1800s. I was welcomed and treated as a serious collector. I had read the only books I could find on British coinage, and I knew what I was looking for. This was nothing like going to coin shops in America, where the bigger the sale, the better. The British dealers were, in contrast, discreet and low-key. I had the strong feeling that if I said I wanted to buy in large quantity, they would have ushered me out.

The oldest firm, Spink, occupied a multistory building with different departments on each floor. They were primarily dealers in military decorations, paintings, and other artifacts. They focused on gold coins and medieval British coins, but they had a good supply of what I wanted: copper coins of the last 300 years. I bought 75 or 80 coins.

The second dealer, Seaby, was like an American coin shop in atmosphere— a retail shop—but not in attitude. The shop sold various artifacts as well as coins, but in a much smaller setting. It also had more of the types of coins I was looking for—ones I thought I could accumulate and create a market for at a multiple price of my cost. They were more commercially minded than Spink and seemed pleased that I bought so many pieces.

The third firm, Baldwin, was in a tall building of apartments where George Bernard Shaw had lived. Walking in, I felt like I was entering Victorian England. The decor was from the later decades of Queen Victoria, and Messrs. Baldwin were dressed in formal Edwardian suits. Their coins were kept in trays in large, polished wooden cabinets. They had what I was looking for, and in quantity, but again I believed that if I tried to buy too much, they wouldn't sell me anything. Over a period of days I went through their whole inventory and bought hundreds of British copper coins from the last 300 years. The prices were also modest.

I was having a very successful trip. Then, right after Christmas, we read in the newspaper that the British farthing was going to cease being legal tender, and on January 1 the coin would be withdrawn from circulation. Normally, you

cannot export quantities of a country's current coinage, but since the farthing would no longer be legal tender, we could ship as many as we wanted out of England. There were 960 farthings to a pound sterling, the equivalent of four to an American cent. We teamed up to buy as many farthings as we could at banks, where we were met with astonishment and amusement. The banks asked if we knew what we were doing since the farthing was going to be worthless in another week.

We managed to buy farthings for well under face value from banks that would rather get rid of them than do the paperwork and ship them across London to the Bank of England. We kept piling bags of farthings into rented taxis until we couldn't fit any more, whereupon we returned to our hotel, the Strand Palace, and loaded the bags onto a porter's four-wheeler and carted them to our fifth-floor rooms. As we purchased hundreds of thousands of farthings, our piles grew to the point that we started to worry about the weight. We changed our rooms to the first floor, rationalizing that if our hoard did fall through the floor, the farthings would land in the basement and not all over the street.

Soon we had millions of farthings. My partner kept rationalizing that if all else failed, we could punch holes in the coins and market them as washers. The farthings were costing us $2,650, plus expenses, per million. A friend of his gave us the financing to keep buying and we ended up with about six million of them.

Then we faced the next problem: Nobody collected farthings! Our primary idea was to convince a manufacturer of coin boards, which collectors use to organize their coins, to issue boards for English farthings. We had to guarantee a large order, but as we had predicted, once these English farthing coin boards were available, we started to sell our farthings in units of a thousand at a time.

It was a wild adventure, and 1959 came to a spectacular and profitable end!

My years in the rare-coin field in the mid-1950s to early 1960s were a time of great change. Coin collecting was emerging from an eccentric and arcane pursuit to more mainstream. In the mid-1950s, if there were more than one rare-coin dealer in a city, they were likely located close together in an inexpensive part of town. By the end of the 1950s coin dealers started appearing in more retail-orientated locations in many local towns. It was becoming more common to see dealers' shops where the general public could be enticed into the collecting hobby.

When I first came into the field, the dominant dealers were of the 1940s generation—my father's generation—and were surprisingly spread out in large cities all over the country. Abe Kosoff, regarded as the "dean" of American coin dealers, was just outside Los Angeles; his former partner Abner Kreisberg was in a storefront in Beverly Hills (coincidently, decades later, I opened my Beverly Hills gallery across the street from where I first met him). The pair had been located in New York City, but Kosoff told me Abner always liked the retail trade and he did not, so after selling "the world's greatest collection" they split up and headed to sunny southern California. Aubrey Bebee was located in Omaha, Nebraska; Max Mehl, for decades the dominant dealer, was in Fort Worth, Texas; Art and Paul Kagin seemed oddly based in Des Moines, Iowa. Hans Schulman, from Holland, who preached about the joys of coin collecting, especially European, at clubs around the country, was based in New York City, along with Max Kaplan (who started as a toll collector in the subway, a brilliant idea that gave him endless days of being paid to look at the dates of coins passing his tollbooth counter). Lester Merkin, who left the music field for his passion in rare coins, was a gentleman dealer upstairs on Madison Avenue who was very helpful to me. New Netherlands Coin Co. was principally an auction house owned by John Ford and Charles Wormser, with their catalogs written by Walter Breen in his unique and extremely thorough style. (They were never a good source for me; Breen's cataloging missed nothing and collectors of colonial coins were comfortable buying from his descriptions.) The most prominent name was Stack's, who operated a street-level gallery on 57th Street that was designed and fitted out to appeal to wealthy collectors.

One of the things that everyone seemed to have in common was the sale of King Farouk's collection. The deposed dictator of Egypt had used state funds to form an incredible collection which was thrown into an auction conducted by Sotheby's in Cairo. The lot descriptions were comically inept and there were great bargains, a subject those attending seemed to always be talking about.

An important dealer out of the mainstream was Worthy Coin Corp of Boston. They ran ads in prominent national publications offering high prices for coins no one could find in circulation. They offered for $1 their buying list of other dates. While Corrado Romano, the owner, did buy quantities of the coins he offered to buy, his fortune was made by selling the want lists for $1. Eventually he became a major buyer of truly rare coins at the New York auctions.

Abe Kosoff saw the future more optimistically than others. He dealt with the biggest and wealthiest collectors and, with his lack of any retail pretense, created an aura of exclusiveness. Nevertheless, he knew that what was good for the overall field would be good for him, and in 1955 organized the Professional

Numismatists Guild of dealers, which promoted ethics, standards, and its members to the general public. The aura of professionalism and trustworthiness was an important part of the rare-coin business becoming more mainstream.

The youngest member of this elite group was Dave Bowers, a few years older than me, who had a serious interest in my specialties of colonial coins and interesting non-traditional numismatics. He also had important family financial backing, so was an important dealer in regular-issue federal coins. Dave's geographical location was probably more remote than any of the other big dealers—Johnson City, in a corner of New York on the Pennsylvania border. There he formed an on-again-off-again partnership with Jim Ruddy, who lived in Johnson City. Their firm, Empire Coin Company, paved the way to the future of coin collecting. Their monthly publication, *Empire Topics*, had articles written by Dave and their monthly offering of new acquisitions. Ruddy, while older than Dave, was still substantially younger than the other dominant dealers.

Jim Ruddy would, in 1965, make one of the greatest strides forward for rare-coin collecting with his book *Photograde*, which showed every type of American coin with enlarged photographs of the details in all the varying condition grading stages. Suddenly, a collector could compare what he was being offered with a standardized grading system.

Also emerging rapidly was the small and intense group of collectors/dealers interested in what many termed the "serious numismatics," generally focusing on inexpensive but historically very interesting coins, tokens, medals, and paper money. I'm not sure whose idea it was to form a group—it likely was Dave Bowers—called the Rittenhouse Society after the first director of the United States Mint. The first gathering was at the American Numismatic Society annual meeting in Boston in 1960. I was the youngest, but everyone was basically just four or five years older. To be a member you had to have published original research in some aspect of numismatics, and the Rittenhouse Society members had seemingly written the basic reference works, led by Walter Breen in all areas of colonial coins; Grover Criswell, who wrote the standard reference book on Confederate currency; George Fuld, noted for his book on Civil War tokens; Dick Johnson, a specialist in medals and just appointed editor of the new newspaper *Coin World*; and Ken Bressett, who authored articles and books in many numismatic fields. We decided at our first meeting that an additional qualification was that you couldn't be over 40 years old, which we realized would exclude the great numismatic researcher and publisher, Eric Newman, who had reached that exalted and, to us, distant age. We passed a resolution to make a single exception for him at our first meeting.

Rare-coin collecting was erupting like a volcano. In addition to coin dealers seemingly in every town, rare coins were becoming story lines in TV shows and movies. Coin conventions and shows were multiplying, as were coin clubs everywhere. People could meet other collectors and share their passion and enjoyment.

Inevitably, some dealers began to promote *investing* in rare coins, and the collecting of original rolls of new coins began to take hold. Nevertheless, it was very exciting seeing, in the span of less than ten years, so many new people appreciating the romance, history, and pleasure of coin collecting. When I held that 1806 half dollar my mother gave me, and I learned there actually were dealers in old coins, I could never have imagined that this tiny corner of the collecting world could explode into one of the dominant collecting fields in less than a decade.

RITTENHOUSE SOCIETY NEWSLETTER

-November 15, 1960-

The first meeting of the Rittenhouse Society was held August 26, 1960 at the American Numismatic Association convention in the Statler-Hilton Hotel in Boston Massachusetts. Present at this organizational meeting were:

Q. David Bowers
Binghamton, N.Y.

Dr. George Fuld
Baltimore, Md.

Walter H. Breen
New York, N.Y.

D. Wayne Johnson
Sidney, Ohio

Kenneth Bressett
Racine,Wisconsin

Kenneth W. Rendell
Medford, Mass.

Grover C. Criswell
St.Petersburg Beach,Fla.

At the meeting Walter Breen presented the "charter" originally proposed for the Rittenhouse Society several years ago. This contained several suggestions for the society's name, including the adopted Rittenhouse Society. After review-ing other proposals in the old charter the members decided that many of the idea (age requirements for members, for example) were obsolete and needed revision.

A slate of officers for 1960-1961 was nominated and voted on. Elected were: Q. David Bowers, president; Walter H. Breen, vice president and D. Wayne Johnson secretary-treasurer. All of the members present contributed $1.00 each to give the treasury a beginning.

Before we convene again it would be advantageous to have some of the ground-work completed. A number of the ideas, requirements and policies already discus-sed or to be decided upon are enumerated below. Sometime during the next month take an hour or so and write your comments and suggestions for each of the items listed. Also mention any new ideas or suggestions that have been overlooked. Mail your comments to: Q. David Bowers; c/o Bowers Coin Co.,Inc.; 70 Court St.; Binghamton, N.Y. The combined results of all the comments received will be then printed and distributed to the members for voting or further discussion.

Chapter 3

The Caribbean Coin Hunt: The Craziest Adventure

In 1961, when I was 18 years old, a coin-dealer friend noticed, during his honeymoon in Bermuda, several rare-date English coins in the change he received in a store. As soon as he mentioned this to me, a lightbulb went on.

In a normal year in England, 68 million pennies were minted, but that would drop as low as 150,000 in a year when new coins weren't needed. This happened several times in the previous decades, and one would assume that some low-mintage coins would turn up in England, but they never did. It suddenly occurred to me that perhaps when England didn't need the coinage, it minted a small number and shipped the coins to former colonies where English coins were still used.

My friend had only found a few rare dates in Bermuda, so I decided to go to Nassau in the Bahamas. I had never been to the Caribbean, and Nassau struck me as straight out of a 1930s mystery movie. I checked into one of the least expensive hotels in the downtown harbor area. The British expatriates hanging out in the bar assured me that if I stayed there long enough, my work ethic would also disappear and I would spend all day hanging out in the bar with them. I didn't intend to stay that long.

I hadn't realized how small Nassau was, with a small economy and a relatively small number of coins in circulation, but there were a lot of scarce and rare dates. The local Barclays Bank didn't have any significant quantity of coins in storage, just the amount that went back and forth from businesses. Each day, I took out as many bags of pennies and sixpence as they would give me, carried them up the outside hotel stairs to my room, poured them out on the table, endlessly turned them over to see the dates, and sorted out the ones I wanted to keep.

As I found a diminishing number of scarce coins, I needed to find coins I hadn't already seen. I bought a pass on Air Bahamas, giving me unlimited flights to the other Bahamian islands. Flying was an adventure in itself. I would show up at the airport in the morning, tell the person behind the desk where I wanted to go, and he would tell me if a plane was headed in that direction and could drop me off.

There weren't many other islands that had banks, but the banks I did find were very friendly. They assumed that I was some kind of eccentric, and on many days I agreed. At each bank I would find a place to sit outside, sort through their coins, and then replace what I wanted with coins I had brought with me.

I did this on Eleuthera, Andros, Little Exuma, Great Abaco, Cat Island, and Long Island. None of these islands had anything more than a grass landing strip, which was conveniently within walking distance of the town. At the end of the day I would stand on the landing strip and the plane returning to Nassau would land to get me.

My Bahamas experience, while an adventure, wasn't a profitable one. I thought I should try Jamaica. It is a much larger country and would have vastly more coins in circulation. With my budget for expenses running on the edge, I found a rooming house listed on the tourist information board at the Kingston airport. My room, outside the center of Kingston, was very hot with no air conditioning. But enduring the less-than-ideal conditions was practical. When I walked to a local store my first day, I bought something inexpensive and looked at the change; every coin was a scarce or rare date. I bought something in a second store, and then a third, with the same result. I couldn't possibly spend any of these coins. They were worth too much on the rare-coin market. Bonanza!

My "home" and office in Kingston, Jamaica: The Sheraton Hotel.

The hotel's social center.

I realized Jamaica was going to be a money-making venture and asked the kind landlady in the rooming house what the best hotel was. It was the Sheraton just outside of downtown. I used her phone to book a room and took a bus to get there. The hotel was in a garden setting of palm trees and tropical plants, with a swimming pool and large outdoor bar. After the depressing walk-up room in Nassau and the sweltering heat in the Kingston rooming house, it was paradise.

I took a taxi to Barclays Bank on King Street in downtown Kingston. The grand colonial building reinforced that I was now in a bigger financial market than Nassau. I met with a middle-aged manager and told him I wanted to go through all of the bank's coins. He looked at me as if I were crazy. I told him that I would compensate him for his help by matching his weekly salary, which he said was 20 pounds. Suddenly all the obstacles disappeared. This eager-to-please manager even agreed to order coins from England to replace coins that I wanted to keep if the quantity became a problem.

Ernie, a friendly taxi driver with an old Cadillac, was usually stationed at the hotel, so I hired him to take me to Barclays first thing every morning to get the coins I thought I could go through that day. Flipping coins right side up is the very definition of tedious and boring work. I had nightmares about thousands and thousands of coins inundating me, helpless as I desperately tried to control the flow. I started hiring people at the hotel to help me sort in another hotel room and my life definitely improved.

One day the Barclays manager told me that he had come across four bags of English silver threepences that should have been sent back to England when they had been withdrawn from circulation in the 1950s. They had been overlooked. I bought the coins from the branch at face value, sold them to a buyer in New York, and made quite a good profit. This was timely, as my hotel bill was coming due.

I had been paying a lot of attention to the Jamaicans and their culture. I had expected resentment of white people, since England had run the country with the type of upper-class people I had no use for. But that was not the case. I never felt any animosity from the Jamaicans. They really were friendly, helpful, and accommodating.

I was, however, about to get a real lesson in human nature.

Ernie, my taxi driver, was an energetic worker, and as I kept recruiting workers to help me with the overload of coins that I was now processing every day from the transit company, I put him in charge as manager. Everyone quit. I was told that Jamaicans would never work for an African. Ernie was considered a "black" while everyone else was a "brown." I had to give Ernie a different job.

It was an important lesson in how different societies create their own hierarchies.

I also got to know Jamaica's English upper-class social world. These people seemed eager to have someone new in their midst, especially someone doing something as unconventional as I was. For me, even this class of people, whom I normally couldn't stand, were a relief from the traveling salesmen at the Sheraton bar. One weekend I was invited to stay at the St. Ann's Bay Yacht Club on Jamaica's North Shore. The name greatly exaggerated the reality. The only yachts were 13-foot sailboats. The "society," while hospitable toward me, was a class of expats who all remembered better days and never forgot titles. Everyone seemed to have been the captain of something.

The main subject of conversation on the North Shore was a film in production a few miles away. The movie was said to be based on a book by an author who lived there: Ian Fleming. Many people had read Fleming's books and had an interest in what the new movie would be. Local people filled out the cast as extras. Sometime later, when I saw the first James Bond film, *Dr. No*, I recognized a lot of faces.

As I traveled throughout Jamaica, a beautiful country, I visited every major town that had a bank, and I saw almost every coin in the country. Inevitably, we were sorting the coins we had imported. It was time to move on.

My next stop was Trinidad, which had a different feel. My base of operations, the Hilton in Port of Spain, was also different. Unlike the Sheraton in Kingston, there wasn't much of a social scene, except for a locals' dance hall where I went every night to listen to a steel band. People came to Port of Spain, the country's capital, to do business with the government oil company. One day at the rooftop restaurant, I was startled to see David Rockefeller at the next table, having lunch with Trinidad's prime minister.

The partner I had brought into this venture was operating out of New York, selling the coins that I found. He started to warn me that we were accumulating more than he could sell. In fact, we were acquiring tens of thousands of coins at face value and having to sell them for less and less profit as we flooded the markets. The result was ever-declining cash flow. We knew that in the long term we could make a lot of money on the coins, but in the short term we couldn't afford to hold out. We had to sell out for a small overall profit to someone who had the cash for a long-term investment. It was a valuable lesson.

Ever since, my business model has been to always try to wait until I can get what I believe something is worth, instead of having to sell it "at market" because I can't afford to hold onto it.

My first big opportunity to put this into action came a decade later in the 1970s, when I had the chance to realize what I hoped would be a great long-term profit. I was doing appraisals at Syracuse University's archives facility. One day I noticed the director throwing out a pile of unissued stock certificates from railroads that had been part of the New York Central system, founded by Cornelius Vanderbilt. I looked through the certificates and thought they were very attractive and interesting. All had been printed in the latter part of the nineteenth century, and they bore engraved vignettes of railroad scenes.

The director told me that he couldn't give the certificates to me, but if I wrote a letter making an offer to Syracuse University, he would agree to it. My letter went off, and I received a response that the university was accepting my offer of three cents apiece for approximately 100,000 railroad stock certificates.

There was no market for stock certificates that were not signed by important people. My many boxes of railroad stock certificates were piled high in my basement office, and I was constantly ribbed by fellow dealers about the $3,000 I had wasted. After about ten years there was some speculative dealer interest, and I had a few offers around $10,000, but I was committed to hold the certificates until someone developed a significant market for them.

Eventually, someone did. In 1980 a pioneering dealer published an illustrated catalog of antique stock certificates with a minimum price in the vicinity of $20, and suddenly a number of dealers wanted to buy me out. I wasn't in any hurry. I sold about a quarter of my 100,000 certificates for $100,000 and was determined to sell the rest in small quantities and individually over the remainder of my life. They didn't last that long! By being able to wait until the market developed, I realized more than 100 times my original cost.

In the field of historical letters and documents it is unusual for a big group of similar documents to turn up. But during the past 60 years some have—most notably a cache of American Express stock certificates signed by the founders, Wells and Fargo. These certificates are very attractive, with an engraved train in the center, and they originally cost me $15 each. A dealer I had worked with for many decades bought the same quantity as I did and sold them for double and triple his cost. I patiently waited until all of his certificates were off the market, and only then did I begin to offer mine at $150 each, increasing the price incrementally as they sold, eventually reaching $3,500 after 40 years. This was a rare enough opportunity that the letter from the dealer, offering them to me for $15, is framed in my archives!

Chapter 4

Family Disaster

In 1959 Dave Bowers told me he was starting to collect letters of presidents of the United States, and I was very intrigued. He was buying from the dean of dealers in historical letters and documents, Mary Benjamin. Her office in New York City was on the second floor of a building on East 77th Street, just off Madison Avenue. Thirty-five years later I established my street-level Madison Avenue gallery within sight of her former office.

Mary Benjamin was an impressive character in every way. A tall and large woman in her early 50s with prematurely gray hair, she had a personality that was even more imposing than her physical being. She exuded knowledge and authority, and she inspired confidence. On my very first visit with her, I became a collector.

I had not thought of historical letters and documents as a business opportunity. Quite the opposite. I appreciated how enormously complex this area of collecting was. In the following months I thought more and more about the power of letters written by prominent people in history. Colonial coins are great historical artifacts that were created by the early settlers of the country and then passed through the hands of future generations, and I have continued to collect them all my life. My collection, which includes all of the issues that circulated in America from the 1652 New England shilling to the 1787 Fugio cent, is a wonderful connection to the founding of this country. Historical letters offer a different insight into the writers' lives, times, and locales. There is no more intimate view into their thoughts, their hopes, their concerns—their souls—than the handwritten letters they wrote.

I fell in love with the intimacy these letters convey. On a visit to Dave Bowers's home in Pennsylvania, he showed me his collection of presidential letters. I traded Dave a collection of British coins in exchange for his collection of letters in 1960.

Soon after that, I spotted an ad for an estate auction of historical documents, books, antiques, and artifacts. The home was outside Nashua, New Hampshire. I went and found myself in my element, with many boxes of books and documents spread out on the lawn as well as inside the house. In one box I found manuscript pages that appeared to have been written by Henry David Thoreau, which I knew were rare and valuable. What I didn't know was that there was a pecking order among the rare-book dealers, and if the old established bookseller Goodspeed's was bidding on something, no one else competed.

I never encountered anything like this in the rare-coin business and wasn't aware of it until after I bought many lots. Several antiquarian booksellers told me I had surprised Goodspeed's representative, Arnold Silverman, who had expected to buy all the documents at low prices without any competition.

I had spent a lot more money than I intended and knew I needed to think about selling most of what I had bought to replenish my business capital. I was inadvertently becoming a dealer, though my passion had certainly made it inevitable. I reasoned that I would rather be the temporary owner of historical letters and documents than only acquire those that I could afford as a collector. I made a practical, but less rational, business decision to sell my inventory of rare coins—a field of collecting where I was well established—and embark at the bottom of the totem pole in my new passion. I knew little about the structure of the business, the dealers, or the best methods to find collectors. I had no business plan for the first time. But I knew that this was what I wanted to do, and I took the plunge. I had done well enough financially that I could coast for a while.

Then, in the middle of the night of March 28, 1961, disaster struck. My mother woke me to tell me that she thought my father was dead. I ran downstairs to my basement office and found that it was true.

I was panic stricken. His financial problems were over, our gut-wrenching fear when he didn't come home on time at night was over, the alcoholism that was his only escape from bankruptcy would no longer be rotting away his life. At 51 years of age, it was over, but he left us behind to face poverty, regrets, abandonment, and, for me, more than a decade searching for an understanding of him, the failures in his life, and how they drove him into alcoholism and prescription-drug abuse.

My father had escaped, but we had not.

After the failure of my parents' drugstore, my mother completed studies to become a nurse. She now had to work two eight-hour shifts per day to bring in enough money to survive. While I had been, for a few years, successful enough in my coin business to help out financially, I was now moving into a new field and my income was at a standstill.

The effect of my father's death on me was monumental. I felt tremendous guilt about giving up a lucrative coin business and going, at the age of 17, into a new field that might not be financially successful.

My father had been instrumental in my success and encouraged me in every idea I had, and I buried my anger that he died. My mother, always the stable parent, showed tremendous mental and physical strength at a horrible time, and the only thing I could do to help was to make meals. Losing a parent at a young age is devastating under any circumstances, but under these circumstances—with tremendous regrets about feelings not expressed, taking his unconditional support for granted, guilt at being angry at what had happened, and the decade-long, almost-debilitating challenge of reconciling the combination of his strengths and weaknesses—made it very difficult to come to terms with who I was during my 20s.

Shortly after my father's death I received a draft notice for the Army. In the process of trying to figure out how not to go, I met a psychiatrist named Gerry Davidson and spent years in psychotherapy with him. He changed my life, saving me from a life of debilitating regrets and the enormous conflict I felt between my father's and my own love of people, and how my father's weakness in business led to his ruin. Thanks to my years of working with Gerry Davidson, I was able to settle in myself the feelings of caring about people without letting those feelings lead to my own destruction the way my father's had led to his.

Chapter 5

Entering the World of Historical Documents: The 1960s

The spring of 1961 was an extremely transformative time for me. I had made the intellectual and financial decision to leave my successful rare-coin business to enter a completely new field, where I knew I was starting from the bottom. I had quite literally fallen in love with my venture into the world of historical letters and documents. I was, at heart, a collector.

I was turning 18 years old, and for the first time since I was 12, I had no income. I was graduating from high school and assumed I would go to a local college in Boston and carry on my business pursuits. The balance of academics and business had worked well during high school.

My father's death changed everything, and there was now no alternative to working full time and attending school at night. I enrolled at Boston University's night school.

Night school was a tougher grind than I expected. Working all day and going to class at 6 o'clock at night, and then sitting in another class at 8 p.m., was exhausting. Plus, I was studying difficult subjects that required detailed attention but did not ignite my passions.

Contrary to common assumptions, I studied business in college. I did not study history and literature there. These subjects were and are still my passions, and I could learn everything I needed to know by doing my own reading. I was practical about my formal education: I focused on accounting, business law, advertising, office efficiency, and business planning—all subjects that I knew would be critical, especially since I was operating with very limited capital.

I faced such a monumental self-education task in my new field that my own time was the most valuable asset in my business plan, and I had to carefully eliminate every activity that wasn't worth the expenditure of my time.

Office efficiency was particularly important. I had to invest my profits into inventory and keep expenses at a minimum, while running a business that required high levels of service to collectors and efficient buying, cataloging, and selling of letters and documents. It wasn't until I was in my new business for a full two years that I hired a part-time secretary and bought a dictation machine.

My focus on business efficiency was inspired by reading biographies. People read biographies for a variety of reasons: inspiration, escape, fascination with other people's lives. I read them first and foremost to learn how people became successful. When I was young my favorite book was *The Age of Moguls*, and I put the businessmen profiled in it on pedestals. I was in awe of these men and thought that they must have superhuman qualities and no concerns about the ordinary trials and tribulations of life that everyone else was concerned about.

When I first encountered original letters written by some of the great presidents, I enjoyed them for the same reason: These letters were insights into the lives of extraordinarily successful people. But beyond being able to get a sense of why they succeeded, I felt a deep and personal connection with these great men. Their letters were about their real lives. Their handwriting ignited my excitement about these great men being actual human beings, not just characters in history.

This emotion that I felt was practically overwhelming—and ultimately life-changing in greater ways than I ever imagined.

The world of historical letters and documents is a virtual time machine that takes us into the lives of individuals in culture and history whose genius has touched us, whose accomplishments have inspired us, and whose efforts have influenced our present-day lives. History and the people who made it are the keys to who we are today and who we may be tomorrow. These men and women of history confronted many of the same feelings and fears that we all do today, and they persevered to achieve in exceptional ways.

While many people may think of collecting as an intellectual pursuit, it is an emotional one as well. The most significant factor in this area is the individual interpretation and assessment of the importance of the content of a letter or manuscript. Every piece, except those of a routine nature, is unique, and there can be enormous differences of opinion as to the significance of individual pieces. As I entered the world of historical documents, I saw this was both good and bad. Since everything was unique, I could apply my own interpretation to a piece, and if my interpretation of the importance was agreed to by a collector, I had a good chance of selling it. If no one else agreed with my interpretation, then I would have tied up scarce capital that I could not afford in something I couldn't sell.

Getting started in this new business was daunting. Unlike rare coins, there were no shows where collectors and dealers met. The only dealer in Boston was Goodspeed's and they would be as hostile toward me, I assumed, as they were when I outbid them in the New Hampshire estate auction. My best hope was the Manuscript Society, a national organization that had a quarterly publication and an annual meeting that rotated around the country. The Manuscript Society had about 1,300 collectors, archivists, and a few dealers as members, and their membership directory was readily available. It was a viable way for me to get started.

I cataloged the letters that I had collected from Dave Bowers and Mary Benjamin. I wanted my first catalog of presidential letters to be finely printed with good illustrations, well-written descriptions, and prices that were essentially what I had paid. Mary Benjamin's prices represented the market, and I didn't see how I could add a profit.

I included some Revolutionary War letters of John Hancock and

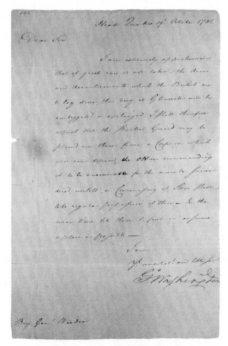

A Revolutionary War–era letter written by George Washington.

Paul Revere. The last page of the catalog described the Henry David Thoreau manuscripts purchased at the New Hampshire auction. Those manuscripts resonated with me—Thoreau wrote that culture comes from nature, not from manmade implements, and embellished his proposition with lengthy philosophical arguments.

I sent the catalog to the entire membership of the Manuscript Society. It was very successful. The first order I received was from the University of Iowa Library, which bought a George Washington letter for $650. I was on my way in my new business!

My second catalog was devoted to nineteenth-century prints, almost all by Currier and Ives. Because color printing was prohibitively expensive, I had to print the catalog in black and white. I failed to appreciate that I could not adequately convey the quality of lithographs in black and white.

I had moved my business from the enclosed back porch of our family house to the basement, and I installed paneling to display the Currier and Ives prints. This was naive and not thought out—I don't think anyone ever came to my basement office to look at prints. My efforts with Currier and Ives prints turned out to be short-lived. I kept several of my favorite prints and sold the rest to New York galleries. I learned that just because I found a field of historical

My first catalog.

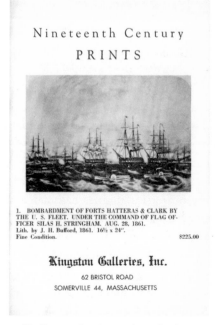

My first and only catalog of prints.

artifacts exciting and interesting did not mean that I could create a viable business in that area.

Overall, the historical document business was the opposite of rare coins. Finding out who the collectors were was easy; it seemed almost everyone was a member of the Manuscript Society. Finding material to buy was much more difficult. I endlessly went to estate auctions, used bookstores, and antique stores all over New England. At that time, there were many specialists in autograph material. While these dealers were not very excited to sell important pieces to another dealer, they were very happy to get rid of letters by less important historical figures. Inexpensive historical letters and documents are time consuming, and less interesting, and they were all happy to have me buy as much as I could. There were also many rare-book dealers throughout the country who handled autograph material, though they were not specialists.

I had to identify areas where I could fulfill a need. I realized dealers likely didn't go to visit collectors or travel to smaller university libraries and historical societies. Photocopies hadn't been invented and dealers made the collectors come to them. I decided to drive around the country to meet potential clients.

I had to be ruthless with my expenses and camped out everywhere I went. During my first stop at Syracuse University, one of the librarians asked me at lunch at the Faculty Club where I was staying. "In Green Park," I replied. Someone commented that they hadn't realized that a motel had been built there.

"I don't know about that," I replied, explaining that I was staying "in" Green Park—at a campground. I don't know whether they were impressed or horrified, but they were astonished!

As I drove thousands of miles to visit collectors and librarians, I developed a useful knowledge of where you could camp reasonably near big cities and universities. An exception was Indiana University in Bloomington, where I had to stay in a Howard Johnson motel—until I was kicked out for cooking in my room.

Apart from the inconveniences of camping, this trip was invaluable. Numerous university libraries had budgets to collect archival material in their geographical areas. The University of Kentucky, for example, collected letters by Henry Clay and other Kentuckians. Also, many historical societies had budgets to collect relatively inexpensive letters and documents relating to the history of their areas. I could readily find this material in the dormant inventories of some of the major manuscript dealers. An example was the Rutherford B. Hayes Presidential Library & Museums, which was interested in everyone associated with his administration.

I created a system for offering inexpensive letters. I sent packages of letters, individually priced, "on approval," and librarians could return anything not of interest. I quickly built a very profitable and viable business, transferring decades of unwanted accumulations of less expensive historical letters from long-established dealers to universities' and historical societies' libraries.

Goodspeed's turned out to be a gold mine for me. I met Gordon Banks, the man in charge of Goodspeed's historical letters department, at a Manuscript Society meeting. He was, to my utter surprise, welcoming and happy to sell me everything he could at a reasonable wholesale price. Gordon was married to George Goodspeed's sister, and his passion was not in making money for his brother-in-law. It was golf.

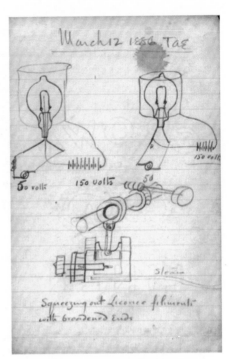

A drawing by Thomas Edison from his experiments in inventing the light bulb, signed with his initials.

The only auctions were at Parke-Bernet, later Sotheby's. They were the major auction house for expensive works of art and antiques, and the historical manuscripts department was a minor part of the overall business. Their manuscript auctions were focused for dealers, not collectors; descriptions were brief, and it was necessary to examine every lot in advance so you knew what was in it and if it was genuine. What they thought wouldn't sell for much was put into large lots, and for me these offered great opportunity. It was rumored that they once offered a lot cataloged as "a box of contents." I attended every auction, and they were a good source of material to catalog properly and offer for sale.

During a second driving trip around the country, I could afford to stay in motels. I focused on visiting private collectors to find out more about what interested them. This was very successful; an unexpected benefit was that many had material they no longer wanted, and I was able to acquire it. In most instances I was the only dealer they had ever met. They had been buying exclusively from dealers' catalogs.

On this second road trip I went to see Philip Sang, the biggest collector of American historical letters and documents. I had heard that he was a tough person to do business with, so I was anxious as I drove to 3900 South Michigan Avenue in Chicago. I arrived early, but couldn't find his actual building. As I drove back and forth between the 3600 and 4200 blocks, I started to panic. Then I spotted, in the center of the block-long brick wall, a single opening with "3900" over a grand entrance. Phil Sang's office was inside an industrial complex that housed his dairy operation, which was the largest in the Midwest.

As I shook Mr. Sang's hand, he immediately struck me as an overwhelming personality. He was an aggressive collector, and he wanted me to know what interested him and wanted to make sure I would tell him about anything I might think important. This giant of the collecting field made this insignificant new dealer feel important, and until his death in 1975 Philip Sang was my most important client for American manuscripts. A crystal paperweight that he sent me as a Christmas gift 50 years ago still sits on my desk.

I was learning, voraciously, about new areas of American history and literature. I was also learning about evaluating historical letters and manuscripts. This includes how important someone was to his or her field, how important the field is to history, how important the content of a specific letter was to the person and their particular field, how rare it was for the person to write about the subject of the letter, and how rare the person's letters are in general. It could be estimated by their lifespan, but it frequently was a matter of how well known they were during their lifetime and after their death. Would someone finding a cache of their letters realize they should be saved? A classic example was the author of *Moby Dick*, Herman Melville. It was not until long after his death, when his novel became widely appreciated, that his name became recognized as a great writer. This was also true of Edgar Allan Poe and many others.

Forgeries were something dealers talked about in the context that they just "knew" what was genuine. Accumulating years of images in your brain of what paper and ink look like at different periods, and what the handwriting of prominent figures normally looks like, creates an instant reaction. There were several forgers who were well known from earlier in the twentieth century; they focused on major figures like George Washington and Abraham Lincoln. Knowing what their forgeries looked like created a false sense among dealers that they couldn't be fooled; more recent forgers were aware of overcoming the aging issues and the skill needed to imitate handwriting. Nothing had been written on the subject of historical forgery detection. Expertise relied solely on the experience of seeing genuine handwritten documents, and not on any conscious forensic analytical ability.

Forming relationships with academic, collector, and library groups was an important part of my developing business in the 1960s. The established dealers acted as islands that everyone had to come to, but no one was going to come to me at first, so I went to where they gathered together. I attended the annual conference of the Association of College and Research Libraries (and later was a frequent speaker) and the Manuscript Society (I became president a decade later), and regularly presented papers at the Society of American Archivists, the American Library Association, and other more specialized groups.

The most inspirational book about the manuscript and rare-book world was and still is a biography of A.S.W. Rosenbach, published in 1960. Rosenbach was a collector at heart but a businessman by necessity. He saw no limit to what his clients could or should collect. He operated in the Gilded Age and moved into prominence around 1910, when enterprising American business pioneers were accumulating tremendous wealth and wanted to bring culture into their lives. They had virtually unlimited money, and Rosenbach had equally unlimited horizons regarding what he could find in Europe to sell to them. His biggest client for many decades was Henry E. Huntington, the streetcar pioneer and magnate. The Huntington Library in California is the extraordinary result of the collaboration between these two giant personalities.

From the early part of the twentieth century to the start of the Depression in 1929, Rosenbach bought almost everything important that came up at auction in America and England. I felt the same passion for historical manuscripts, and the same appreciation for limitless opportunities in collecting. I read the Rosenbach biography several times and fixed in my mind a photograph of his New York office: a double-height, theater-like library with antique furniture, sculptures, paintings, and tall bookcases. I couldn't imagine a better setting for offering great collections to the titans of business.

Baronial splendor: The book room of A.S.W. Rosenbach's last "store" in New York.

This was in my mind when I was invited to meet Rosenbach's successor, John Fleming, who was interested in acquiring some manuscripts I had by the first Chief Justice, John Jay. I still recall the excitement as a butler escorted me into Rosenbach's old "office," that grand stage set in the photograph. Fleming, a plain-looking man about 50 years old, welcomed me and we sat in two of Rosenbach's large antique upholstered chairs. But then Fleming offered me half my price for the manuscripts. He said the man who sold the John Jay documents to me, Frank Monaghan, was his source, not mine, and I was poaching on his turf. Fleming said matter-of-factly that I could sell the manuscripts to him for half my price and he would forget this intrusion, or he would ruin me in business. I was stunned, but I firmly turned him down. Perhaps because I had been through so much in life, I wasn't going to be bullied.

When I told Frank Monaghan the story, he was so incensed and supportive that he subsequently gave me larger groups of letters on consignment. Monaghan's collection became an important source for me. After Fleming died

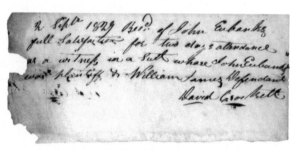

A letter signed by Davy Crockett.

I bought much of the antique furniture that was in Rosenbach's office. Today these symbols of Rosenbach's "golden years," especially the chairs Fleming and I sat in, are part of my office.

The rare-book dealers in the United States were great sources of interesting letters and documents, but once I bought what they had, they were not acquiring anything new. It occurred to me in 1967 that rare-book shops in London could be a similar source. I studied English history, culture, and literature. I also educated myself about the rarity of the handwriting of leading historical figures and the current value of letters of varying importance.

While I was excited to expand my horizon to England, I was mindful of a general resentment against America. People in England appreciated what the United States did in World War II, but they saw Americans as too boastful, too rich, too stubbornly opinionated, and lacking the genteel manners they cherished. I was very careful not to be any of the American stereotypes, and I was welcomed everywhere.

The English rare-book dealers never socialized with each other or even did business with each other, yet they took me to their clubs for lunch and invited me to their country houses on weekends. I was the young, new, and respectful dealer and was well treated by these well-established dealers. They showed me their historical letters and documents. In many cases I saw pieces no one had looked at for decades, and they bore prices established two or three currency devaluations earlier. If I bought a letter signed by T.E. Lawrence or Charles Dickens for $500, for example, I could price it $600, but I was also shown boxes of letters from minor authors—200 letters by the same author priced at a dollar each. I could sell them as a collection at a rate of

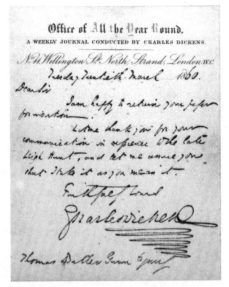

A hand-written note by Charles Dickens.

$10 per letter to university libraries. While other American dealers focused only on buying the most prestigious pieces, I focused on what gave me the best return on my limited money. During the second half of the 1960s I averaged 18 trips a year to London. I also exhibited at the London Antiquarian Book Fair, the first American to do so, and while I neither bought nor sold very much, the dealers appreciated my support and could claim that it was an "international" book fair for the first time. They were very helpful in referring collections to me that were not on the level they wanted to handle.

The only specialist in historical letters was a young man named John Wilson, who worked at Maggs Bros., a venerable old firm in Mayfair. They had an excellent inventory, priced higher than the non-specialists. We had a great chemistry, and John invited me to stop by his flat before we went to dinner. He was living in one room, with a shared bathroom down the hall, and cooking on a hotplate that was fueled by putting shillings in the gas meter beside the bed.

This was a man who knew the historical letter and document field

John Wilson in my basement office in the mid-1960s.

better than anyone in England and was selling tens or maybe hundreds of thousands of dollars' worth of material each year. Over the course of a few visits I offered to start a business with him. Putting up about $14,000 was a very big investment for me. I knew that John would be shunned if other English dealers knew he was in business with an American, so I was the silent partner. Our partnership lasted for decades, and our friendship for life.

I exhibited at the Los Angeles Antiquarian Book Fair around 1961 or 1962.

At the same time that I was developing my sources of material in England, I was also relentlessly expanding in every way I could in the United States. I exhibited at the New York and California Antiquarian Book Fairs. Both were good sources to meet collectors. My client base had begun to include some well-known leaders and businessmen. Many interesting and successful people are fascinated by other interesting and successful people in history.

I was also studying the French language, history, and literature. I reasoned that Americans would be interested in the major figures of French history but not the lesser-known figures. Everyone knew Napoleon, Marie Antoinette, Louis XVI, Louis Pasteur, and Marcel Proust, and I thought American university libraries could have an interest in French literary letters. The most respected dealer, Michael Castaing, had an office that dated back to the middle of the nineteenth century. He spoke reasonably good English, but always with the same initial greeting: "But I have noth-ing, I have noth-ing," before pulling out half a dozen important and fairly priced manuscripts.

At the other end of the spectrum of business attitudes was Jacques Lambert, who was not at all friendly and spoke not a word of English. He had made money in the fashion business and invested heavily in his extraordinary inventory. He had at least 300 letters of Napoleon and hundreds of letters of almost every major figure in French history and literature. I bought vast quantities of letters from him and found my limit when he told me I was buying so much I had to pay him in gold bars (which I learned I could buy at a French bank). The few rare-book dealers did have documents for sale, but not on the level of the English.

My lack of major capital turned out to be a problem in Paris, where I was interested only in major historical figures, and my profit percentage was therefore less.

My catalogs very quickly started to integrate the French material and I found a very good market for it. The French dealers didn't send catalogs to America, few Americans could write or speak French, and if they visited Paris they never ventured into any of the dealers' shops, assuming they would be as aloof as other Parisians. I started to hear about American university libraries that collected French authors. These contacts came about at library conferences where I asked many people I knew if they were aware of any French collections in America. I found out, for example, that the University of Illinois had an interest in Marcel Proust. Lambert had approximately 75 excellent-content Proust letters in stock which, over a period of years, I sold to them.

John Wilson told me about an interesting character who was advertising for historical documents. In 1970 Ray Rawlins was a retired British colonial governor of several African colonies, who lived on the Isle of Man. Wilson was interested in a more important level than what Rawlins was finding, and suggested I contact him. Rawlins invited me to come to the Isle of Man, a summer holiday island in the Irish Sea. He told me it was easy to get there, but that depended on your perspective, and while the Isle of Man might be a wonderful summer holiday location, I first went there in the winter.

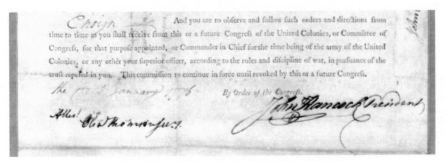

Portion of a document signed by John Hancock,
appointing an ensign in the colonial army.

Rawlins, with all the affectations of the British upper class, was basically a friendly and charming character. He had the ruddy face of a life in Africa.

Listening to his stories about his career, I thought "African adventurer" described him. While he was certainly pompous, being sent to these countries held no glory and the living quarters for the governor sounded quite primitive.

Rawlins, through his advertisements, was offered a lot of material not of interest to him for his collection, so he was buying this to sell. He had no interest in dealing with collectors and was very interested in our working out a relationship. I was also interested because he could be an important part of my concept of creating a supply system from attics, through me, to collectors. I wanted to have as few steps and bottlenecks in this process as possible, and having a good agent dealing with people who found the documents in their family papers was a major step. I bought, quite literally, hundreds of documents and letters on this first visit and for many years went to the Isle of Man at least once a month.

The second time I went there I was invited to stay in his guest room in his comfortable and pleasant house, set on a hillside overlooking farm fields and the ocean. I learned, uncomfortably, that the heat of Africa had made Rawlins and his family love the cold of the Isle of Man, and they had the windows and doors open so that the wind blowing up the hillside went through their house. I kept insulated long underwear in London for my visits. Apart from the enormous amount of material I was purchasing from him, I always enjoyed my visits. His wife prepared picnic lunches, which we took to dramatic cliff tops overlooking the Irish Sea and to beaches that, if you lived in a British city, must have seemed heavenly. Their social life was very active, and I attended many parties. In preparation for my first one, I was told we were going to a party of "eyewuzzes" and I asked what that meant. They told me I would find out, and within a minute or two of arriving someone introduced themselves with "I was the director of" something or other. The island was a tax-free financial refuge of retired British people.

As a young teenager, I had put many people—especially political leaders and businessmen—on pedestals. A person who came into my business life in the latter part of the 1960s changed my view of some of them. Seymour Halpern was a congressman from New York City and the Republican chairman of several important House committees. He was a very personable politician. He loved collecting historical letters and documents, and I went to Washington to see him several times a month. He arranged for me to stay at the Congressional Hotel, where he was living, and every night I socialized with him and his circle of friends. These were senators and congressmen who I frequently saw in the news and thought impressive. Getting to know them night after night, when they were not performing for the media, was a rude awakening. As they spouted opinions on subjects they knew nothing about, they fell off their pedestals. This was my first time seeing living public figures as private people, and I was shocked.

Halpern walked me onto the floor of Congress for many historic events, including the astronauts returning from the moon in July 1969. I was in awe of the people I shook hands with on the floor of Congress, but my overall indelible memory is learning that behind the public images of so many politicians were human beings with the same inconsistencies as the rest of us.

Harry Truman was the great exception. He stayed on his high pedestal. As a kid, I had read several of Truman's books and thought him a real and unpretentious person. I have no idea where I got the nerve to write him a letter saying that I would like to meet him, but I received a personally signed response that if I was in Independence, Missouri, his hometown, when he was also, he would be happy to meet me. In 1963, at the age of 20, I drove cross-country, and Harry Truman met with me for more than an hour. He answered every question I had. I asked him how he thought he would be evaluated by history.

President Harry Truman wrote me a short note and signed this photo in 1962.

He told me that he had no idea—no one could form an accurate historical perspective until 50 or 75 years after the events—but he had done his honest best in an impossible job. Truman was amazingly humble.

When I asked about his relationship with Eisenhower, Truman said he liked him up until the point he became president. He disliked the way Eisenhower, as president, dropped his old friends in favor of big businessmen, who

Congressman Seymour Halpern and President Dwight Eisenhower.

became his new social circle. Decades later I asked John Eisenhower, Eisenhower's only child and a close friend of mine, what he thought of Truman's assessment. John told me he thought there was a lot of truth in it.

Toward the end of the decade a new source of material developed for me. Charles Hamilton, a flamboyant New York City dealer who had a midtown street-level gallery, had mainly offered framed documents for sale and wholesaled less expensive pieces to me. He decided to use his talent for attracting publicity to start a new auction business, and it successfully brought in consignments from people who hadn't realized the potential value of what they had. Catalog descriptions were minimal, which gave me the opportunity to research what was offered and frequently buy many underrepresented documents. Additionally, after each auction at the Waldorf Astoria, he held a large party for everyone, and it became a good chance to meet the new collectors his extravagant publicity had attracted. He and I could not have been more unalike in our business attitudes. He shot from the hip, with quick opinions on everything to get publicity. Still, we became good friends and had monthly luncheons right up to the week he died in 1996.

As interesting as all the personalities were, the practical issues of the business were never far from my mind. My first catalog, in 1960, was expensively produced, and almost everything was priced at what I had paid. I knew I would lose money in the short term, but the goal was to establish myself with an impressive first catalog. After that I issued typed price lists on 8" by 10" sheets, printed on a hand press by a local printer. Costs were even lower because I did some of the press work myself, pulling the just-printed page from the press and

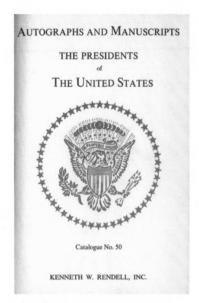

AUTOGRAPHS AND MANUSCRIPTS

THE PRESIDENTS
of
THE UNITED STATES

Catalogue No. 50

KENNETH W. RENDELL, INC.

New York City dealer Charles Hamilton.   *Catalog 50*, published 1969.

inserting a new piece of paper before the press closed again. By the latter part of the decade I was selling approximately $300,000 a year, which likely was exceeded only by one or two other dealers. Eventually I produced catalogs on reasonably good paper, with attractive covers. In 1969, as I approached Catalog 50, I wanted to commemorate my progress. I published an 82-page catalog of "Presidents of the United States"—the same title as my first catalog. For the first time I wrote a preface:

> During these nine years, I have derived much enjoyment from rela-
> tionships with collectors and librarians, and satisfaction from placing
> autograph and manuscript material in collections where it is appreci-
> ated. These past nine years have also provided a source of frustration:
> the disappearance from the market of much of the fine material avail-
> able when I began. Such lamenting is an "occupational hazard" for
> collectors and dealers alike. The Roman scholar Pliny complained of
> the scarcity of letters by Julius Caesar; chroniclers of the manuscript
> business in 1920 and again in 1930 lamented the disappearance of the
> "good old days." I recall that in 1960 collectors and dealers were speak-
> ing of the "good old days" of the 1940s and 1950s. Today, the early
> 1960s are spoken of in these terms. It is sometimes difficult to realize,
> but today will be "the good old days" in a few years.

Chapter 6

The 1970s: The International Decade

Ten years after starting in the historical documents business, I thought developing clients in Europe would be the next logical step. This was 1970 and all my sales, at this point $325,000 a year, were coming from the United States. I knew Europe would be a much greater challenge, but I was thriving on challenges. No American dealer made any effort to reach European collectors, but I hadn't gotten where I was in business by listening to conventional wisdom.

I read in the Rosenbach biography that Martin Bodmer was the most important collector of European manuscripts and rare books in the world. He was extraordinarily rich, lived in Geneva, Switzerland, and collected on an institutional scale. With no expectations, I sent Bodmer the first catalog I published in this new decade—an interesting array of material, mostly American but also important European letters and documents. I received in return a typewritten postcard ordering four pieces, including a letter Benjamin Franklin wrote to his grandson while he was in Paris to negotiate the treaty to end the American Revolution. Franklin had enrolled his grandson in school in Geneva and gave him advice on what he needed to learn to be successful in life.

Bodmer also ordered a signature of John Milton and a lengthy Henry David Thoreau manuscript from the initial New Hampshire auction. Thoreau extolled the importance of silence, the annoyance of people who talk too much, and, reminiscent of Walden, the value of being alone to think uninterruptedly. The fourth piece was a George Washington letter about the pending war with France and his return from the presidency to lead the American army.

I had already sold the Milton, but Bodmer's total came to $20,000. This was the largest catalog order I had ever received.

Assuming Bodmer was elderly, I decided not to send the package by air mail, which would take ten days, but to pay $100 for Pan American Airways' air freight for overnight delivery. A week later, after a long day, I opened *Time* magazine with a glass of wine and saw at the top of the "Milestones" page: "Died: Martin Bodmer, manuscript and rare book collector." *I* nearly died!

I stayed up to call his office once it was morning in Geneva. I was told that Bodmer had opened my package, reviewed the letters, and approved payment. I would get a check shortly.

If I had sent the package by regular air mail, it would have arrived after his death. Bodmer's postcard sits framed on a shelf in my office. It is both a souvenir of my first major catalog order and a constant reminder to never hesitate and never take the future for granted.

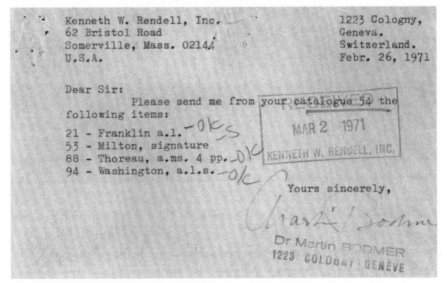

The postcard I received from Martin Bodmer in 1971, ordering several documents.

Soon after this I went to Geneva, at the invitation of Bodmer's librarian, to see his collection. I was hoping he had a family who intended to continue his collecting.

Bodmer's library was magnificent, situated down the hill from his extraordinary mansion overlooking Lake Geneva. There were two classical buildings facing one another on each side of a courtyard and fountain, surrounded by beautiful gardens. The librarian walked me around display cases holding spectacular manuscripts and rare books from ancient times to the early twentieth century. I was not yet over the shock of seeing all that when he ushered me into an elevator, and we went down to what turned out to be the main part of the library, underground.

It was amazing—complete musical manuscripts of Mozart, Beethoven, and Wagner; literary manuscripts of Goethe and the major French writers; and many more. Ancient manuscripts, including early gospels, were beyond comprehension in a private collection. Bodmer had arranged for his collection to become a public foundation and for his archives to be available to researchers.

It was an extraordinary start to the business of selling to collectors in Europe, but totally misleading. My first experience, with the pinnacle of collectors, abruptly came to an end.

I went back to my fundamental concept of determining where I could add value. If I wanted to be successful developing collectors in Europe, I had to improve the process and make it easier for collectors to buy and sell.

France, I believed, was not likely to be successful. Everyone in France could easily visit the very competent Paris dealers who also published catalogs. I did exhibit at one Antiquarian Book Fair in Paris and met several Arabs who had been educated in France and were interested in collecting European manuscripts. One in particular later bought several Mozart manuscripts from me, making the venture financially successful. Brussels and Amsterdam were cities I periodically visited to see if the rare-book dealers had found any new manuscript material, but I never thought of them as possibly having a significant collector market I could develop. It was impossible to either buy or sell historical documents in Italy. An export license was necessary, along with other government regulations, and because of that there were no dealers in Italy, and without them, collectors didn't develop.

One Italian couple had moved to southern France to start their business. Renato and Rosine Saggiori exuded excitement for the material. When I first met them, they were living in a very small, rented house on a busy street in the town of Apt, outside of Marseilles. They had a very small inventory and very big personalities. Within a few years they had bought an old house in Gordes,

Richard Wagner's autographed manuscript of *Tannhäuser* (left), and an autographed manuscript of Ludwig von Beethoven (above).

Renato and Rosine Saggiori with their children and my son Jason, at their home in Geneva, Switzerland.

with an extensive garden. They were buying French material from French people, similar to Rawlins on the Isle of Man, and I started visiting them almost every month.

My visits with the Saggioris were always good business and great fun. We all spoke French reasonably well, but they had heavy Italian accents and spoke rapidly. I frequently had trouble understanding them; when we reached an impasse, we resorted to German. None of us spoke it quickly, but we understood each other well enough.

Over the years we did a huge amount of business together and enjoyed our personal relationship very much. They regularly went to Paris for auctions at Hôtel Drouot; these auctions were not like those in any other country. Frequently there were no catalogs or listings; material was just put into lots, and you had to go and see what was going to be auctioned. The Saggioris worked very hard going to every auction, which became a major source for them, and consequently for me.

My passport became so full that I had to get another.

My dealings in Europe included many important French documents, including a letter signed by Napoleon Bonaparte.

A 1776 marriage agreement signed by Louis XVI and Marie Antoinette.

The prices of German historical manuscripts were the strongest in Europe. Germans were avid collectors of their cultural history, especially music, and there were good German dealers they could buy from. There was also an excellent auction house in the university town of Marburg. I didn't see anything in Germany that I could improve upon.

I did exhibit at an International Antiquarian Book Fair in Cologne to look for collectors interested in non-German culture. The summer before the fair, I put myself through a Berlitz total-immersion program to speak German.

A week before that Cologne book fair, in the offices of a rare-book dealer in London, I was leafing through a book on a table. The dealer told me that it was the most important woodcut book of the Italian Renaissance. Half a dozen of the 75 woodcut pages of the *Hypnerotomachia Poliphili* had been damaged, so the book was unsaleable. The dealer said a complete version would sell for $150,000, but this incomplete copy, a "cripple" in the trade, was available for $3,500. He added that I would be crazy to buy it because I'd never be able to sell it.

On an instinct that I could sell some of the individual pages, I bought this "cripple" copy, with a broken spine and loose pages. On the second day of the book fair the London dealer came by my exhibit, noticed half a dozen pages displayed on a bookshelf, and told me not to waste the space exhibiting them because no one would buy them. I said I appreciated his not having told me the day before; not knowing I couldn't sell any, I had sold 27. While I did do well selling German manuscript material, mostly bought in Paris, my instinct that there would be rare-book collectors who could never hope to own a complete copy of this book, and would want a woodcut page from the most important illustrated Italian Renaissance work, was borne out. The experience would be similar to many others in my career: I didn't believe I couldn't do something that everyone else assumed was impossible, and since I didn't know I couldn't do it, I did it.

As I realized I could build a viable business in Europe, John Wilson and I decided to buy a flat in London. This was around 1970. Our large apartment was on Wigmore Street, parallel to Oxford Street, near the top of Bond Street in Mayfair. This put us in an excellent position to invite private collectors to visit, as well as people who wanted to sell. John had a strong following among collectors in London, and I gave him pieces on consignment from my inventory in Boston to offer to his clients.

My first major client in London was Alistair McAlpine. He was 31 years old, with a cherubic face, multiple chins, a prematurely receding hairline, and a permanently rumpled appearance. McAlpine told me that he was interested in some of the French artists' letters I had displayed at the New York Book Fair in 1973. I went to see him in the London headquarters of the construction company founded by his grandfather, Sir Robert McAlpine. The McAlpine family was the biggest contractor in England and owned the largest private airline and properties such as the Dorchester Hotel. I brought an attaché case full of letters by French artists, as well as some French authors McAlpine had

POLIPHILO QVIVI NARRA,CHE GLI PARVE AN‑
CORA DI DORMIRE,ET ALTRONDE IN SOMNO
RITROVARSE IN VNA CONVALLE,LA QVALE NEL
FINE ERA SERATA DE VNA MIRABILE CLAVSVRA
CVM VNA PORTENTOSA PYRAMIDE,DE ADMI‑
RATIONE DIGNA,ET VNO EXCELSO OBELISCO DE
SOPRA.LAQVALE CVM DILIGENTIA ET PIACERE
SVBTILMENTE LA CONSIDEROE.

A SPAVENTEVOLE SILVA,ET CONSTI‑
pato Nemore euaso,& gli primi altri lochi per el dolce
somno che se hauea per le fesse & prosternate mébre dif‑
fuso relicti,me ritrouai di nouo in uno piu delectabile
sito assai piu che el præcedente.Elquale non era de mon
ti horridi,& crepidinose rupe intorniato, ne falcato di
strumosi iugi. Ma compositamente de grate montagniole di non tro‑
po altecia. Siluose di giouani quercioli, di roburi,fraxini & Carpi‑
ni,& di frondosi Esculi,& Ilice,& di teneri Coryli,& di Alni,& di Ti‑
lie,& di Opio,& de infructuosi Oleastri, dispositi secondo lapecto de
gli arboriferi Colli.Et giu al piano erano grate siluule di altri siluatici

A woodcut page from a "cripple" copy of the *Hypnerotomachia Poliphili*, which
I sold in Cologne, Germany. While the book's damage reduced its value as a
complete book, I guessed—correctly—that I could sell the individual pages.

asked me about. He quickly thumbed through the several hundred pieces. Then he asked, "How much for everything?"

I typically planned for every possibility, but I had never imagined that possibility. I had to rapidly add the pieces up in my head because he had called his assistant into his office and moved on to another subject.

I feared that I was going to make a mistake and tell him too low a figure, but I also worried that if I erred the other way, he would say no and I would lose the opportunity for future business. Whether I was accurate or not, I will never know. McAlpine agreed to my price, seemingly on gut instinct, and buzzed someone to come in and pay me. I left, dumbfounded.

This was the beginning of my relationship with Alistair McAlpine. Soon I was buying hundreds of letters in France written by French artists—Monet, Cézanne, Renoir, Gauguin—and immediately selling them to McAlpine. I was going back and forth between London and Paris weekly. Our relationship became intense. I went to his house in the country most weekends, had Sunday lunch with his family, and dined regularly with him, but beneath his charm was a steely character.

His marriage ended soon after I got to know him, and he bought a new country estate he named West Green. I was a regular fixture at his Sunday lunches, where he entertained acquaintances from his social and business worlds. He collected paintings, as well as antiques, and a very frequent Sunday conversation centered on where Alistair bought all the wonderful things in his house. He always told people about particular galleries in the Mayfair section of London and, after everyone had left one Sunday, I commented to Alistair that he must be getting a good commission from the galleries. He corrected me: He wasn't getting any commission; he secretly *owned* the galleries. He was a real operator in everything he did, and it made me particularly pleased that he took me into his confidence and proudly told me about many of his schemes.

Alistair McAlpine with
Margaret Thatcher in 1975.

McAlpine's country house was blown up by the Irish Republican Army (IRA).

Alistair is one of the most interesting and contradictory personalities I have known. He could be impervious in his upper-class attitudes and yet express sincere concern for the plight of the lower economic class. One night at the exclusive London club Annabel's, he was lamenting the plight of pensioners who had to choose between food and coal, and said the government had to do much more to help them. I told him that he didn't sound like the treasurer of the Conservative Party (and Margaret Thatcher's patron); he replied, "I think the government needs to do all of these things, but just don't take my money to do it with." I told him I thought he was the only honest politician.

I was buying so aggressively that the supply of letters by French artists and authors eventually ran out. Alistair's interest in what he had collected also waned. The excitement of pursuit and conquest, not possession, was what interested him. He wanted me to sell his collection, and I was well positioned to do so.

Coincidentally, I was working on what turned out to be a 205-page catalog of letters and manuscripts of French authors and artists. I bought back McAlpine's collection and then sold most of it to the new Getty Museum in Los Angeles and to an American in Paris, Daniel Sickles. A wealthy descendent of a Union general in the Civil War, Sickles greeted me at his home on the Île Saint-Louis, in the middle of the River Seine, with a paper bag full of French currency and a declaration that he would not be buying anything further. He considered his collection complete!

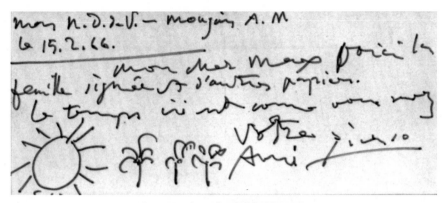

A note written by Pablo Picasso.

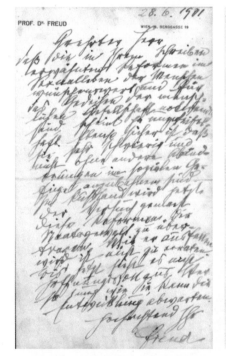

A letter by Sigmund Freud.

A letter by Paul Gauguin.

Meanwhile, my base in Boston was strengthening. In 1973 I moved my business from the basement of the house I grew up in, which I was paying my grandfather $100 a month to rent, to a new office building where rent was $1,200 a month. The new offices allowed me to double my staff, primarily researchers, and create a conservation laboratory, specializing in removing poor restoration work that would eventually harm manuscript paper and ink. It was the only one in the world operated by a dealer. I was also researching the forensic issues of modern forgery detection and set up a laboratory with these essential forensic tools to analyze handwriting, typewriting, paper, and ink.

Assembling an extensive file of facsimile handwriting of well-known individuals, I developed an ability to authenticate historical documents that was considered unmatched and unprecedented.

It is an important rule to recognize mistakes quickly and adjust to the unexpected reality of a situation. I have always applied this to documents I purchased: If I paid $100 for a document I later realized was worth only $75, I priced the document at $75. Conversely, if I paid $100, based on a belief that a fair sale price would be $150, but then discovered that the

Working conditions in the basement, as seen in this 1970 photo, became difficult.

From the basement of my family home to a suburban office park, 1973.

document was more important than I thought, I would price it at a fair price, regardless of what I had paid for it.

While the English dealers had welcomed me, the hospitality of London auctioneers was very different. Sotheby's and Christie's, the important auction houses, both had rare-book departments that sold historical letters and documents. The cataloging was a bare minimum and assumed dealers would view the material on site and arrive at their own opinions. Collectors never bid, except through dealers who charged a 10 percent commission. Official viewing times of the lots were very brief, but as I was to find out, the favored dealers could examine the material whenever they wanted.

London dealers explained to me the operation of "the ring": The dealers did not compete against each other at the auction (unless representing a client); they collectively agreed on the lots that the group would bid on as well as the specific amounts of the maximum bids. One dealer in this group was designated to buy all the lots without competition from the other dealers. After the official public auction the dealers in this group would, in a private and exclusive auction, bid against each other. This private auction was, in effect, the real auction. The monetary difference between the official auction and the "ring's" auction was divided among the dealers.

Theoretically, I could just bid against the ring, but, as I found out the first time I went to Sotheby's, it wasn't that simple. I attended the sale of manuscripts by the English composer Arthur Sullivan, of Gilbert and Sullivan fame. I was in full view of the auctioneer, but he ignored my bids. I was an outsider and, in retrospect, should have asked John Wilson to bid for me. The following day I went to see the dealer who bought them. He sold them to me for double what he paid at the auction. Even at double, they were a great bargain and found a home in the J. Pierpont Morgan Library in New York.

Notations by composer Arthur Sullivan.

While I was learning how English auctions really worked, I was also becoming directly involved in a situation that would shake up and revolutionize the system. A dealer who specialized in medieval manuscripts told me he employed a cataloger who was so good, and so fast, that he didn't have enough work for him. The dealer feared he would go to work for Sotheby's or Christie's, and he would lose his source of under-cataloged and undervalued manuscripts. He wanted me to hire the cataloger in Boston.

When I first met Roy Davids, the vaunted cataloger, in 1970, our chemistry was instant. We shared our views of the current market situation and the future. I was enormously impressed, but also realistic. He had learned about a very difficult area to catalog, he had enormous respect for the importance of manuscripts, and he shared my belief that efficiency was necessary to develop any business in the field. He would rapidly outgrow any job that I could offer him, and having learned the details of my business, potentially could be a dangerous competitor. We left it that we would maintain a close personal relationship.

The dealer's worst fear came to pass, and Roy Davids was hired as a cataloger at Sotheby's. His new job was the lowest on the totem pole. The head of the department, a titled Englishman referred to as Lord John, saw himself as the god at the top, and it was a totem pole, not a ladder where someone had the chance to climb up. Roy quickly shook up Sotheby's cataloging. Now it wasn't just the medieval dealer; it was all the dealers in London, including me, who were affected. Roy and I remained friends and Lord John did everything he could to block him, but Sotheby's had been bought by an American who introduced meritocracy, which gave Roy hope.

I always met Roy for lunch at the Westbury Hotel, the usual restaurant for Sotheby's executives. At one memorable lunch he told me he had asked Lord John for a raise, as he was doing the work of several experts; not only was he turned down, but he was told that he had no future there. Roy thought merit should be rewarded. I had noticed Lord John having lunch with a group, but neither of us paid

Roy Davids.

particular attention. We talked about what Roy would do after leaving Sotheby's and whether Christie's could be an option, though we both felt it was more poorly run than Sotheby's. We agreed to continue our conversation at dinner.

When Roy walked into the restaurant in the evening, he had a great smile on his face and said that he had been called into his boss's office after lunch. and Lord John said, "All right, all right, we don't want you going to work for Rendell—you'll get the raise."

We celebrated and joked about whether Roy would be able to take over the department. We should have taken the subject more seriously. Roy started writing memos about how the book and manuscript department could better serve private collectors directly, and how they could bring collectors from other departments into the world of historical manuscripts. Roy uniquely combined his personal enthusiasm with realistic analysis of the possibilities and a detailed plan. Since he knew that his boss would never agree, he sent his plan to his boss's superior, who saw the future along the lines of the new owner, a man determined to make Sotheby's friendly toward collectors and root out incompetency. Roy's memos resulted in his boss being fired and his own appointment to the overall head of rare books and manuscripts.

Roy and I both shared the belief that the future was in communicating better with existing collectors and developing new collectors with outreach and greatly improved services. He took on more and more challenges at Sotheby's without leaving his two positions in the rare-book and manuscript department. He created the position of marketing director, which he also assumed, and started the *Sotheby's Magazine*, perhaps his most brilliant marketing idea. We worked together on several major private, not auction, transactions, including one of Winston Churchill's manuscripts of his World War II speeches. Roy was also selling pieces I owned directly to Sotheby's clients in private-treaty sales, a concept pioneered by him and now of major importance to auction houses. Eventually the overall chief executive of Sotheby's retired and Roy Davids and the president of Sotheby's New York, Dede Brooks, were the two contenders for the job. When she was picked over him, she wanted him to retire. Roy Davids was not a good potential competitor to have waiting in the wings. He didn't really have a choice, and for a very substantial payoff, he retired. He immediately announced that he was becoming a dealer. He went on to enormous success in building collections of manuscripts and selling them for extraordinary prices. Our personal friendship, and business dealings, were based on our shared belief in the importance of what we were doing and that it was critical to introduce more people to what had always been an iconoclastic collecting area.

Over the ensuing years Roy was virtually a member of my close family, stayed with us for a summer on Maui, and was best man at my wedding. His remarkable life and great influence on the manuscript world, especially in England, came to a tragic end with a devastating stroke, just as his personal life was about to bloom. He said he had finally met the love of his life, an Italian woman, while searching for and finding an Italian villa. He left his personal collection, and a hard-earned large estate, to the Bodleian Library at Oxford University.

I continued to think constantly about expanding my business into new geographic markets. My most challenging idea was suggested by Mitsuo Nitta, Tokyo's leading rare-book dealer. I met Nitta at an antiquarian book fair in New York. He wanted me to come to Tokyo to participate in an exhibition he was planning. He said he would invite his clients, handle discussions with them about documents and manuscripts, and take care of all payment arrangements. This meant that all transactions would go through him, and he would earn a commission and would also control the relationships.

Roy with my son Jason during a vacation.

Japan's economy was booming, and I was excited about the prospects of becoming a part of it. Nitta and I agreed to continue our discussions over dinner, and I booked the best Japanese restaurant in New York. When we met at his hotel to go to dinner, he said, "Me have club, me have club." I assumed we were going to a private Japanese club. His wife, who spoke no English, was with him, and as the three of us got into a taxi he told the driver, "Playboy Club, Playboy Club."

This was the most bizarre setting for a business discussion. The three of us were seated at a tiny table, with girls dancing on platforms above us and loud music making it difficult to carry on a conversation or eat our dinner.

The next day, in a quieter setting, we completed arrangements for the exhibition in Tokyo.

ボストン事務所

マサチューセッツ州ボストンにあるレンデルの事務所には世界で最も大量の、最も多様な未整理のオートグラフ資料——著名人書簡、原稿、文書などを保存しています。このボストンの事務所には、鑑定のための科学実験室、および正確な分類のための調査資料を備えた図書室を有し、総ての調査、保存、分類、管理を行っています。

日本常設コーナー

レンデル社では、欧米の学術文献および稀観書の輸入に定評と実績のある株式会社雄松堂書店を通じ、1966年より日本へのオートグラフの紹介をして参りました。1988年春よりこの雄松堂書店と共同で日本橋三越本店にオートグラフ・コーナーを常設し、日本になじみ深い著名人（学者、政治家から俳優やポピュラー歌手まで）のオートグラフをたくさん展示しております。この常設コーナーを通じ、オートグラフの魅力をご理解戴ければ幸いです。

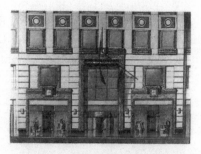

ニューヨーク・ギャラリー

ニューヨークのレンデル社は美術品や骨董品街の中心地である Place des Antiquaires と呼ばれる地域にあります。このニューヨークのギャラリーでは、音楽、芸術、歴史、政治、軍事、文学、科学、医学、演劇、歌劇などあらゆる分野にわたる、古くは1500年代のルネッサンス・ヨーロッパの時代から今日にいたるまでの世界中の著名人のオートグラフを顔に入れ展示しております。

なお、詳しくは、下記へお問い合わせ下さい。
株式会社 雄松堂書店 古書部
〒160 東京都新宿区三栄町29 ☎03(357)1411 (fax03(351)5855

Our Japanese brochure.

Tokyo was a thoroughly foreign experience for me. While Europe was foreign for me as well, European languages have some fundamental commonalities with English, and I didn't feel as isolated in Europe as I did in Tokyo. Nevertheless, fortitude is one of my strong points, and over the next few years I continued to do these joint exhibitions in Japan. I got into a routine of arriving in Tokyo five days early, so I would have plenty of time to overcome jet lag, visit stores to learn about current Japanese culture, and assess what in Western culture would interest Japanese clients. Music stores were particularly important. Seeing the phonograph records for sale indicated which composers' autographs could be of interest. Typically, in foreign countries, bookstores are useful, but since I couldn't read titles, bookstores were of no use. Video stores were helpful for understanding taste in movies.

During discussions with Nitta as well, a pattern of interests soon became apparent. Douglas MacArthur was a hero to the Japanese because he gave them a constitution as well as opportunities to succeed after World War II. John F. Kennedy, Abraham Lincoln, and Buffalo Bill Cody were the only other Americans, besides pre-World War II movie stars, who were popular with the Japanese. Economists, including political economists such as Adam Smith and John Stuart Mill, were of great interest, as were German composers, Italian operatic composers, French authors, scientists of all nations, all royalty, and world leaders.

My Tokyo Gallery at Mitsukoshi Department Store.

After a few years of working with Nitta, I started to do solo exhibitions at Mitsukoshi, Tokyo's leading luxury department store and a prestigious venue for art exhibitions. These lasted several weeks and were very successful. During this period I was able to acquire a number of musical manuscript pages in the handwriting of Mozart. Though expensive, they sold extremely well. My sales were impressive enough that Mitsukoshi offered me a gallery space for a permanent sales exhibition. Nitta provided the knowledgeable staff.

A client I met through the Mitsukoshi gallery, Jiro Tokuyama, mentored me in doing business in Japan. He was a graduate of Harvard Business School, well connected, and generous with both his advice and introductions to important people. Through Tokuyama, I was invited to decorate Tokyo's new opera house for opening night with 75 framed manuscripts of operatic composers.

It was a wonderful opportunity and experience designing that exhibition. Everything had a price on it. The only disappointment was that nothing sold. Later I realized why: I had too carefully decorated the lobby, placing framed groups on the walls, and the Japanese sense of design and respect for orderliness prevented people from disrupting—ruining!—my exhibition by even thinking of removing anything.

Tokuyama also introduced me to the CEO of Shiseido, the cosmetics giant. The CEO didn't speak any Western languages, and we conversed through his executive assistant about his desire to use a large gallery on the ground floor of Shiseido headquarters in the Ginza district to create an exhibition commemorating the 200th anniversary of the French Revolution. My immediate reaction was that this would be a very small exhibition, and a very violent one. Privately, I was horrified by the idea.

Our Shiseido Exhibit commemorated 200 years of French culture.

I suggested I create an exhibition of documents commemorating French culture over 200 years. The Shiseido CEO was enthusiastic, and I was impressed with his knowledge of French art and literature. I had a fascinating time developing the list of people to include and writing the literature to promote the show. The exhibition was very successful.

My biggest challenge in Japan was getting used to people's dislike of saying "no" to offers. I was expected to understand the inflection in their voice when they said "yes," and to interpret whether they really meant "yes" or they actually were being polite and meant "no." In one particular case, I offered an expensive collection of John F. Kennedy manuscripts to the owner of Meisei University in Tokyo, Dr. Mitsuo Kodama. He asked me to bring the collection to Tokyo so he could see it in person. For a full week I couldn't decipher whether he was going to buy it. While Dr. Kodama didn't speak English, he had assistants who did, and every day I was told that he couldn't decide. I finally told him that I had to return to Boston, and if I did not have his commitment to buy it, the collection was going back to Boston with me. The morning I was leaving for the airport, his assistant phoned to say that in a dream Dr. Kodama was told to buy the collection.

This was the most unusual basis for a purchase I have ever had!

The publisher of *Forbes* magazine became one of my most interesting clients in America. I received an order for $1,750, handwritten on Forbes stationery and signed by someone else with the last name Forbes. I didn't know who "Kip Forbes" was, so I called *Forbes* magazine and asked for Malcolm Forbes. He was a regular, but not major, client at the time. His assistant told me that Christopher was Mr. Forbes's son. When she told me to go ahead and process the order, I replied that I needed to confirm that the transaction was okay for $1,750.

Suddenly, a booming voice came on the line. It was Malcolm Forbes, asking what his son had purchased. He laughed loudly when I told him that Christopher had ordered a French document. Malcolm said he wanted his son to follow in his footsteps, and Kip evidently had his good taste in collecting documents.

This was the beginning of my relationship with this unusual entrepreneur, who modestly ascribed his success to inheritance. Malcolm Forbes believed that people were the most important factor in assessing a company, and he explored their character and their potential via elaborate luncheons in his townhouse, attached to the *Forbes* office building on lower Fifth Avenue. These lunches were the basis of articles for the magazine. Here Forbes got to know executives, and he and his sons got to know me as well at one of these lunches.

In his office Forbes worked at a large desk that was made more impressive by his magnificent Faberge desk set and his jeweled picture frames. These items reflected his opulent lifestyle. He owned yachts of various sizes, a commercial-sized jet, the "Capitalist Tool," and many houses around the world. Forbes wrote a fascinating book, *More Than I Dreamed*, about his collections—from toy soldiers and boats to Faberge eggs, trophy paintings, and actual trophies once awarded to now-forgotten people for now-forgotten accomplishments. But he described his collecting of historical letters as the most important and meaningful to him, and it was easy to see the connection between his personal focus on letters of historical personalities and his magazines' focus on the leaders of companies.

His magazines were famous for his socially progressive and fiscally conservative editorials. Forbes expressed great concern for the welfare of the poor and harshly criticized people who sat on their birthright. His editorials exuded common sense and criticized his own lack of it, particularly when he attempted a record balloon flight, spending $1.2 million and traveling only 20 feet. He also chronicled his worldwide motorcycle trips, which he considered business trips. When asked about his death-defying sports, Forbes responded that he was very careful because heaven couldn't possibly be as good as what he was already living on earth.

In the early 1970s Forbes bought interesting but not expensive pieces. In 1976 he became a major historical document collector. Phil Sang, the Chicago entrepreneur in the dairy and pharmaceutical fields, had been the most important collector of American historical autographs. When he died, Sang's estate put his collection up at auction. Forbes bought with wild enthusiasm. One of many great acquisitions was the logbook of the pilot of the *Enola Gay*, the plane that dropped the atomic bomb on Hiroshima. He also bought an expense account from Paul Revere for one of his rides.

In the 1970s, I was offered the most incredible Thomas Jefferson letter I had ever encountered. Jefferson wrote about the future of the United States and the problems it faced with slavery; he offered his ideas as to how America needed to solve what he saw as its greatest threat. The owner of this letter wanted $20,000, a great sum in those days. I bought it without hesitation. When I showed it to Forbes and told him that he could have it for $25,000, he told me he couldn't imagine paying that much for a letter. Then he read Jefferson's powerful thoughts and agreed to buy it.

After Forbes died in 1990 and his collection was sold at auction, that Thomas Jefferson letter, which he had bought from me for $25,000, sold for more than $700,000. It was irresistible to two bidders at the auction, and it was a critically important lesson about investing in collecting areas. If your criteria were technical collecting issues, you probably weren't destined to sell your collection for a lot more than you paid, but if you bought what you really found exciting, chances are other people would get carried away as well.

In *More Than I Dreamed*, Forbes shared his excitement for collecting the documents of history:

> Unquestionably, my favorite among the collections are the autograph ... documents. Such documents give us in many ways a better conception of a person than it is possible to get from a formal portrait or, in later years, from a photograph. They remind us that these are more than historical figures—they were people pouring out their hopes, sadness, reactions and directions onto paper. Their letters and documents are what makes flesh and blood of key figures in our country's history.

Forbes wrote about his acquisitions in his magazine and displayed them in the *Forbes* building, where he eventually built the Forbes Museum to show them off. His enthusiastic sharing of what he collected made sales to him very satisfying. I found him an exceptionally engaging and enjoyable person.

Chapter 7

Branching Into the Ancient World

In 1970, as I was developing European collectors for historical documents, I learned that the Folio Society, which published classic books in fine editions, had opened a gallery in their headquarters building in London's West End. My interest was that they were selling historical documents, and I might be able to sell to them. Since London dealers were passive and unbusinesslike, I thought my personal service would appeal to them.

The founder, Charles Ede, had created a club-like gallery for the subscribers to his Folio books. In addition to documents, the gallery offered medieval illuminated pages, antique maps, Old Master prints, and various types of ancient antiquities and writing.

I was mesmerized by Ede's idea of making all these areas available to a much wider audience. His concept—the history of mankind as seen through artifacts that could be collected—resonated within me. Instead of my selling documents to them, I bought examples of early writing in the form of clay tablets, incised with cuneiform symbols, written between 3000 and 2000 B.C. in Mesopotamia; pieces of Egyptian papyrus with pictographical hieroglyphic symbols; several small Greek pots from the fifth century B.C.; and illuminated manuscript leaves dating from before the invention of printing in the late fifteenth century.

These illuminated manuscript pages, written by hand on vellum, had exquisite small paintings of religious scenes. The complete manuscript had been sufficiently damaged in the past and was unsalable, so the undamaged leaves were sold individually. They predated when letters and documents were signed by prominent people, and I thought they could have great appeal with collectors. I located several long-established dealers in London and New York who had quite a few pages in stock, all quite reasonably priced, and bought what they had.

I soon realized I would not be able to create a significant business in this area. I had acquired virtually everything on the market, and what I found had been accumulated over decades. If I created sufficient interest to sell everything I had bought, I would have no sources to acquire more. Nevertheless, I was having a wonderful time learning about medieval illuminated manuscripts, as well as medieval history and culture.

What excited my interest even more were the ancient antiquities, especially the early writing from Mesopotamia, beginning about 3000 B.C. The clay tablets and cones recorded business transactions and were used as receipts for agricultural crops, bread, beer, and oils deposited at main storage areas, as well as donkeys and oxen. They also paid tribute to gods and arranged sacrificial offerings. The Egyptian early writing that the Folio Society had for sale began about 2000 B.C., was written in hieroglyphics, and involved the afterlife and the various Egyptian gods. I knew that if I were to make ancient writing part of my business, it would never be financially important, but I thought it was a natural extension back in history and I was fascinated with it.

My inquiries at the Folio Society led to an introduction to Ede. He was a generation older than me and had left Oxford University to join the Army in World War II. After the war he decided great books deserved printing worthy

The Egyptian *Book of the Dead*, 1567-1085 B.C.

An illuminated manuscript page from before the invention of the printing press.

A Mesopotamian clay tablet, 2113-2006 B.C.

of their importance. Ede was particularly tall and distinguished looking, with sharp facial features. He was always casually but well dressed in tweeds with a neck scarf. His fast pace of speaking was refreshing to an American accustomed to the British slow and pedantic conversations. We were intellectual compatriots from the beginning, and over seemingly endless drinks in the Folio Society bar he educated me in these new areas I knew nothing about. We shared a basic interest in human history and an attitude of trying business ideas others had not. He was my kind of person!

As Ede showed me pieces of Greek and Roman pottery that especially interested him, I started buying for myself. I felt almost emotionally overwhelmed when I looked at a vase from ancient Greece or Italy and saw the paintings of people on them. Their clothing was different, but the people looked like people. Just as I was thrilled to read letters written from different time periods and identify with those people, I felt very connected to people more than 2,500 years ago who

A Greek vase, 500 B.C.

were represented on this pottery. They were portrayed in activities easily related to today: music, dancing, eating, and drinking.

One day Charles Ede and I were coming back to London from his country house. He was driving and asked me to hold in my lap a spectacular Greek cup from the fifth century B.C. The artistry was amazing, and I asked how he was going to price it. By the time we arrived in London I told him I couldn't give it back to him. It has been in my office ever since.

In 1971 Ede decided to go into classical Western antiquities as a full-time profession and retire from his publishing enterprise. He always thought of himself more as an academic than a businessman. He asked if I would be interested in being his minority partner, bringing the American business-like approach that he thought he lacked. I accepted.

The initial location for the Charles Ede Antiquities Gallery was just off Bond Street, a block from Claridge's Hotel. The street-level gallery had large windows and attracted many people walking by who had no idea that they could collect ancient art, well cataloged and guaranteed, at such reasonable prices. Ede's lack of pretension showed in the way visitors and clients were treated and in the way catalog descriptions were written. He wanted the business to be welcoming, in stark contrast to the exclusionary atmosphere in other London galleries. Ede's source of supply, the British archaeologists and academics who brought extra pieces back from excavations for their own collections, lasted for many years and provided us with a sufficient number of new pieces for our gallery.

For the first time in my life, I was in a position to consider expanding my business into new areas, not to make money but for my own knowledge and enjoyment. I knew that none of these areas that Ede had commercially pioneered could ever be major sources of revenue. There was too limited a supply, and I personally could not take a disproportionate amount of time to cultivate new clients. My core business was my principal source of income. Nevertheless, the personal enjoyment and satisfaction was important, and I decided to create a new bimonthly series of catalogs offering selections from all of these new areas. This catalog series, called, appropriately, *The History of*

Jamie Ede at home with my son, Jason.

Mankind, did introduce many new people to these fields but the success was, as expected, personal rather than business.

At this time I expanded my staff in Boston to include two exceptional researchers and catalogers who enabled me to undertake a series of extraordinary catalogs. Mei-Ying and Pat Bozeman worked with me to publish, between 1979 and 1980, large-format catalogs on *The Ancient World, 3100 BC to 800 AD*; *Early Writing from Mesopotamia and Egypt* (140 pages); *The Medieval World, 800 AD to 1450 AD* (287 pages); and *Renaissance Europe, 1450–1600* (354 pages). No one could ever do anything like this again—the original material is not available.

The *Ancient World* catalog did very well because of three orders. The Xerox Corporation bought a number of pieces, across all areas and time periods, to create a museum on the history of writing in their headquarters in Connecticut. Dave Karpeles, a great collector in Santa Barbara, bought a selection of pieces that became part of the Karpeles Museum. A prominent French collector bought the most expensive piece in the catalog, an Egyptian papyrus document written in 232 B.C., partly in Greek, one of the earliest surviving examples. This document, a contract involving embalmers, was written on a scroll 45 inches long, which had been flattened and posed a major shipping problem. The collector wanted it delivered to Paris, and while there would be no customs duty, getting something this unique through French customs would be a nightmare. I offered to personally deliver it within a few days. It was winter, and I realized the Plexiglas-encased papyrus, with packing, could easily fit inside a ski bag. The collector burst into applause when he realized why I was standing in front of the hotel with a ski bag. We set off for his house with the bag sticking out the car windows.

Our company's catalog series included *The History of Mankind,*
The Medieval World, and *Renaissance Europe.*

The *Renaissance Europe* catalog did particularly well because of so many major pieces. It began with a manuscript in the hand of Michelangelo and continued with major historical figures such as Martin Luther, Henry VIII, Elizabeth I, Hernán Cortés, Ferdinand and Isabella of Spain, Niccolò Machiavelli, Peter Paul Rubens, and Sir Walter Raleigh.

After more than 30 wonderful years of friendship, Charles and his wife Liz Ede passed away. I eventually sold my minority interest to their son, Jamie, who has done a spectacular job of expanding the business far beyond what Charles or I ever imagined.

Xerox's catalog for their exhibition
on the history of writing.

A manuscript written
by Michelangelo.

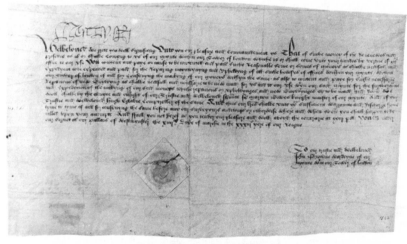

An official document of Henry VIII.

Chapter 8

The Hitler
Diaries Hoax

T he initial telephone calls from *Newsweek* in early April 1983 were
ambiguous and gave no hint of the true importance of the inquiry.
Ted Slate, *Newsweek*'s librarian, was asking about the types of handwritten materials that can be authenticated and the procedures necessary to do
so. While I treated his inquiries seriously, I was also adamant that I was not
interested in becoming involved in a news story based upon authentication. I
had steadfastly avoided involvement in news stories about whether an important
document was authentic. There seemed to be any number of so-called experts
available to testify on both sides.

Slate persisted, particularly wanting to know whether or not European
handwriting from the beginning of the century could be positively authenticated. After giving him an overview of the problems involved, he said *Newsweek*
wanted to hire me as a special consultant and that this would be a major story
worldwide. He told me that there would be considerable travel involved and,
based on what people told him about my sports activities, he thought I would
be in the physical shape needed. I told him that what was involved must be
more than an important document whose content was already known, but the

discovery would be the news story. The news that it had been found would only be temporary, not what he was describing. Therefore, it must be an unknown manuscript, probably a journal or diary, and the only person I could think of who would merit such attention would be Adolf Hitler. I told him Hitler was frequently forged, but if there was handwriting beyond a signature it would be very difficult to create a good forgery. There was a long period of dead silence on the other end of the phone, and finally Slate said it was really important that I come to New York and talk to them in person.

Several days later, on April 13, Slate reached me again, this time in Washington, where I was giving a lecture at the Library of Congress on forgery detection. *Newsweek* wanted to pursue the authentication subject further, and I agreed to visit their office the following Saturday before a lecture at New York University. Despite desperate urgings to come sooner, I wouldn't change my schedule. I kept telling Slate that there was little chance I would be interested in working on their project.

Arriving at *Newsweek*'s skyscraper headquarters building on Madison Avenue, I was taken to Slate's comfortable, book-lined corner office. He looked like the classic librarian: as well dressed as necessary, but not businesslike. He was middle-aged, with a very friendly manner that belied his sharp understanding of overall issues. I agreed to sign a secrecy agreement and was very impressed with how strongly they wanted to hire me. They told me the German magazine *Stern* had acquired approximately 60 volumes of Hitler's handwritten diaries, that they had survived a plane crash at the end of the war, and that *Newsweek* was in active negotiations to purchase the English-language publication rights. I was literally speechless for a few minutes as I considered the potentially enormous historical importance of Hitler's diaries.

For the next several hours *Newsweek* gave me details of the discovery amid constant interruptions with discussions of television ads, the first Hitler diaries cover, and the question of whether to reveal Hitler's writings about the Holocaust in the first *Newsweek* installment or chronologically to keep building interest among readers. I pictured a train rolling at high speed, with the engineers discussing which tracks to steer it on while I was back in the station trying to get them to listen to my concern that there wasn't enough information to let the train leave the station in the first place. It was days before they began to focus on the real issue: were they genuine? Forgers devise many diversions to get the victim's focus off the critical issues—where a forgery is vulnerable—and onto side issues, where the victim's own needs take over and propel the forgery into a full-scale hoax. *Newsweek*'s librarian had an open mind, but everyone else thought that the authentication issue had been dealt with by *Stern*, and their focus was on publication.

Newsweek had already begun to investigate the crash of Hitler's plane on the way to his mountain retreat, just before the Russians captured Berlin. According to *Stern*, among Hitler's personal belongings was a trunk containing the diaries. Hitler's valet, Heinz Linge, had referred to this trunk in a book he authored just after his release from a Russian prison in the mid-1950s. Also, Hitler's personal pilot, Hans Bauer, had stated previously that when he told Hitler that this particular plane had been shot down, Hitler became very upset and told him, "Everything I have written for posterity was on that plane." I was impressed that the trunk also contained many letters written to Hitler, drafts of letters by him, his handwritten outline of the program of the National Socialist German Workers Party, a large quantity of photographs by his personal photographer, Hitler's World War I Iron Cross, and several paintings by him. All this lent circumstantial credibility to the diaries. If Hitler had shipped his personal belongings from Berlin, these would be the type of effects I would expect to find.

We left Slate's comfortable office and met with the editor of *Newsweek*, Maynard Parker, in his significantly smaller and crowded office. Parker, tall and slim, exuded an aura of commanding one of the two most important news magazines in America. He explained why *Newsweek* believed the diaries to be genuine and described the many trips he and others had been making to *Stern*'s

Hans Bauer, the personal pilot of Adolf Hitler.

headquarters in Hamburg and Zurich (the location of the diaries). I was shown summaries of *Stern*'s three authentication reports and statement that they "showed three independent experts an excerpt from the diaries. The origin of the text was not mentioned. The only thing to be examined was whether it had been written by Adolf Hitler personally. For comparison, five samples of Hitler's writing, the authenticity of which is undisputed, were obtained from the Federal Archives in Koblenz. The experts examined not only the writing but also the text. The officially recognized American expert, Ordway Hilton, by comparing the handwriting between the diary and the Koblenz documents,

A map of the route taken by Hitler's plane—possibly carrying important documents—in the final days of World War II. Its goal was Salzburg, but it crashed near Börnersdorf.

concluded: '[It] was written by Hitler.' Even the experts of the Federal Archives ascertained that, on the basis of the documents present, 'with the probability bordering on certainty, the manuscripts in question come from Hitler.' The former head of the forensic division of the Zurich City Police, one of the most prominent European handwriting authorities, made the following analysis: 'The range of forms and psychological characteristics of authentic handwriting features and signatures of Adolf Hitler also occur in precisely the same configuration in the documents examined. There can be no doubt that these documents were written by Adolf Hitler personally.'"

After perusing the authentications for a few minutes, I informed Parker that they were meaningless. The experts had seen only three pages and had not been told of the existence of more material. Even if these three pages were genuine, it did not prove that all of the diaries were genuine. In a case as important as this, every page of every volume would have to be carefully examined. I also noted that the three pages had nothing to do with diaries: two consisted of a statement concerning Rudolf Hess's flight to England and the third was a telegram. They might have been written in a notebook by Hitler, but that notebook might later have come into the hands of a forger who added the diary portions and created another 59 volumes. I found photocopies of three manuscript pages in *Newsweek*'s papers and asked what they were. No one knew. They didn't look anything like Hitler's writing.

I hastily formulated a plan for my own examination of the diaries and discussed with Slate and Parker the many possibilities. A contemporary forger may have wanted either to enhance the Führer's image or embarrass him. A modern forger would know that the value of the diaries was in their publication, and the German population wanted to forget that their parents' generation had voted the Nazis into power. The only text they would pay to read would confirm that their parents' generation voted for a leader who made Germany great again, who was betrayed by his fanatical followers.

I reviewed the technical problems of forging Hitler's diaries: little of Hitler's handwriting exists and a forger would have difficulty assembling a sufficient number of prototypes. We made plans to fly to Zurich, where I planned to spend the week examining the diaries and write a detailed report for the next issue of *Newsweek*, describing how they had been proven genuine or fake.

We adjourned to the suite of offices of Katherine Graham, owner of *Newsweek*. I observed to Slate that he seemed to have more power than a librarian, and he told me Mrs. Graham always wanted to be certain that they were on solid footing with stories, which is why they wanted their own independent expert confirming authenticity. Eleven years earlier, in 1972, Mrs. Graham, who also owned the *Washington Post* newspaper, had been meticulously careful with the Woodward and Bernstein Watergate story. We discussed the work being done by several historians hired by *Newsweek*.

One, Professor Gerhard Weinberg, had gone to Zurich and examined several of the volumes. Slate showed me his report and I again found that none of the points arguing in favor of authenticity were valid. Weinberg noted that the more than 100 signatures of Hitler in the diaries argued against their being forgeries; but it is well-known that the forger can become so convinced of their skill that

Professor Gerhard Weinberg examined the diary pages for *Newsweek*.

not only do they not hesitate to forge numerous signatures, but in some cases actually create opinions not known to have been held by the subject. I stated I wanted a report from Weinberg and the other historians listing every point in the diaries that was not contained in any printed work or archival record. It would be illogical if every fact and detail in the diaries had already appeared in print or was available to researchers. This report was never made.

Finally, Slate told me that the diaries were being smuggled from East Germany, the site of the plane crash, and that *Stern* was receiving them a few at a time. They didn't have all of the diaries in their possession.

My trip was repeatedly delayed. According to *Newsweek*'s schedule, I would have the week of April 18 to examine the diaries and the next week to complete the report for publication the following Monday, May 2. The delays in my departure were caused by difficulties with *Stern* over the publication agreement.

I contacted the National Archives in Washington, the principal repository of Hitler's archives, and spoke to the archival specialist in the Third Reich archives, who I knew, and asked for photocopies of all Hitler handwriting. A courier from *Newsweek* picked them up. I also asked if anyone had used the Hitler archives or requested photocopies in the past three years; no one had. We constructed comparison sheets, on which we mounted identical letters or letter patterns from genuine examples: 26 sheets of capital letters, 26 sheets of lower-case letters, approximately 20 sheets containing common German words in Hitler's handwriting, and a chronological arrangement of Hitler's signatures.

Midweek, *Newsweek* said that *Stern* executives had, in a meeting with them and Rupert Murdoch, raised the price they wanted for publication rights; Murdoch and *Newsweek* thought their handshake deals were firm and refused. *Newsweek* would now treat the diaries as a major news story; they had the text of the planned first issue of *Stern* from the negotiations and both considered it fair game. *Newsweek*, anticipating the publication of the diaries, had designed a very dramatic cover with Hitler, which was altered, at my insistence, with the addition of the significant subtitle, "Are they genuine?" In that issue I reiterated what I had been telling *Newsweek*'s editors: there was no proof the diaries were either genuine or fake, and only a complete examination of every volume would provide conclusive answers. Saturday, April 23, 1983, the front pages of newspapers throughout the world covered the discovery of the Hitler diaries. Murdoch's *New York Post* declared, "World Shattering Documents from the Mind of a Madman . . . Hitler's Secret Diaries Found . . . Revealed Dictator 'Virtually Unaware' of the Holocaust." The noted British historian Sir Hugh Trevor-Roper described what he considered to be conclusive evidence of the diaries' authenticity.

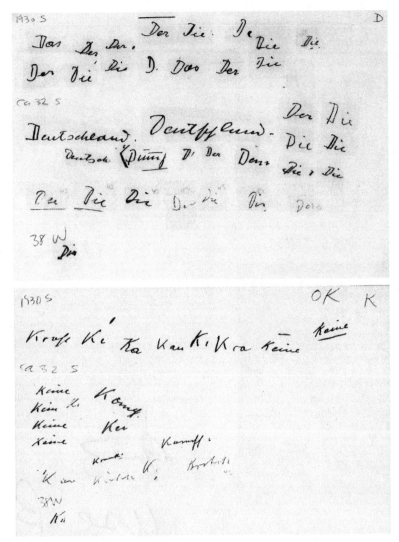

Hitler's genuine handwriting, cut up into capital "D" and "K."

The following day, Sunday, *Newsweek* issued a press release concerning its cover story for Monday. Headlined "Leading Historian Who Has Examined Hitler Diaries Believes They Are Authentic," it outlined what *Newsweek* would be reporting. This included my interview "Are They Genuine?"

That night I was shocked at the storm that was developing. Within an hour after the publication of *Newsweek*'s press release, all three networks called to invite me to appear on their news programs the following morning. CBS wanted to discuss the subject that night in preparation for an in-depth interview, and I chose their approach.

Rendell: Taking a closer look at paper, ink—and Hitler's signatures

ARE THEY GENUINE?

Are the Hitler diaries genuine or a brilliant, diabolical fraud? Stern magazine says historians and handwriting experts have firmly established their authenticity. But Stern's experts saw only one page from the Hess volume and a few other documents, not their full contents. And Stern's rush to press was sure to raise doubts, not settle them. The German experts would not discuss their procedures last week. Ordway Hilton, a South Carolina document examiner who worked with Stern, told NEWSWEEK *that the documents he tested were genuine. But a great historical paper chase was clearly just beginning.*

In his 45 years in the handwriting and document business, Ordway Hilton, 69, has had some fascinating tasks. He accurately denounced Clifford Irving's "autobiography" of Howard Hughes as a fake and cast doubt on the controversial Hughes "Mormon Will." Last April Stern editor Thomas Walde and acting publisher Wilfried Sorge came to his door bearing a handful of notes, letters and autographed photos—all known to be in Adolf Hitler's hand. They also brought two pages whose authorship was less certain: a document concerning Rudolf Hess and the text for a telegram to Miklós Horthy, Hitler's Hungarian regent. Hilton's job was to determine if the pages were in Hitler's handwriting. The Stern executives "didn't say where the documents came from," says Hilton, "and I didn't ask."

Since Hilton knew only a few words of German, he asked for typed transcripts of the pages. "If you don't know the language, you can go wrong in guessing what somebody meant," he explained. He photographed the pages, enlarged some photos to make a chart and examined others under binocular microscopes. The papers were in good condition, but the handwriting was nearly illegible, an odd mixture of old German and Latin script. Hilton noted that the "s's," "f's" and "h's" were virtually indistinguishable, the "n's" and "m's" were little more than wavering lines and the "i's" and "e's" were so short they were almost invisible. "These are the individualities that help to identify," he said. He compared the signatures—the curious "Adolf" resembling a double 7; the stylized H, followed by descending zigzags. He looked for telltale signs of forgery, such as odd breaks between letters. After two weeks, Hilton said he reached the point "where there was just no question": both documents were written by Adolf Hitler.

Experts in Europe went through the same process over the following weeks. Dr. Max Frei-Sulzer, former head of forensic services for the Zurich police department, reported that there could be no doubt that both of the documents were written by Adolf Hitler personally. Experts at the Landeskriminalamt, the German FBI, looked at a different set of papers, but their conclusion was the same: the originals could be called authentic with a probability that verged on certainty. Like Hilton, neither knew the historical issue at stake or of the mystery involving Hitler's pilot, Hans Bauer, a plane crash, postwar gatherings on Hermann Göring's yacht or a pipeline into East Germany. None claims to have "authenticated the diaries." "What I have verified is two samples of writing," said Hilton. "I don't know what's on [other pages] or whether the writing is the same."

The official German criminal lab also conducted a chemical analysis on a sample of notebook paper from the diaries and reported that the sample was "typical of paper used by Germans in the 1930s and 1940s." Other document experts said that

NEWSWEEK/MAY 2, 1983

British historian Sir Hugh Trevor-Roper.

The *Newsweek* cover announcing the discovery of the supposed "diaries."

I questioned the authentication statements in the initial issue.

In CBS's control room the next morning I watched the satellite feed of a press conference taking place in Hamburg. *Stern* was unveiling the first issue and Trevor-Roper was acting as the principal proponent of their authenticity. David Irving, the right-wing British historian, was ejected from the press conference for attempting to shout down Trevor-Roper with statements that the diaries were fake. It was an embarrassing scene, with the two well-known historians taking opposite sides but neither basing their opinion on definitive and obtainable facts.

The circus had begun.

Almost by the hour the situation became more bizarre. My opinion that the media should focus on *Stern*'s refusal to make the diaries available for examination was not only a minority view, it was mine alone. Everyone was intent on wild speculation, resulting in misinformed and irresponsible opinions.

Those attending *Stern*'s second press conference, intended to promote the content of their next issue about Rudolf Hess, were shocked by Trevor-Roper's statement: "A final judgement cannot be given until the whole text has been examined. . . . As an historian, I regret this process has been sacrificed to the requirements of the journalistic scoop. . . . It is always possible for one man to be deceived." Trevor-Roper, his reputation perhaps contributing as much as any factor to the initial success of the hoax outside of *Stern*, had quickly changed his position when he realized that the handwriting was being seriously questioned.

David Irving immediately brought the surreal atmosphere back by shouting that he had changed his mind as well, but now he was convinced the diaries were genuine.

Speculation that the diaries had been faked in East Germany, for political more than monetary reasons, dominated the news on April 26. The *New York Times* reported, "[Experts] say a central thesis that might be developed in such a manipulation by the East German and Soviet Secret Services would be that the West turned down opportunities to end World War II, prolonging the

The cover of *Stern*: "Hitler's Diaries Discovered."

Stern's second cover story on the Hitler Diaries.

suffering it created, and holds the historical responsibility for the eventual division of Germany." A West German official was quoted as saying, "If I were faking such a diary for the East, I'd want Hitler to be a bore, a monster and a fool, but I'd like England and America to have given him the chance to make things worse."

By the middle of the week *Newsweek* had obtained an original copy of *Stern*'s first issue on the Hitler diaries, and I immediately saw that everything illustrated was forged. Almost certainly none of the diaries were genuine. The debate over authenticity had, however, become so emotional and theatrical that another voice making a statement for or against the diaries without having examined them would only add to the circus-like atmosphere.

In an attempt to bring some semblance of order and intelligent opinion to the situation, I issued a press release: "I am involving myself beyond the scope of my work with *Newsweek*, because the present situation is a tragedy for the integrity of many journalists and publishers and . . . historians who not only are fighting over the contents of the diaries but more importantly are issuing press statements concerning authenticity which are at the least uninformed and at the worst irresponsible. . . . The authenticity of historical documents is not a guessing game. It is a scientific and factual procedure involving the careful examination of all materials, from the ink, paper, binding, printing and adhesives to the individual characteristics of handwriting and writing habits. Hundreds of pieces of evidence are checked. . . . Many archives have contained forged sections placed in with genuine writing. I believe the Hitler diaries can be proved authentic or false and that this can be accomplished and reported to convince both scholars and the public. It is time for *Stern* to allow a definitive investigation of the original diaries. *Newsweek* disagrees with presenting the Hitler diaries as a soap opera—spreading them out over a number of years. This whole situation has evolved into a soap opera with new twists and characters every day, the old ones changing their minds and many others displaying an appalling lack of competence."

Speculation began to subside the following day. Whether the historians had simply run out of hypotheses or my press release had some effect, news reports did begin to concentrate on the need for a complete examination of the diaries.

The saga took a dramatic new turn when *Newsweek* told me that Peter Koch, editor-in-chief of *Stern*, had arrived in New York with the first and last volumes of the diaries. Koch was meeting with *Newsweek*'s Parker, who was attempting to arrange for my examination of the volumes. Later that night, Parker informed me that Koch had an appreciation for my approach and, while not specifically agreeing, had no fundamental disagreement with my seeing them. On Sunday,

May 1, I finally had an opportunity to delve into an area that had been puzzling me. If all of the diaries were forgeries, which was certain to me, how could three competent handwriting experts have authenticated the three pages? I read again *Stern*'s statement to *Newsweek* that they had "showed three independent experts an excerpt from the diaries. . . . As materials for comparison, five samples of Hitler's writing, the authenticity of which is undisputed, were available from the inventories of the Federal Archives."

Stern editor-in-chief Peter Koch.

I had also obtained complete copies of the experts' reports. After carefully going over and over them, I came to the startling conclusion that they had relied principally on examples that were in the same handwriting as the diaries. The forger had somehow placed forged Hitler letters in *Stern*'s dossier.

With little prospect of examining the diaries with *Newsweek*, I called CBS News. I told them that some of the diaries were in New York and Peter Koch was staying at the Plaza Hotel. They said if they were able to get him to appear on CBS News, I could be on the set to handle the diaries while they were photographed. In return I would give CBS an exclusive interview describing how the hoax had been perpetrated. I met late that night, somewhere around 2:30 a.m., with Parker to confirm an agreement whereby *Newsweek* and CBS would simultaneously break the story of the forgeries in *Stern*'s own files that were used to authenticate the diaries.

In the middle of the next day CBS called to say Koch had no objection to my being there Wednesday morning and would like to meet me. The following morning Koch appeared on both ABC and NBC but did not show the diaries. Wolf Hess, the son of Rudolf Hess, Hitler's deputy Führer, appeared with Koch and dominated the conversation, stressing the inequity of his father's continued imprisonment. He was urging that his father be released and shown the diaries, which he would be able to authenticate. (Rudolf Hess had been sentenced to life imprisonment.)

I felt well prepared when I met with Koch, Hess, and another Stern editor at 6 a.m. There was no offer to show me the diaries, but at 20 minutes to 7:00, as pre-arranged, a CBS producer asked Koch for the volumes so that still photographs could be made. Koch handed them over, and three or four minutes before airtime they were given to anchor Diane Sawyer, who was planning to show the diaries during the opening of the program. I had just three or four minutes to examine them while they were being set up. It was immediately apparent that the 1945 volume did not even resemble Hitler's handwriting. I asked Diane Sawyer to turn as many pages as possible while on the air so that these would be recorded on video, and I then went through the 1932 volume and noted which pages she should illustrate. We had a rapid discussion as to why the diaries were forgeries; I literally stayed on the set until the last possible second, dropping down behind her desk as the show went on the air.

Wolf Hess with one of the forged diaries.

The interview with Koch was very well handled by both parties. When Diane Sawyer pointed out the handwriting discrepancies I had shown her just minutes before, Koch replied that Stern had had three eminent experts authenticate the diaries and added that since a person could be sent to prison on the testimony of one of those experts, he could not see why it was necessary to pursue the matter any further.

After the interview Koch discussed with me my request to examine the diaries, but he could see no reason for them to be examined a fourth time. It was clear it would be difficult to convince him, so I suggested we all adjourn to breakfast, where we might discuss some of our experiences in dealing with the press coverage. Koch was to appear on CNN three hours later, and I spent the intervening time avoiding the subject of the diaries' authenticity. I would have to have hard evidence, actual comparisons mounted next to genuine examples, to convince him. Probing for some other areas of conversation, I discovered that Koch was an avid jogger, and one of his complaints was that he wasn't able to run every day. After we discussed various running routes through Central Park, we found a mutual interest in ski racing. In another part of my complicated life, I was a serious ski racer. My coach, the U.S. ski team coach Harald Schoenhaar, was German and had grown up with Wolf Hess. After updating Hess on my coach's life in recent decades, the conversation turned to helicopter skiing, and we discovered that Koch and I had been on the same trip in the Bugaboo Mountains in western Canada four years earlier. We were both so out of context at CNN that neither of us had realized this. The three of us talked for two hours about skiing. I was invited, without any agreements, to examine the diaries after the CNN appearance for as long as I thought necessary. I immediately understood how they had gotten into this colossal mess: this was the biggest story in the world, and because of our personal connections in the ski world, I was being given unrestricted access, with no agreement about how I would use the information.

We went to *Stern*'s New York offices. While I was assembling the comparisons of Hitler's handwriting, Koch was spending the afternoon shopping for toys and a car telephone. When I asked that he and I meet later that evening, I was told it was impossible because he would be attending a Broadway play. A meeting for the next morning was established.

That evening I assembled the overwhelming evidence necessary to convince even the staunchest supporters that the diaries were forgeries. I presented my handwriting analyses to the other editor of *Stern*, who had accompanied Koch. I showed him that the three questioned documents experts had been shown forgeries from *Stern*'s own files; he immediately telephoned the editor in charge in Hamburg, who went to *Stern*'s offices to locate this file. The originals of these forgeries had to be located, he said, before those involved could remove them.

We met again at midnight in the fantasy-like setting of the Four Seasons Restaurant. We sat next to the pool, with the fountain creating a celebratory atmosphere for a dramatic conversation. The editor, who I was convinced held a much more important position than was apparent, told me that the next issue of the magazine, which had gone to press earlier that evening, had been halted and that more than 20 people were already working on a revised issue. While *New York Times* food critic James Beard celebrated his birthday with friends at nearby tables, we discussed the personal tragedies that were about to befall various editors at *Stern* and the tremendous loss of prestige the magazine would suffer. The editor also told me in great confidence, and which I have never before disclosed, that he and others at *Stern* were sure the diaries were fake, but the owner of *Stern* was behind their publication, and they thought it would only be a local German story, covered for four or five issues at most. He said they had no idea the story would explode on the international scene the way it had.

When he arrived at *Stern*'s office the next morning, Koch in no way indicated that he didn't believe the diaries were genuine. He was visibly shocked when I showed him my handwriting analysis; his several arguments were overwhelmed by the physical evidence laid out on the conference table. The scene was described in a later issue of *Stern*: "Koch turned as pale as the paint on the wall. With a stunned, 'That's that, I guess,' Koch called the chairman of Gruner und Jahr, the parent company of *Stern*, to break the news." He told him that while he had expected me to deliver another affirmative opinion, he had to concede that my examination was conclusive and that the diaries were fake—he could see it for himself. The chairman told Koch to have me come to Hamburg to look at all the other material and bring the hoax to a conclusion.

Koch's immediate worry was that I would speak to television and print reporters waiting outside *Stern*'s offices. I assured him that if the entire archive was made available to me, I would hold back the story. My main interest was in determining if any of the other materials were genuine, who was involved at *Stern*, and who the forger was.

We agreed that I would fly to Hamburg the following Sunday. *Stern* would, I was told, put me up in a safe house. I would not agree to that; I wanted to stay in a luxury hotel in Hamburg. We compromised on a *Stern*-owned guarded apartment near a luxury hotel, where I could use the restaurant. I would have the week of May 9 to examine the archive and write a detailed report, which would be released by *Newsweek* the following Monday. This would give *Stern* sufficient time to plan how they would deal with the story of the hoax.

At this point no one knew that I had protected the integrity of the whole story against a double-cross by *Stern*: I had secretly made a duplicate set of photocopies of the diaries and taped them around my legs. Right before my dinner at the Four Seasons, I had stopped at my room at the Regency Hotel and quickly stripped them off. If *Stern* decided to break their agreement with me, I had the duplicates and could proceed with a story illustrating the extensive comparisons that I had made and shown to *Stern*.

My analysis of the "diaries" was essential to uncovering the forgery, which was then publicized in *Newsweek* and *Time*.

A tense meeting with *Newsweek* was my next complication. The magazine's editors wanted me to release my evidence in time for their next issue, coming out on Monday, May 9. They feared that if they waited more than a week, the story, which they had worked so hard to develop, would be scooped by their European competition. I promised *Newsweek* that they would have my story the following weekend.

Unknown to *Stern*, *Newsweek*'s Ted Slate would also be coming to Hamburg. Each day I would use a small camera to photograph the material I was working on and pass the film to Slate at the hotel bar. As my report was being completed, *Newsweek* would be assembling a duplicate copy of the evidence. My agreement with *Stern* would not be violated; *Newsweek* could not use the evidence until the day *Stern* had agreed. If *Stern* violated our agreement through delays, or refused to release my report, it would still be in *Newsweek* as agreed.

At 7 o'clock the next morning, Friday, May 6, Melissa Ludke of *Time* magazine called with the news that a wire service reported that the German Federal Archives had declared the diaries forgeries. I had been working with her on *Time*'s cover story on historical forgeries, and she had known since earlier in the week that I considered the diaries forged.

At *Newsweek* I read the wire service reports. *Stern* editor Henri Nannen stated, "The magazine will not accept the statements from the Federal Archives but will take them into consideration." Twenty-three minutes later the wording was changed from "will not accept" to "cannot ignore." I was dumbfounded; for the previous 48 hours *Stern* had known, and the editors had accepted, the fact that the diaries were forgeries. Several weeks later, when *Stern* published its own version of the hoax, it wrote, "Koch's call reached Schulte-Hillen, Chairman of *Stern*, in Hamburg—early enough to be the first to flash the 'false alarm' over the wire services, early enough to be the first to reveal this gigantic flop himself. . . . But for Schulte-Hillen. He just couldn't accept the fact that he and his predecessor . . . who . . . had spent 10,840,000 deutsche marks . . . on a gigantic fraud. Just the same, Schulte-Hillen asked Koch, 'Bring Rendell to Hamburg as fast as you can so he can examine all the volumes.' But for Koch the race was over."

Most of Friday was spent working with Russell Watson, the chief correspondent of *Newsweek*, and Steven Strasser, the senior writer. We prepared a cover story for Monday, May 9, with Watson working on the overall hoax and Strasser and I outlining the points that *Newsweek* wanted me to cover in my article. That evening I did an interview with *Stern*, and at midnight one with *Time* magazine. A little after one o'clock Saturday morning Strasser arrived at my hotel with additional points *Newsweek* wanted covered. It was to be a night without rest, as *Stern*'s Hamburg office called at 3 a.m.—the beginning of their day—to reiterate that they wanted to hire me to investigate how all of this happened. Finally, at 5 a.m. I began to write the story; it was delivered to Strasser three hours later. Perhaps my greatest satisfaction in the whole affair was that *Newsweek*'s editors printed my full two-page article virtually unchanged. I had been warned that it would be heavily edited, but in the end only six technical terms were clarified. At the beginning of my article I came right to the point: "*Stern*'s experts' conclusions that the diaries and *Stern*'s samples (from the Federal Archives) were written by the same person is certainly correct. The problem is that that person was not Adolf Hitler."

Newsweek's issue "uncovering the Hitler hoax."

As I left New York City Saturday afternoon, I believed that the Hitler diaries saga had come to an end, but I was mistaken. On Sunday evening I returned to New York to appear on Monday's CBS News to discuss that day's *Newsweek* cover story declaring the diaries a hoax. As before, my appearance spawned a large number of requests for interviews, which occupied much of the

The diaries "were written by the same person. . . . The problem is that that person was not Adolf Hitler."

following week. In Germany Gerd Heidemann, the *Stern* reporter and source of the diaries, had disappeared, but he surfaced several days later to deny any complicity. The *New York Times* quoted him as saying that "it was not his fault that in the two years *Stern* had had access to some of the diaries it had not properly authenticated them." But Heidemann's story of how the diaries were obtained—through an East German general—was quickly coming apart. During the course of the week they were traced to Konrad Kujau, a dealer in Nazi memorabilia in Stuttgart. Upon arrest,

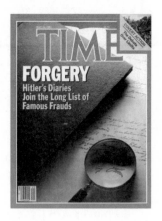

Kujau immediately implicated Heidemann in the hoax. I had agreed to *Stern*'s proposal to investigate how all of this happened at *Stern* and to write my report for a future issue of the magazine. Neither I, nor I think anyone else, could anticipate the circus that had gone on behind the scenes at *Stern* magazine leading to their buying the diaries.

Discovering the Behind-the-Scenes of the Hitler Diaries Hoax

As I began thinking about my new assignment from *Stern* magazine to examine how this fraud was perpetrated, I reflected on the previous weeks' news stories. The bizarreness of the circus created by the historians and journalists was stunning. The thrust of the news media's coverage should have been on the need to examine the diaries physically. Unfortunately, it was diffused into speculations, many wild and absurd, by historians and others. After seeing the illustrations in *Stern*'s first issue it was evident that the diaries illustrated, and probably all of the others, were fake; I needed only to examine the physical evidence of the diaries to prove this conclusively and complete my assignment for *Newsweek*. I could not understand how a major European publishing house had been swindled out of more than $5 million. How could *Newsweek*, the Rupert Murdoch organization, *Paris Match*, and others have invested so much time, effort, and money pursuing publication rights to such outrageous fakes? How did such bad forgeries become such a great hoax?

The paper, ink, and handwriting were not the key elements in the success of the Hitler diaries hoax. The human elements of ambition, secrecy, and greed propelled these inept forgeries into a major journalistic scandal.

Konrad Kujau, a minor Stuttgart dealer in military memorabilia and documents, readily admitted, boasted even, that he forged all the diaries. But his role in the hoax was relatively minor. For the hoax to be successful, it was necessary to overcome many journalistic business checkpoints, and this had been accomplished through the emotional reactions of the victims themselves. At many points the hoax could have and should have unraveled, but once out of the hands of the forger, the victims themselves played the major role. They carried the hoax onto the front pages of magazines and newspapers throughout the world.

The story of the Hitler diaries begins in 1973, when Gerd Heidemann, *Stern*'s investigative reporter, known as Der Spurhund ("The Bloodhound"), bought Hermann Göring's yacht, the *Carin II*.

His purchase of this yacht, in need of extensive repairs, was in keeping with Heidemann's lack of common sense in his journalistic pursuits. At *Stern* he was considered a too-thorough researcher. He had no sense of when to stop. Editors would find that he had spent many months futilely pursuing a point of no great importance in an investigation. He was also considered extremely gullible, never questioning information. It is a wonder he was not fired years before, but he seems to have been very adept in dealing with *Stern*'s bureaucracy.

The *Carin II* was a financial nightmare. Heidemann had mortgaged his house and had no funds to restore it. Its ownership did lead him into the world of retired Nazis, including an alleged affair with Göring's daughter, Edda. The boat became the meeting site for many characters from the Third Reich, including former SS generals Wilhelm Mohnke and Karl Wolff, and the intensity of the reminiscing convinced Heidemann and *Stern* that these "deck conversations" would be a viable book. *Stern* gave him a large advance on this book, and he spent it on the boat's restoration. He taped conversations of Third Reich personalities, but their conversations were frequently incoherent as they drank more and more heavily, reliving old times, and the project had to be abandoned.

In 1979 Heidemann married a woman who shared his interest in the Third Reich (during a live radio

Stern reporter Gerd Heidemann with the Hitler Diaries.

broadcast in Germany, when I made a remark she didn't like, she burst out, "you don't know our Führer, you don't understand what he was really like!"). The newlyweds had what they undoubtedly considered a romantic honeymoon in South America at *Stern*'s expense. They were accompanied by SS general Wolff, and the threesome pursued both Josef Mengele and Martin Bormann, while visiting with the likes of Walter Rauff and Klaus Barbie.

Upon his return Heidemann faced strong criticism within *Stern* for pursuing Bormann; *Stern* itself had published a major story giving conclusive proof that Hitler's former secretary was killed during the Russian assault on Berlin. He was also forced to face the financial reality that he could no longer keep up Göring's yacht.

Efforts to sell the boat led him to a major collector of Nazi memorabilia, German industrialist Fritz Stiefel. Stiefel decided not to pursue the yacht but showed Heidemann one of his prized possessions: a diary written by Hitler. It came, he stated, from a plane crash during the final days of the war.

The provenance was a reasonable deduction by Stiefel. It was the first of many pieces of the puzzle fitted into place by the victims while the forger, unable to answer their questions, simply confirmed the answers they themselves came up with. The provenance was logical because it was well documented that Hitler sent metal trunks of papers out of Berlin for his mountain retreat in Berchtesgaden just as Berlin was falling to the Russians.

Heidemann reported seeing the Hitler diary to his editors and was told by Henri Nannen, the founder and publisher of *Stern*, that he did not "want to hear or read about your Nazi Scheisse." Editor Peter Koch was even more blunt: his memo forbade Heidemann to pursue any Nazi stories and called Heidemann "mentally deranged." Rational people would assume this would be the end of Heidemann's enterprise, but Heidemann was able to "disappear," with the editors not caring what he was doing as long as they did not have to deal with him. Thomas Walde, the head of the history section at *Stern*, however, listened to Heidemann's story and secretly authorized him, despite the direct and clear orders from the publisher and editor-in-chief not to pursue Nazi stories.

Heidemann located the source of Stiefel's diary: Konrad Kujau. Heidemann had had Stiefel's telephone tapped and asked him to call his source to see if there were more diaries. Kujau had a very profitable relationship with Stiefel and had sold him about $75,000 in Hitler memorabilia, mostly forged watercolors and paintings that he claimed had been created by Hitler. Stiefel had not blindly trusted Kujau; he hired a reputed art historian named August Priesack, who had been employed by the Third Reich to catalog Hitler's watercolors and paintings between 1934 and 1939. Kujau must have held his breath while

Priesack examined his fakes, and his relief must have been incredible when Priesack not only authenticated the forged paintings but recalled fondly having last seen many of them in the 1930s!

Heidemann contacted Kujau directly and asked where the diary was found. Kujau didn't know what to say, and Heidemann responded it must be a secret because it came from East Germany. Kujau agreed. Heidemann asked how it had come out of East Germany, and when Kujau again responded that he couldn't answer, Heidemann said that only a high-ranking East German could have gotten it out. Kujau agreed. Heidemann asked if there were any more diaries, and when Kujau hesitated he said that Hitler must have written more than just one, and, of course, Kujau agreed. Heidemann suggested that he must have written one every year and Kujau, appreciating the situation, suggested Hitler would have written more than one each year. Heidemann then had no hesitation in offering Kujau two million deutsche marks for all the diaries.

Heidemann and Walde now faced the dilemma of raising the two million deutsche marks (the price would escalate as "additional" volumes were found, to over 10 million deutsche marks). They could not go to the editors since they had both defied direct orders. They decided to go to the supremely self-confident managing director of Gruner und Jahr, *Stern*'s parent company, Manfred Fischer. Fischer did not like Peter Koch and was delighted to scoop his editor by personally securing the Hitler diaries. Fischer authorized payments in cash and the diaries began to arrive at *Stern*.

The diaries presented Hitler in a more acceptable light, which would appeal to contemporary Germans whose parents likely voted the Nazis into power. The diaries portrayed Hitler neither as a monster nor as a munificent leader, but rather a leader the German people put into power at a time of great economic hardship, a leader who would repudiate the terms imposed upon Germany at the end of the first World War, a leader who might only be guilty of not controlling his fanatical followers. The forger created a Hitler that many people would want to believe was real, which meant that *Stern* magazine would sell more copies.

The text about Kristallnacht, the nationwide anti-Jewish riots in 1938, are indicative of a revised Hitler when he is quoted as complaining about the fanatics who have caused "millions and millions in damage to the German economy, and I don't just mean the broken glass." He frequently makes entries concerning the "Jewish problem" but suggests that Germany could ship them to other countries if they would accept them. The "final solution" in the diaries was his idea that perhaps Hungary, or another area in the East, could be given to the Jews to settle there and feed themselves. Heinrich Himmler, the head of the

SS, comes under severe criticism. Quoting from *Stern*'s memo describing the diaries: "Hitler's attitude toward Himmler . . . ranges from gruff to antagonistic. Himmler is spying on him, mistrusts the SS Chief's mythical idealization of the Germanic people and doubts his military capabilities. After the assassination attempt in . . . 1939, Hitler considers himself the victim of a plot, behind which he also suspects Himmler, and threatens, 'this duplicitous animal breeder, with his drive for power, still has a lot to learn from me.' . . . (Himmler) is living in another world. . . . I'm beginning to think he's out of his head." Following the invasion of Poland: "Hitler notes in his diary that he gave Himmler strict instructions not to carry out any reprisals against the Polish population. The merciless treatment of Polish civilians under the German occupation—an instance of high handedness by subordinates?" *Stern* adds, "[Is this] a macabre confirmation of the popular saying, 'if the Führer only knew about that'?"

The German people, *Stern*'s management thought, were going to want to read about this rehabilitated Hitler, and they could not have been more pleased at the prospect of the business the diaries would create.

Heidemann negotiated an extraordinary contract with *Stern* for the publication of the diaries. He was granted a very large advance, a veto over the historians who would work on the diaries, and a relatively large percentage of the publication profits. According to Fischer, Heidemann was also the person in charge of checking the diaries' authenticity.

At the same time that Kujau was defrauding Heidemann by selling him fake diaries, Heidemann was cheating Kujau by only giving him 25 percent of the money *Stern* thought it was paying for the diaries, and *Stern*'s management, in turn, was deceiving the editors.

Heidemann then used his investigative talents to track the flight path of the plane carrying Hitler's personal possessions from Berlin, and he found a crash site in Bornersdorf, East Germany, with graves nearby that led to the identification of the plane. Part of the cockpit windshield was found being used in a shed. Heidemann had now pulled the whole history of the diaries together.

The third major opportunity to prove the diaries false occurred when Heidemann, unable to keep the secrecy of their existence, showed one to SS general Mohnke. This particular diary referred to events that Mohnke was part of, and Mohnke told Heidemann that it could not possibly be genuine because the events did not happen. Heidemann explained to Mohnke that the diary entries must have reflected what Hitler intended to do but never carried out!

In May 1981 Peter Koch wanted to assign Heidemann to investigate the attempted assassination of Pope John Paul II, and he had to be brought in on the managing director's scoop. Koch and the other editors who were let in on the secret were angry but did not question the diaries' authenticity. Koch stated they must have been genuine because Fischer had paid millions of dollars for them, and it was unthinkable that they had not been authenticated. Koch visited Heidemann at home to discuss the diaries and was shocked at his incredible lifestyle: he had purchased two new apartments in which to put Hitler memorabilia, he had a new BMW and a new Porsche, and he told them that he was negotiating to purchase Hitler's boyhood home. Koch was shown, among other artifacts, what Heidemann claimed to be Hitler's suicide gun. Koch realized that it was both the wrong make and the wrong caliber. Despite these visits, and the questions they raised concerning Heidemann's sudden wealth, the hoax marched on unimpeded.

By the end of 1981, despite an almost complete lack of interest on the part of the editors, Schulte-Hillen decided that it was time to begin publishing the diaries, whether or not all of them had been smuggled out of East Germany (in reality, Kujau was still writing them). While he thought there could be no question of their authenticity, it was agreed they would bring in outside experts (who Heidemann would select) because their genuineness would be questioned by the publications *Stern* wanted to sell the rights to. This should have been the end of the story, but the three experts recommended by the Bundesarchiv (German Federal Archives) all presented reports that either authenticated the pages examined or allowed *Stern* to interpret them as authenticating the diaries.

The handwriting in the Hitler diaries is certainly the most inept attempt at imitating another's handwriting since William Henry Ireland's absurdly fake Shakespeare manuscripts in the late eighteenth century. With the exception of imitating Hitler's habit of slanting his writing diagonally, the forger failed to observe or to imitate the most fundamental characteristic of his handwriting, though Kujau managed to slightly imitate the capital H in Hitler's signature. He made the classic error of using that same form of the H in the text of the diaries. It is extremely rare for an individual to use the same form of a capital letter in both their signature and in the text. Obtaining the materials to create the forgeries was accomplished with an equal lack of skill. Even superficial research would reveal that Hitler always used beautifully bound leather writing folders and desk appointments. Kujau's imitation leather notebooks, with their crude wax seals, are comical. The use of a mechanical pencil (never used by Hitler) for many consecutive entries and the consistent use of the same modern blue-black ink are only overshadowed by such colossal errors as mistaking an F for an A in selecting the large metal initials to put onto the cover of one diary.

Stern provided all three experts with copies of Hitler's writing that they stated were from the Federal Archives and known to be genuine. But I discovered that the critically important ones were actually obtained from what was referred to as the *"Stern*/Heidemann dossier." The examples from the Bundesarchiv were almost without value for comparison purposes. The examples the experts relied upon for comparison were those later traced to the *Stern*/Heidemann dossier.

The situation is remarkable for its absurdity. *Stern*, in attempting to accomplish an objective verification of the 60 diaries' authenticity, showed their experts only three pages from notebooks, not the diaries, and gave them for comparison examples controlled and provided by their own reporter, who had a major financial stake in the diaries' authenticity.

The three experts, for their part, naively accepted *Stern*'s word that what they were being given as genuine examples were indeed that. In two cases the experts noted that there were differences in the signatures of the supposedly genuine examples but stated that the preponderance of evidence provided by the long, handwritten letters was sufficient to declare the questioned pages genuine. There was a complete lack of suspicion on the part of the handwriting experts—they made no attempt to independently verify where the supposedly genuine examples actually came from.

Stern magazine's issue explaining how the hoax had happened bore a very appropriate photograph of Konrad Kujau on the cover aiming a rifle at the viewer. The issue is notable for exposing its own management's gullibility in what it labeled "the biggest flop of the German press history." *Stern* wrote under a photo of me working in their office, "Rendell is doing what the

Stern's magazine issue explaining the Hitler Diaries hoax.

higher-ups at the publishers and in the editorial offices had failed to do for two years out of exaggerated secrecy and fear for the exclusiveness of their 'super scoop' . . . The 'biggest journalistic scoop in postwar history' had become even bigger than the few people in on it had ever hoped in their fondest dreams. It was the biggest journalistic blunder of all time. In their blatant presentation of Heidemann's hoax, the people responsible had correctly predicted a sensation à la Watergate. Unfortunately, it was a Watergate for *Stern*."

In keeping with the atmosphere of the whole story, the criminal trial of Kujau and Heidemann took on its own circus atmosphere, with Kujau writing out, in the courtroom, sections of the diary and signing them "Adolf Hitler." When the judge asked him what happened to the millions of marks he had received, Kujau replied, "I remember buying champagne but don't remember anything after the champagne." The judge said he wasn't sure whether Heidemann had conspired with Kujau in creating the diaries, or whether he had just defrauded *Stern* of most of the money they thought was going to Kujau (he kept 75 percent of it), and sentenced both of them to 4-1/2 years in prison.

Throughout my life I have always been very analytical. For me, it was the way to understand business situations as well as people, and myself. The events of the Hitler diaries left my businesslike and analytical approaches in shock. I knew the facts of how it happened—I experienced them firsthand—but I couldn't understand how these men in responsible journalistic and business positions could have behaved the way they did.

In watching a friend of mine, a professional close-up magician, perform, it suddenly all made sense. His performance is based on causing people to focus on one thing and not see the deception. The difference with the Hitler diaries was that the victims were both the magician and the audience. They didn't look at the critical events; they skipped over them, to what they wanted to see: news scoops, outdoing fellow employees, windfall profits, beating the competition, personal fame, a sense of following orders, and, perhaps, a revisionist view of Hitler.

Hugh Trevor-Roper, the British historian and author of *The Last Days of Hitler*, who was widely considered very arrogant, had initially authenticated the diaries in print and at *Stern*'s first news conference, but at the second news conference he stunningly admitted that he may have been too hasty. Within a few weeks of the declarations that the diaries were a hoax, he wrote to me from his home in Scotland, saying that if I was in London, he would come to meet me if I wanted. We had a private dinner at the Dorchester Hotel, and for someone described as an aloof elitist, Trevor-Roper was the most forthcoming and analytical of those involved. He described going to Zurich to look at the diaries on behalf of Murdoch's *Sunday Times* newspaper, on whose payroll he was dependent as a director. When he returned to England, he went to stay at Windsor Castle at the invitation of Queen Elizabeth, an invitation, he said, he had spent his lifetime hoping for. His head "was in the clouds" and he was detached from outside reality, he told me, when Murdoch called and said he was going forward immediately with publication. He wanted Trevor-Roper's statement that they were genuine, and he said he couldn't be sure. Murdoch said that wasn't good enough; what was his best guess? The historian said it was the biggest mistake of his life in caving into his employer's pressure.

Trevor-Roper told me his second great mistake was in not understanding how the news business had changed so dramatically from when he was in the news spotlight at the end of the war. He was overly confident he could handle and control the news with the Hitler diaries and was shocked at the circus in *Stern*'s first press conference. David Irving, the right-wing historian, was screaming that the diaries were fake. He knew then that he didn't understand what he had gotten himself into.

Trevor-Roper was not the kind of person I personally had an affinity for, nor a good chemistry with. But that night, in the splendor of the Dorchester's dining room, I thought he was probably the only participant in the hoax who understood why and

Robert Harris's 1986 book about the hoax, *Selling Hitler*, later became a TV mini-series.

how he had been so wrong. Six months later I ran into him at a party in the Parliament in London, and while he gave me a warm greeting, he was back to his lofty self and brushed off my compliments about his honesty and self-understanding. Another year or two later we were both at a dinner, where he recognized and greeted me but seemed to no longer remember the Hitler diaries. It is doubtful that the other participants in the biggest journalistic fraud of modern times would ever forget them.

Chapter 9

Exploding Onto the Public Stage

As the 1970s came to a close, I was on top of the world. In 20 years I had gone from starting out with less capital than any other dealer to developing my business in America, Europe, and Japan, far beyond what I, or anyone else, imagined. I had followed, unknowingly, the advice of the founder of computer science, Alan Turing: "Those who can imagine anything can create the impossible." I had challenged every fundamental tenet of the antiquarian manuscript business and found the dealers were all thinking and living in the same box. By being genuinely excited about the insights historical letters gave me into people and times past, being basically interested in the people who did or could collect, and having the attitude that I would go to them, I had built a thriving business. My catalogs were written for intelligent people who did not have an advanced degree in the subject, not for institutions that presumably already knew the historical background.

During the 1970s I had spoken at many universities on various aspects of the historical letters and documents field, and usually at the annual meetings of all the professional organizations: the Manuscript Society, the

American Library Association, the Association of College and Research Libraries, the Society of American Archivists, and others. I had co-authored *Autographs and Manuscripts: A Collector's Manual*, the most comprehensive reference book on the subject.

My research staff had continued to grow, and despite our modern office building, we were becoming as crowded as we had been ten years earlier in the basement of my family home. Mei-Ying and Pat Bozeman now both had their own research assistants, and we added a specialist in Western American history, Dave Warrington. Another anniversary catalog, number 150, was devoted to presidents. This was now a large-format, 237-page catalog, opening with 12 George Washington letters (my first catalog had only one). Working with our new Western American specialist, I was well under way on a series of three catalogs on the American frontier, in large format, totaling 727 pages. These were published in 1981.

In the spring of 1983 I completed writing the first volume of a series of catalogs of English and French literary authors. I was beginning work on the first volume of a catalog focusing on the American Civil War, 287 large-format pages, published the following year. I thought there weren't any new approaches to take, no more voids to fill in giving everyone outstanding information and service, nor any improvements in our very well-researched catalogs. Sales were more than $1 million a year.

I didn't realize that while I thought I was on top of the world, it was only my "known" world.

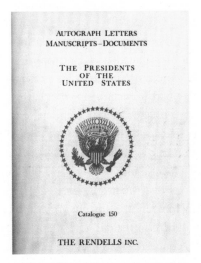

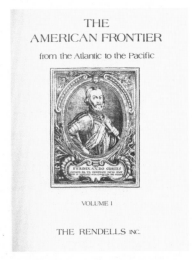

Our Catalog 150 featured documents related to the American presidents.

The first of three catalogs I produced about the American West.

For the past 20 years building my business had been a marathon where I was constantly thinking about how I could create new opportunities, new clients, more efficient administration, and more thorough searches to buy historical letters and documents. For years I had heard dealers say that if only more people knew about the excitement, wisdom, and enjoyment that this field of collecting brought, it would explode with new collectors. The worldwide publicity of the Hitler diaries, specifically the methods of forgery detection that I used, and

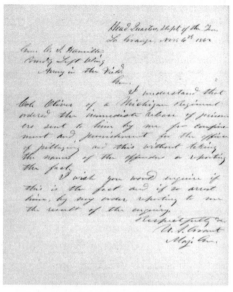

A letter written by Ulysses S. Grant.

the seemingly endless publicity that I received, opened up the world of collecting historical letters. Suddenly, I was no longer running a marathon but seemingly endless sprints reacting to opportunities, rather than my seeking them out as I had been doing for my whole career.

It was difficult to comprehend everything that happened. I was deluged with invitations to speak, though I had no interest in becoming an entertaining speaker. One proposal by a team of two producers at CBS was sufficiently flattering that I had to consider it. They wanted to create a TV series based on my character as an Indiana Jones of the art world. I have to admit it was flattering enough that I looked into the practical issues of what they were proposing. I would be the technical consultant, and they would use my real life as a background for storylines. The initial screenplay had my character uncovering a ring of scholars dealing in stolen antiquities to finance their cocaine habits.

I contacted several of my clients who were television producers. One of them, Leonard Stern, had created several successful series, including *McMillan & Wife*, starring Rock Hudson. He told me I could expect a maximum of $50,000 per episode, and in reality I would have no control over what they created. In the context of my business, I had to consider my image. Also, my clients would be worried their private dealings with me would turn into a public TV episode. I knew otherwise, but thought that would be a concern. It didn't make economic sense. What I would be paid as a technical consultant was far less than what I was making as a private dealer and consultant.

Above all, I wanted to get my life back on track after the Hitler diaries. All of the publicity had affected others' views of me, especially in the ski racing world. No one knew what I did outside of that world because to serious ski racers there isn't any other world. I enjoyed the anonymity, but mostly I enjoyed being judged, like everyone else, on my racing performances. Suddenly, racers wanted to ask me about Hitler, being on television, and having a successful business rather than how I had planned to attack a particular slalom course that day. I had enjoyed escaping into this different world, and now that was changed.

I learned that publicity was cheap if you were willing to say what the news media wanted you to say. I didn't believe news should be entertainment. My entire career had been based on the reality of facts, and I found myself rushing to re-embrace the academic world I felt comfortable in. I accepted speaking invitations at a number of journalism schools and at universities that were my clients. "How Bad Forgeries Became Great Hoaxes" was a serious appraisal of my direct involvement and everything I had learned at *Stern*.

My lecture was, invariably, covered by local television, and I was always asked the same question at the end of the interview: "What is the most important legacy of the Hitler diary hoax?" I always gave a serious journalistic answer. While reeling that off every time, I had another answer running through my mind and one day, after a lecture at the UCLA journalism school, I gave my real answer: Because of the Hitler diary story I had met a fantastic television journalist, my age, who lived in Boston. I went on to say I found journalism full of interesting women who, it seemed, couldn't find men with big enough egos to publicly be in their shadow. My ego, I explained, was big enough to find this amusing. The television reporter looked shocked at my answer; I told her I knew it was on tape, and then gave her the answer she expected to hear. A great relief came over her face!

Shirley McNerney was the ABC affiliate Boston reporter whose specialty was live breaking news stories. She had recommended they do a story on me when the news of the diaries first broke, but the news department said I was getting so much national coverage they didn't see a local angle except that I lived in Boston. The next day, Shirley's day off, they changed their mind and Shirley's best friend, along with reporters from other network affiliates, did interviews focused on the local person being involved in this major international story. Mary Richardson, her friend, exuded personal warmth as well as professionalism, and over the next two weeks I alerted her to new developments; she sometimes came to New York to interview me. I gave her the exclusive TV interview of how the diaries were forged. Some of these telephone calls were in the middle of the night, and after the story was over she invited me to dinner, saying her husband was anxious to meet the person making those midnight phone calls. When she invited me to bring my wife, I said I didn't have one, and her reaction was, "Have I got the woman for you!" And she did.

When I picked Shirley up at her apartment in Boston, I noticed the books on the shelves in her living room. This was a habit of mine. Many of Shirley's books were by sophisticated French authors, in French, and she had read them all. Our chemistry was immediate and we literally talked all night, until she had to go to work in the morning. I had dated a lot of successful women, so I could appreciate the rarity of our mutual magic, which was like wildfire. We were engaged two months later, and it was the beginning of the most remarkable romantic and, later, business partnership.

The worldwide publicity over the Hitler diaries had brought unimagined public attention to the field of historical letters and documents, to my business, and to me personally. There were feature stories about my business in popular magazines, including *Town & Country*, *Architectural Digest*, *Vanity Fair*, and others. Newspaper features were very frequent. Events that would not have received any notice in the past suddenly were covered. When I bought a collection of documents by the signers of the Declaration of Independence for $352,000 at an auction in New York, this was a story because the "Hitler diary expert" was the purchaser. I was careful to make sure the stories focused on my business, not on me personally, and, without question, there was a business benefit.

Of a much greater value was Shirley's belief that the interest in the items I was offering for sale would be dramatically greater if more people had direct access to them. She had the academic background, the personal interest in culture, and the firsthand knowledge of national news and was very excited to see my world introduced to a larger audience. My first gift to her was a letter by Madame de Sévigné, the seventeenth-century author of a book I saw on her bookshelf, whom I had hesitatingly asked her about at our first dinner. Shirley had read everything by her, and it was the start, and the cornerstone, of her collection of letters and manuscripts by prominent French women from the seventeenth to twentieth centuries. Her enthusiasm, from a different perspective, inspired me to successfully pursue her many suggestions about expanding my business to a vastly wider audience.

At about this time Roy Davids, my close friend at Sotheby's, contacted me about some diaries he had seen, which the owner adamantly insisted were written by Benito Mussolini, the World War II Italian dictator. Roy thought they were forged because consecutive entries were written at the same time. The owner said his father was one of the Italian partisans who stopped Mussolini's car and executed him, and he had taken the diaries from his luggage. Roy asked me to look at the diaries. Perhaps my saying they were not genuine would convince the owner. The two of us went to an apartment in London that was notably dark and old-fashioned, in a 1940s way. The Italian man animatedly told us the story of his father, and the other Communist partisans, stopping Mussolini's car while he was trying to flee to Switzerland, shooting him, his mistress, and the others, loading their bodies in a truck, and driving them to Milan, where they were famously hung up in the square.

When I looked at the diaries, it was clear Roy Davids was correct: multiple daily entries were written at the same time, not on different days, but otherwise the handwriting was likely that of Mussolini. The former Duce's handwriting was always quite clear, and I was able to understand enough of the content to begin to realize what they likely were. Mussolini wrote about his great love for his wife and their wonderful marriage (never mentioning his mistress), his devotion to the Catholic Church and the Pope, and his love for the Italian people. He recognized that he had made mistakes but claimed he was forced into decisions by Hitler, whom he detested, but who was capable of the utmost terror toward Italy if he didn't do as Hitler directed. I realized I was reading a text that was fictitious but likely written by Mussolini, who—having been

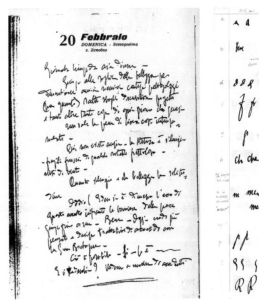

A diary page written by
Benito Mussolini.

Handwriting comparisons
of Benito Mussolini.

overthrown by the Italians in 1943 and imprisoned at a ski resort, and realizing his power was gone and all he had left was his reputation and legacy—wrote a version of his life for posterity. The diary wasn't a forgery, but the story was, and both were the creation of a desperate former dictator longing for redemption.

In my view the diaries had a relatively modest value, nothing like the amount the owner wanted. He thought the Italian media would buy publication rights, but I saw them as not only being untrue, but also boring. I encouraged him to find out for himself but, without an important authentication, he had little chance of finding a buyer. I also raised the issue of who owned the publication rights since several of Mussolini's children were still alive and, in America, would have inherited those rights.

The new worldwide interest in historical documents led to a former Hollywood agent, Leon Becker, leaving Beverly Hills to pursue his interest in historical documents as a business. He had great personal flair and was a very large man who visited the health spa La Costa, south of Los Angeles, on a number of occasions. He reasoned that many wealthy people were overweight and while staying at La Costa were being starved on a minimal diet. There was a small shopping mall within walking distance of the spa, and he thought giving them an opportunity to spend money and gratify themselves would be a good business model. It was, and Leon's business was very successful. He spent a great deal of time designing frames and mats for each piece and, while he probably didn't make a lot of money, he certainly enjoyed his business. I enjoyed providing him with his inventory.

On the other end of the spectrum, both geographically and in design, was a section of the B. Altman department store on Fifth Avenue in New York. They framed dozens of pieces in many fields, with portraits, in frames that were minimal in cost and design. Altman ran full-page ads in the *New York Times* offering framed historical documents, something they could afford because of the discounts offered by newspapers to businesses that bought advertising space in bulk. Altman developed a large business offering routine documents, signatures, and letters, and I was their principal supplier. It was an ideal relationship—I was interested in pieces with interesting content and less interested in routine documents and signatures, so I was happy to sell the routine material to them.

Meanwhile, potential major clients were coming to me. I was working with a new and very enthusiastic client from Dallas who was interested, at first, in collecting important letters of presidents and then expanded into Civil War and Revolutionary War personalities. He was ten years younger than me, and we had an instant chemistry. Our backgrounds could not have been more different. His father was the legendary real-estate developer Trammell Crow, the biggest commercial real-estate owner in the world who, when his son Harlan introduced me to him as a forgery expert, responded, "Keep him away from our legal files." Over the years I developed a very warm personal relationship with both of them, and they introduced me, socially, to the worlds of real-estate development and high-level Washington insiders.

Trammell wanted to establish a yearly gathering on his "farm" in East Texas, and Harlan invited me as one of the 25 people included the first year, 1983. Harlan said this was

Trammell Crow.

going to be camping, but based on the attire of most guests that first year, the message evidently didn't get to them. Gucci loafers, cashmere sweaters, and general elegance were not in keeping with tents, sleeping bags, and campfires. It was the start of a yearly gathering with special speakers, many of them leading Washington figures, that lasted until Trammell's death in 2009. I had the distinction of being the first speaker, but I didn't quite feel that way when Trammell put his arm around me and said, "Ken, what we need is a speaker." I agreed with him, and he said that was good, because I was it. When I asked him what he wanted me to speak about and when, he said, "Right now, and you figure it out." Over the next 26 years I never missed one of his "campouts." I met a number of people whose paths I never would have crossed otherwise. Many of them had started in the real-estate business with Trammell and it was very interesting, and impressive, to hear how they built their businesses over the decades.

On trips to Dallas I stayed in one of Trammell's first hotels, The Anatole, where he first pioneered the use of atriums, and I visited office buildings he had designed to be pleasant, convenient, and people friendly. It was no wonder his office buildings rented faster, and for more money, than competitors, who did not build in all of the personal amenities he did. Knowing him for the several decades I did, it was not surprising. Trammell really enjoyed everyone he had at his campouts, and I remember well the last one he was able to attend as Harlan, affectionately, helped him get around so he could visit with everybody.

Harlan took over the family business at a crucial time during a real-estate downturn. Much has been written about how he reorganized the company and put it on a solid footing for the future. I'm sure it gave his father enormous satisfaction that his son could take over the empire he built and continue its success with a new business plan for the future.

Harlan Crow and myself hiking.

During the past 40 years Harlan has built the most significant collection of American historical manuscripts from early explorations through later centuries. Some years ago he decided to collect books as well. His library building, which he meticulously designed himself, is one of the most beautiful and atmospheric in the world. I was standing with Harlan in his new library before it was

The boathouse at Harlan Crow's estate in the Adirondacks.

finished, and he modestly said that it was not as important as one that I was putting together for another client. I told him that the difference was that he, Harlan, had personally selected and made the decisions on everything in his library, from the manuscripts he collected to the architectural design, and everything reflected his own ideas about what was important.

Our families have spent time together at Harlan's Camp Topridge in the Adirondacks, and we have shared many mutual business and personal changes over the decades. It is a relationship I continue to enjoy.

Shirley and Chris DeMuth, CEO of American Enterprise Institute, at Harlan's Adirondack estate.

Another opportunity arose that reminded me of my younger self and reading biographies of successful businessmen. I read J. Paul Getty's *How to be Rich*, and now I was about to benefit directly from him. When he died, then the world's richest man, Getty left his fortune to his museum in California, which expanded dramatically from the villa in Malibu to the mountaintop art museum in Los Angeles. The museum developed well-funded archives and bought artists' letters from me. My buying in France, to sell to Alistair McAlpine in England, caused many collections to come onto the market. After McAlpine stopped collecting I continued to acquire letters of French artists because they represented an opportunity for collectors to have something from the hand of artists whose paintings were unaffordable. The Getty agreed it was an opportunity and acquired my entire artist inventory. They also purchased, through me, the remainder of McAlpine's collection, which had become dormant in the pantheon of his collecting interests.

In 1985 I took on a challenging situation, in large part because I was fascinated with the archive. Admiral Richard Byrd, the first person to fly over both the North and South Poles, who spent an Antarctic winter alone at the South Pole and wrote a classic book about the experience, died in Boston in 1957. His archives were inherited by his wife, Marie, who died in 1974. There were several surviving children and grandchildren. All had inherited undivided interests in the papers and were not able to agree on anything. I was brought in to appraise the fair market value for an actual sale, not a donation, and to negotiate with the descendants so the papers could be sold. I arrived at a value and the Polar Archives of Ohio State University agreed. Still, the descendants couldn't agree. One was blocking the sale, and even in a face-to-face meeting he would not tell me why. He considered agreeing only if the papers couldn't be seen for a period of years. I told him no one would buy them for $155,000 with that restriction. I had gone through everything and told him there was nothing scandalous or embarrassing to the family. Finally, he said he was concerned about his school reports, the ones his father would have received, and he didn't want anyone to see them. I offered to take these from the archives the next day, which I did, and the papers went off to the Polar Archives.

Everything in the archives concerned the basic administrative and business operations of Byrd's expeditions, which were important from an exploration standpoint. The logistics, contingencies, supplies, and all of the very complex planning that went into them were important research archives. What was missing was a sense of Admiral Byrd, the man. I wrote in my appraisal report

Admiral Richard Byrd.

that "the heart and soul of Admiral Byrd is not found in the archives." The Polar Archives knew of this and went through the papers before agreeing to the price, but we shared the sense that the personal Admiral Byrd was missing.

The sale of the papers, and my involvement, was covered by the Boston media, and as a result a man contacted me who had bags of Admiral Byrd's papers and had held onto them because he didn't think they should be thrown away. He was a responsible person and brought everything from his storage area to me, saying he wanted what he had to go with the papers he had read about. The first bag had every Christmas card Byrd ever received. I was disappointed, but when I emptied out the next trash bag, everything that had been missing was there: his personal journals, his letters, everything that showed who Byrd was as a person, and how he coped with all of the challenges and problems of Antarctica. Of particular importance was his journal for his flight over the North Pole. There had always been questions about whether he had actually made it as far as the North Pole. It was clear from what Byrd wrote in his journal that he certainly thought he was over the North Pole. I made inquiries in the family about this discovery in an abandoned storage facility, and I learned that one of his sons had early dementia and had probably stored the papers and forgotten about them.

In July 1985 Shirley and I were married with, in a sense, appropriate drama. TWA flight 847 was hijacked after takeoff from Athens in June, and Shirley was assigned to cover the story from the standpoint of a Boston area businessman, Bob Brown, who was selected by the terrorists to be held along with the crew until the release of other terrorists held by Israel. Unbeknownst to them, Brown was a former Army Special Forces officer in Vietnam, an identity that was important to keep secret. They had already killed a U.S. Navy seaman who was on the plane, and Brown was an obvious target if they knew his background.

Shirley became very friendly with his wife and family as they awaited news of this international ordeal. As the plane was being flown around repeatedly from Beirut to Algiers, Shirley completed our wedding plans in the Browns' living room. As our wedding date approached, Shirley thought she might be sent to Europe to continue coverage. At the last minute Ronald Reagan negotiated the release of the hostages and Israel, a short time later, released the terrorists. Bob Brown arrived back in Boston just in time to attend our wedding with his wife. Many media people were guests, and for everyone who had been following the dramatic saga of flight 847, Bob Brown was our most popular guest.

Shirley and I on our wedding day.

Jason and Jeffrey at our wedding.

July 14, 1985, was the cementing of an already incredible union in every way. Personally, our union was the most important decision I ever made, and professionally it led to a rapidly developing, though unintended, business partnership combining my knowledge of the field, my reputation, and my experience with Shirley's knowledge and belief that I needed to be thinking of the larger world of cultivated, intelligent, and successful people as potential clients. Neither of us ever dreamed of how fantastically successful this would be.

Throughout the mid-1980s my established business was very strong, particularly with a new collector in Santa Barbara, Dave Karpeles. He wrote out his orders on lined paper torn from a spiral binder, with his name and address rubber-stamped at the bottom. For all the unpretentiousness of his writing paper, what he inquired about was very sophisticated and showed a wide international interest. Dave would always negotiate the price of each document and then want to negotiate the price for everything as a group. It was never easy making sales to him, but intellectually it was very satisfying to work with someone with such a great appreciation for all the sophisticated subjects I was offering. In the days before the internet, no one knew Karpeles was a scientist with Remington Rand Univac and then General Electric Tempo, where he created the first operating optical character recognition program, which revolutionized banking procedures. He also developed an artificial-intelligence program allowing people to communicate with a computer using unrestricted English language.

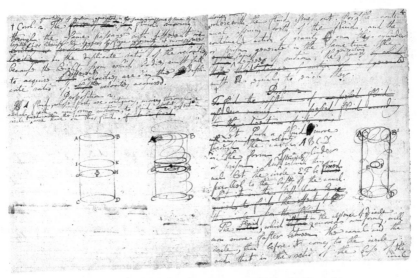

Isaac Newton's corrected manuscript of the *Philosophiae Naturalis Principia Mathematica*.

Karpeles was spending considerable amounts of money with dealers and in auctions, and there wasn't anyone else who was buying across such a wide range of historical periods, countries, and subjects. The first time I went to see him in the Montecito section of Santa Barbara, I was impressed with both his palatial home and the art displayed throughout it. He made it clear that his collection of historical letters and documents was his main interest. He had bought the estate across the street from his home to house his collection and to provide a space for the staff he hired to catalog and exhibit it, and this eventually became his museum. He asked me to speak at the dedication of the Karpeles Manuscript Museum, and I felt honored. When I viewed his initial exhibits, it was more apparent than ever that he had collected in such a broad way to enable his museum to show the development of both American and European history and culture over the centuries. As a dealer, and even more so as a collector, it gave me great pleasure to have a part building this collection of over a million pieces, which is now exhibited in a number of locations throughout the country. Karpeles had enormous foresight, and no one has ever approached his concept of world history.

Another longtime client who was important to me commercially, however, was coming to an end. B. Altman & Co., the department store on Fifth Avenue in New York, which had been buying large numbers of attractive documents and signatures, particularly of the popular presidents and the leading figures in almost all fields, was sold and the new corporate owner eliminated departments that could not be automated.

My wife, Shirley, after more than 25 years on air, was reaching the point of wanting to make changes. In 1987 she covered the teacher-in-space program. She was standing directly under the *Challenger* when it exploded and won prestigious national awards for her continuous and emotional coverage; she was one of the few reporters at Cape Canaveral who managed to stay on the air. Covering the *Challenger* tragedy felt like a capstone to her career. In our personal lives, we had the complication that by then I had sole custody of my two boys, 5 and 16 years old. From a family standpoint, it was difficult that Shirley frequently didn't get home until 8 o'clock at night. She was able to negotiate a new part-time schedule and began to pay more attention to her ideas about how the business could directly reach more people.

My publicity was already making people aware that historical letters could be collected; Shirley's focus was on making the actual historical documents physically available so people could experience them and want to buy them.

A new upscale antique center was being built on East 57th Street, The Place des Antiquaries, between Lexington and Park Avenues, and there were galleries still available. It brought exposure to people walking through, and part of its desirability was that people coming to see a dealer in any specialized field would be exposed to the other dealers as well. It was a logical step for us to take in 1988.

The first New York gallery, on East 57th Street.

In Paris my dear friend Thierry Bodin had risen to become the most important dealer in Europe. We had met in 1970, when he was an assistant to an old and long-established documents dealer, Morssen, in Rue de Seine. We have been very good friends since the day he invited me home for lunch, to meet his wife Pierrette. Over the following 50 years we have had a close personal as well as business relationship. He introduced me to Philippe Zoummeroff, a Frenchman who had been educated in America. Zoummeroff inherited a family tool business, which was very successful but uninteresting to him. Collecting was his passion, and it was almost on a professional level. He bought many documents from me and one day said he wanted to form a collection of letters and documents by the most important Americans. He wanted to limit the number to 100 so it was not unwieldy. Even though he had quite a spectacular house in Paris, space was a factor. He already had 15 or so documents by important Americans such as George Washington and Abraham Lincoln, but creating the list of 100 was an interesting and challenging project. We both developed our ideas, and his education and knowledge of America was such that his ideas were sometimes more interesting than mine. He wanted Al Capone on the list, while I did not, because I didn't like the idea someone would think Al Capone represented some part of American society. We had many fascinating dinners in Paris working over the list, which made me think of who the most influential people were in other areas. In the future I suggested Zoummeroff's concept to many collectors who were concerned that they weren't sufficiently focused and that their collection would get out of control.

Thierry and Pierrette Bodin.

While visiting Paris regularly, I had also developed several Middle Eastern clients who, over interesting luncheons, gave me a better understanding of Middle East issues. Shirley joined me for lunch with one of them at the Crillon, one of Paris's most elegant hotels. I told her I expected to sell him a Mozart manuscript. When he sat down, he told me that he wasn't going to buy it. Shirley later told me that she wondered if I would cancel lunch before running up an extravagant bill. By the end of lunch he had bought two Mozart manuscripts, and Shirley had a better idea of how I operated!

She also gained a new insight when I told her on a Friday night that Paige Rense, the founder and editor-in-chief of *Architectural Digest* magazine, had personally called that day to place an order from our catalog. Previously she had ordered through a secretary, but this time she was on the phone herself, and I asked her what her collecting theme was. She said she had no idea; it was all over the place, there was no order or structure to it. I told her I would be in Los Angeles on Monday, and if she had time for a long lunch, I would tell her at the end of it what I thought her theme was. She was intrigued and said she would change her plans to be available.

Shirley said she had no idea I was going to be in Los Angeles on Monday, and I replied that I hadn't either, but if I had offered to come to Los Angeles just to see Paige, she would never have agreed; since I said I would be there anyhow, there was no commitment on her part. Not only did Paige and I establish the theme of her collecting but as we parted, she commented, "When I find something as fascinating as I have found our conversation, I want to have it in the magazine," and a few months later I was the subject of a feature in

Architectural Digest. Paige and I continued a personal friendship, and regular luncheons, after *Architectural Digest* moved to New York City. Shirley and I were honored to attend her very small wedding, at Robert Frost's former home in Vermont, to the artist Kenneth Noland. Their wedding was held in his artist's studio, which he had built in Frost's barn.

The 1980s were dominated by the monumental fraud of the Hitler diaries, followed by the murders and fraud of the Mormon forger (more on that later), and my encounters with the dark side of people weren't over yet. For many years the FBI had consulted me about potential forgeries of historical documents and the establishment of fair market value to determine federal jurisdiction in criminal cases. They also consulted me about tracing documents that turned up in criminal investigations but were never reported stolen.

Sitting Bull.

It was not unusual when the FBI in Boston asked if they could come to confer with me about some letters they suspected might be stolen. They told me that a man had sold a group of James McNeill Whistler's letters to Goodspeed's Book Shop in Boston and then mentioned having various Abraham Lincoln letters he would bring in another time. Claire Rochefort in the bookshop noted the dates of the Lincoln letters, and in checking found they were listed as belonging to the National Archives. The letters that the bookshop had bought, written by Whistler, were not reported stolen, but the FBI hoped I might know how to investigate further.

Two FBI agents were seated across from my desk, and when they put the letters on my desk in front of me, I put my hands up in the air and said I wanted them to be sure that I had not touched the letters. They didn't understand why, until I pointed to pencil writing on the back of the letters—it was my handwriting. I had owned all of the letters and had sold them to the Library of Congress. I produced the order slips and invoices for them.

When the FBI went to the Library of Congress, they had no record of owning the letters—they had not only never cataloged them but also couldn't find their purchase orders, nor my paid invoices. I had all of the paperwork, and the seller was arrested for grand theft from the federal government. In searching where he lived in Washington, they discovered the Lincoln letters along with many other documents stolen from both the Library of Congress and the National Archives. The total value amounted to more than $1 million.

When they told me the thief's name was Charles Merrill Mount, I vaguely recalled him as a minor buyer of artists' letters years earlier and that he lived in Ireland. I learned from the FBI that he was an art historian and had written biographies of John Singer Sargent and Claude Monet. He was also an artist, and he created a character for himself. His name originally was Sherman Suchow from New York.

Just before he was to go on trial in federal court in Boston, I received a call, at night, from a very friendly man who explained that he was the federal public defender and was representing Mount. He hoped I might have some information that would help his client. Completely taken aback, I suggested that the information I had was that his client was guilty as hell, and he ought to have Mount plead guilty. His lawyer, Charlie McGinty, explained it was a very tough case to defend—my thought was "no kidding"—but that it was his job to do the best he could. Wasn't there something I could think of that might make a jury sympathetic? There wasn't.

Never having met Mount, I wasn't prepared for the person at the defense table. He was dressed as an English country gentleman, including a cane and bowler hat, and exuded all the airs of a country squire. As the government presented its case, he heckled witnesses from the Library of Congress and the National Archives, despite repeated warnings from the judge. When her patience wore out, he was jailed for contempt of court. Yet every morning Mount arrived from jail in all his gentlemanly finery. His spirit of defiance never wavered.

Charles Merrill Mount.

My testimony, on direct examination, was about the sales I had made to the Library of Congress of these pieces he had sold for tens of thousands of dollars to the bookshop in Boston. It was pretty much cut-and-dried testimony. My original invoices, and their purchase orders, were submitted as evidence, and it seemed unquestionable that everything had been bought from me. With that, the government rested its case and then the circus began.

Mount testified that it was known throughout the world that I was a crook, no one would buy anything from me, and no one would believe anything I had to say. I thought it was all irrelevant since the purchase and sales documents proved the case, but in a jury trial you never know what might sway jurors. When I went home that night, I went to my attic where I kept old business files and found dozens of letters that Mount had written and signed to me from Ireland. In them he thanked me profusely for being so reasonably priced and stated what great contributions I made to the field of research by making these inexpensive pieces available. The next day the assistant U.S. attorney entered all of these letters into evidence and forced Mount to read every one of them to the jury. He was his only defense witness, and though the government thought it was an open-and-shut case, they did not want to take any chances and said they would call me as a rebuttal witness the next day.

That night I realized that while I had testified in many courtrooms before, this was the first time I was testifying in Boston. My son Jason, seven years old, wanted to be a trial lawyer, and I thought he might enjoy coming to court the next day. He and I went to the U.S. Attorney's Office on our way to court, and we went over how they would question me. They told my son that the defense would attack me in every possible way because they had no case except to try to discredit me. They didn't want my son to get upset. He assured them he wouldn't. When we walked into the courtroom, Mount showed that his nights in jail had not tempered his spirit. He looked at my son and said in a loud voice, "Who the hell is this, the only character reference you can get?" It was an appropriate start for an unusual day in court.

I contradicted Mount's testimony in numerous areas, and you could tell from body language that the jury had heard enough—there couldn't be any question that he had stolen and sold the letters, but the federal public defender gave it one more try. He announced he was impeaching me and asked me questions about the Mormon murderers. It became an interesting game, as he was not prepared with enough information to ask intelligent questions, and since I wouldn't comment beyond yes or no, every question went down a dead end. It was over pretty quickly, and the jury spent the minimal amount of time in finding Mount guilty.

Mount was sentenced to eight years in federal prison. I thought this was the end of it, but one night at a small dinner party in Washington, D.C., the man sitting next to me, who was a judge on the U.S. Court

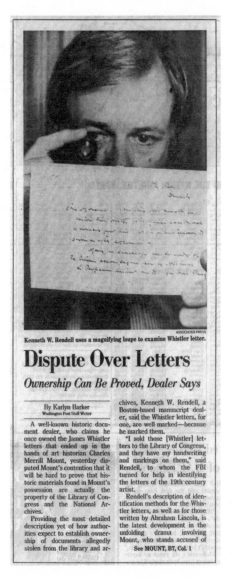

Kenneth W. Rendell uses a magnifying loupe to examine Whistler letter.

Dispute Over Letters
Ownership Can Be Proved, Dealer Says

By Karlyn Barker
Washington Post Staff Writer

A well-known historic document dealer, who claims he once owned the James Whistler letters that ended up in the hands of art historian Charles Merrill Mount, yesterday disputed Mount's contention that it will be hard to prove that historic materials found in Mount's possession are actually the property of the Library of Congress and the National Archives.

Providing the most detailed description yet of how authorities expect to establish ownership of documents allegedly stolen from the library and ar-

chives, Kenneth W. Rendell, a Boston-based manuscript dealer, said the Whistler letters, for one, are well marked—because he marked them.

"I sold those [Whistler] letters to the Library of Congress, and they have my handwriting and markings on them," said Rendell, to whom the FBI turned for help in identifying the letters of the 19th-century artist.

Rendell's description of identification methods for the Whistler letters, as well as for those written by Abraham Lincoln, is the latest development in the unfolding drama involving Mount, who stands accused of

See MOUNT, B7, Col. 1

of Appeals in Washington, said he knew all about me because Charles Merrill Mount filed endless appeals from his conviction, and I was always described as being in league with the FBI in framing him. He died in prison after serving six years.

By the end of the decade Shirley had retired from television and was developing her own ideas on bringing the personal experience of our material to a much wider audience. The general business, both buying and selling, was going very well, and in 1989 three major changes coincided. While our gallery at the Place des Antiquaries in New York was doing well, we were limited by the relatively small amount of wall space, and I was concerned about how long this consortium of dealers could last. Almost all of them were more concerned with their jealous rivalries than with the good opportunities they never would have had in individual galleries.

After much searching and research we found an excellent location on Madison Avenue, between 76th and 77th Streets, to the left of the entrance to the Carlyle Hotel, one of the most prestigious hotels in the city. I had a meeting with the landlords and I was relieved, and impressed, that their attitude was to put together an interesting group of quality tenants, not just merchants who could pay the highest rents. They offered us a very fair deal. We moved in a few months later, after renovating the gallery, and would be there for more than 25 years.

I had also been thinking about a gallery in Beverly Hills. We found the location we wanted just off Rodeo Drive, next to the jeweler Harry Winston and a popular restaurant. Beverly Hills turned out to be a sharp learning curve for us. We deliberately designed the gallery to look like our New York gallery—in fact, the name was The Kenneth W. Rendell Gallery of New York. We didn't want it to look like another

The Madison Avenue gallery.

flashy Beverly Hills gallery with merchandise priced for Beverly Hills.

We were greeted by the local media with many feature stories. The most common question, and an unsettling one, was the surprise reporters expressed that we thought people in Los Angeles would have an interest in culture. Our Beverly Hills gallery was also the scene of the only television segment that embarrassed me. "Lifestyles of the Rich and Famous" did a full program touring through the gallery, focusing on all of the expensive pieces. It wasn't a good omen. Though the gallery did well, the clients were completely different from New York. Our overwhelming success in New York was based on helping people develop their collecting interests once they discovered they could own original historical letters and documents. In Beverly Hills people would come in and buy an expensive piece, but very few turned into collectors. While people in New York seriously considered expensive purchases, in Beverly Hills it was a quick and casual decision, even if the piece was $100,000.

Bill Bell, the creator and producer of the soap opera *The Young and the Restless*, was typical. He bought two expensive pieces, and I contacted him about meeting personally. He invited me to dinner at his palatial estate. It was a fascinating evening, and I recall Bell telling me that the estate next door, which had been Cary Grant's house, belonged to him and he used it as a guesthouse. He was upfront in saying that he wouldn't be interested in

The Beverly Hills gallery.

buying anything else from the gallery, but we talked about why his soap opera was so popular, and he made many realistic literary comparisons to serialized fiction in the nineteenth century, notably Charles Dickens. He and I had many delightful lunches together at a popular restaurant, the Bistro Garden near my gallery, but I could never interest him in collecting on the scale I hoped.

We had a ten-year lease, and by the time it was up our block on North Beverly Drive had changed dramatically, and many national chain stores had located there. Williams-Sonoma and Victoria's Secret were our new neighbors, and our new rent was prohibitive.

Our third major move of the year was our relocating offices just outside Boston. We were very crowded in the building where we had been since 1973, and there was no room for expansion. We had looked into buying and renovating buildings in nearby towns but had not found any good opportunities, when my son asked why we didn't buy the modern bank building that was for sale quite close to where we lived. We normally had no occasion to drive by this building, but once we did, we knew it was what we were looking for. It was a one-story brick-and-glass building, a former bank with a huge modern vault, set on a large piece of land directly across the street from where John Eliot had preached to the Indians in the mid-1600s. The land was large enough to accommodate doubling the building's footprint; we had an architect add a second floor, and in late 1989 we moved into our new custom-designed building.

Our purpose-built office building outside Boston, 1989.

Our new vault to protect the most valuable inventory.

Chapter 10

Selling Ronald
Reagan's Papers

I n 1985, midway through Ronald Reagan's two terms in the White House, I shared the view of many Americans and the media that Reagan's advisors probably wrote everything for him and that he was basically an actor with strong conservative values who knew how to play the role of president. That opinion changed dramatically at the beginning of 1985, when I was offered a group of hundreds of handwritten letters drafted by him as governor of California. His secretary, with his permission, had saved these drafts.

Unknown to anyone outside of Reagan's inner office was his habit of drafting letters by hand, signing the drafts "RR" if he wanted his secretary to sign the typed version with his full name, or "Ron" or "Ronnie" if he wanted her to be more personal. His handwriting was very clear and easy to read; those he was writing to would have been pleasantly surprised to receive a handwritten letter from the governor, so it is difficult to understand why he would then have the letters typed and signed with a machine or by his secretary. (After I sold a significant number of the letters to Malcolm Forbes, Forbes asked Secretary of State Jim Baker if Reagan was still drafting letters in this way in the White House, and Baker said he still did this one night a week.)

Reagan's habit of not signing his letters was established early in his career, when Warner Bros. hired his mother to sign letters with his name (there is usually a similarity in handwriting between parents and children). The most extraordinary letter in this context is one that he personally wrote on July 13, 1969, to an old friend in Illinois:

> I understand someone helpfully answered your letter over my signature while I was laid low by the flu. I just felt old Midwestern friends should still hear from me over the signature below. Best regards, Dutch.

Below this text, he has written, "sign it Dutch."

The letters show Reagan as an articulate, well-organized creator of much of the rhetoric that commentators frequently attributed to his aides and speechwriters. By showing Reagan as the creator of these policy statements, the letters illustrated his character and sincerity, his firm belief in the moral correctness of his own views, his refusal to consider altering his policies because of political pressure or expediency, and his great concern that his opinions and views be understood.

April 24, 1967:

It is not true that my position has changed. . . . I still believe the individual should have the right to ownership, control and disposition of his own property and any invasion of that right by government is a threat to individual freedom. . . . This was not made clear by the press in reporting my answer. . . . The press has not fully explained that the tax increase was made necessary by the eight years of fiscal irresponsibility which left us with a nearly bankrupt state. We are doing all we can to reduce the cost of government but are being opposed by Democratic legislature which would continue their spending ways regardless. Welfare is our greatest problem . . .

May 11, 1967:

If I thought there was ever evidence of a clear and present threat to freedom for our traditional separation of church and state I would understand the ban on prayer in the schools. I don't think such a threat exists. My disagreement with the Supreme Court decision is based on my fear that this is one more step in downgrading our spiritual heritage and encouraging materialism.

October 3, 1967, to Ruth Gates:

In our attempt to make our welfare and health programs more workable we haven't changed the provisions for those over 65 . . . Nor . . . to the blind. . . . Our cuts were in such things as braces on teeth, dentures, reading glasses etc. so that we wouldn't have to deny medical care . . . for those . . . seriously ill. . . . We want to pinpoint those who are cheating so we will be better able to help the deserving. . . . We should do all we can for those who through age or disability now find themselves in need of a helping hand. Certainly no one in this country should be denied a doctor because of inability to pay.

He wrote in January 1967:

First of all I've never used the expression: "welfare which my taxes pay for." You've evidently been subjected to a distortion or misquote. My position has been stated repeatedly that the overwhelming majority of welfare recipients want to work and should be helped so they can become self-sufficient. I have attacked the red tape and excessive administrative cost of welfare but never the amount received by the recipient. . . . Welfare should be directed at salvaging human beings without drying up their confidence and will to live independently. But for those unable to work I have flatly stated we must do even more.

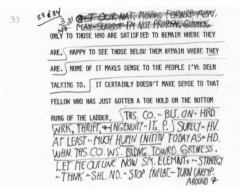

Reagan annotating a typewritten speech prepared for him.

December 19, 1967, to Ed:

I'm sure you know how much I share your concern and your belief in the need for someone to lead us from the present wilderness. You do me great honor and one I'm not sure is deserved when you assigned that task to me. . . . Believing as I do that a path of duty lies before us, a hard road leading to our destiny, I intend to do whatever is asked of me and all that I can to keep us on that road.

June 13, 1967, to Betty and Mac:

This is quite a job I've got for myself but you'd be surprised how little real strain when you actually base all decisions on what you honestly believe is right and not just politically expedient.

January 1967 to Catherine:

I had no illusions about what would happen when I really started to keep my campaign promises. Everyone wants economy until it touches their pet boondoggle. Now everybody's mad at me—except the people.

In a letter that foretold his own future, he wrote to Edward Bromfield on June 28, 1968:

You also laid things on the line and deserve the same in return. We are in agreement about the need to arouse this nation and to remind the people of their greatness. When I was somewhat in your position and had cast my first vote a president (Franklin D Roosevelt) said to us "we have nothing to fear but fear itself." We need to be reminded of this today. I'm aware there are others who have suggested me for that higher office but I have to feel I'm right in my decision to not become an active, seeking candidate. At the convention I will be placed in nomination by the California delegation. At that time if the feeling is widespread enough the convention will act accordingly. It is my conviction that this job seeks the man. You have made me feel better about our nation's future because of the views you expressed.

Time simplifies history. I think that, regardless of political orientation, these letters express a sense of decency, personal warmth, and genuineness that everyone longs for. The most conservative president of recent times quoting the most liberal and progressive president in such a sincerely flattering way seems unheard of today. They made many collectors feel better, and I quickly—too quickly in fact—sold all of the letters.

As interesting as this collection of manuscript letters was, I became more intimately involved with the personal side of Ronald Reagan through a Beverly Hills dealer. Reagan's rebellious daughter Patti had given the dealer on consignment a group of letters her father had written to her, which were full of warmth and thoughtful fatherly advice. My reaction was that these were letters I did not want to see publicized because I felt they were an invasion of his privacy and, even though it

My work with Ronald Reagan's documents included hand-written letters and annotations to prepared speeches.

showed him in a very favorable way, exposed the poor relationship he had with his daughter at the time. I said I would buy all of them, for a total of about $150,000, and prepared to write out a check. I was told that the dealer had already offered two of them to a well-known, disreputable small dealer who we both knew would sensationalize them in the press. No matter how much I argued, the dealer insisted that if that person wanted to buy them, he would sell them to him. I bought everything else and sold them to one of Reagan's wealthy supporters, Helen Copley, who owned the Copley Press newspaper empire. I believed that would be their permanent home, and Mrs. Copley agreed that no one would be shown the letters during Reagan's lifetime.

The other two letters took quite a different turn. The dealer who had bought them offered them directly to Reagan for a staggering price, with the threat that if he didn't buy them, the dealer would make sure they were well publicized. There was nothing embarrassing in them from Reagan's fatherly perspective, only the embarrassment of his daughter selling them. Reagan turned his offer over to the FBI, who considered it extortion and tried to have the dealer prosecuted, but he was let off with a warning. A few years later I was brought into an FBI case concerning Jimmy Carter's papers and was told they were prosecuting this same person for violating a little-known law concerning presidential papers. I told the FBI I thought this was an unfair enforcement of a law I had never heard of and anyone could easily have violated, but they told me it was payback for the Reagan extortion. In the Carter case the dealer was sentenced to federal prison.

Many years later, after the 2004 death of Mrs. Copley and the sale of Copley Press, it became known that the library she had created was actually owned by the newspaper company, and the collection was put up at auction. The letters I had thought best to keep private were suddenly on the market.

Reagan wrote to Patti on White House stationery on May 23, 1983, about a private meeting with nuclear-freeze activist Dr. Helen Caldicott, which Patti had arranged:

> The enclosed appeared in today's Washington Post. It has caused quite a stir in the press. Of course, no such conversation took place, nor have I had any conversation with her since we met in December. And as you know her words about my believing we could win a nuclear war were never part of that visit . . . (I don't believe such a thing). So, her speech is a complete falsehood both as to having a conversation with me at all and as to the subject of the supposed conversation. Patti it isn't easy to learn we misplaced our faith and trust in someone. I know I've had

that experience—once with someone I thought was my closest friend. But when it happens, we must be prepared to accept it and not shut our eyes to the truth. There was a time in ancient days when a messenger bringing bad news was put to death. I hope you won't call for my execution. I'm afraid she is so carried away by her cause she subscribes to the belief that the end justifies the means. Such a belief if widespread would mean the end of civilization. Love Dad

A lengthy two-page letter was written as president on Air Force One, answering Patti's letter of concern about legislation affecting American Indians.

I realize how the plight of these several thousand appears to you and certainly the Bureau of Indian Affairs has not been a howling success. . . . But Patti the whole subject is one that causes great frustration for anyone who comes in contact with it. You see the question of these 8,000 Indians. Sometimes I could be of help. As for instance when I was able to prevent the building of a dam that would have flooded "Round Valley" and displaced the Indians who were promised the Valley was theirs forever.

Most of the time however I knew the frustration you feel because like this instance the Indians themselves were in disagreement among themselves.

You see the "Indian problem" doesn't really exist. The Indians think of themselves as Hopis, Sioux, Cherokee, etc. and rarely do they agree on what should be done. Then within their various tribes there is the great division between those who want to live in our modern lifestyle and those who would continue in their native tradition. Even these latter however want at the same time some of the modern advantages. . . . If this sounds heartless, I don't mean it to. It is frustrating and I'll admit I don't know the solution. Maybe 100 years ago we should've adopted a melting pot policy and made them a part of our society to begin with. You look . . . and see their happiness and total success in the modern world and wonder if that isn't preferable to reservation life. Then you see the reservation Indian happy with his sheep herding and closeness to earth and sky and feel it would be tragic to move him. I don't know the answer. I do know that to agree with the one group in this present problem would cause just as great an unhappiness to an even greater number who see an opportunity to improve their lot with the proceeds of the coal mining. Please believe me the entire matter is much more complex than it appears to you now. We can only do our best to understand and be helpful when we can but not to inject ourselves carelessly when our good intentions can worsen the situation we are trying to resolve.

Some months after originally purchasing these letters to keep them from being publicized, I was contacted about a new letter that Reagan had written to his daughter, which she wanted $10,000 for. This was just after Christmas, and I was upset at both the very personal content of the letter and the appearance that a situation was created where he would write an emotional letter and she would be able to sell it.

It was written on Christmas Eve 1990:

All right I'll quit bothering you but I had more in mind then arguing politics. The line in the song says it all; "the days dwindle down to a precious few." On February 6th I'll be 80 years old.

Your mother and I are hard put to understand the separation between us and our firstborn. It didn't just happen with your growing up and leaving home. I can recall your mother coming home in tears after driving you to school. She couldn't understand your complete silence even to the point of you not saying "goodbye."

Was it having to share with a newborn brother? I remember a loving daughter who never let us leave the house without waving goodbye from the window. We have some snapshots that reveal a difference in a little girl. We ask ourselves "what did we do wrong." We were once a loving family.

Well as I said earlier "I'll stop bothering you" but I don't understand the separation of our family. I recall a little girl sitting on my lap and asking me to marry her. Her mother across the room behind her signaled me to say "yes." So I did and explained would have to wait till she was a little older. Love Dad.

I made it known to Patti that this was the last letter I would buy, and no more appeared.

A few years later my wife and I were invited to an event by Malcolm Forbes honoring the retired president and Mikhail Gorbachev. We were seated quite close to Ronald and Nancy Reagan. I quietly told Shirley that I wished I had the nerve to whisper in his ear, "The next time you want to send a letter to your daughter Patti, please fax it to her." But I did not.

Chapter 11

The Mormon Forgeries and Murders

The morning of October 15, 1985, Shirley and I were getting our day underway. Being a television news reporter, she needed to know the day's national stories, so we had three televisions in almost every room, tuned to the three networks. Shirley could turn the sound up on any story she might need to know about. I saw the video running about a bombing in Salt Lake City, and I recognized the name of the victim. The reporter stated the murder was believed to have involved a business deal.

Steve Christensen, the victim, was not someone I personally knew, but he had bought a letter from Mark Hofmann, a dealer in Mormon historical letters, and I had been asked to authenticate it. My examination of the letter showed no physical signs of forgery, but I stated there was no proof it was genuine either.

The next day, Tuesday, October 16, it was reported that the wife of Gary Sheets, whose financial consulting company employed Christensen, had been killed by a similar bomb. There were again reports that it was believed to be about a failed business deal, but I knew Sheets was also connected to this letter and I called the Salt Lake City police homicide division. No one called me back. Two days later there was another bomb, this time blowing up Mark Hofmann in his car, but he survived. Now I was very insistent with the Salt Lake police that all three victims were related through this questionable letter about Mormon history. Finally, they listened.

I first met Mark Hofmann seven or eight years before at an antiquarian book fair and regularly saw him at major book fairs throughout the country. He was always looking for Mormon historical documents. He had a very withdrawn personality, was always well dressed in Mormon fashion, and was overly polite in a typically Mormon way. If I didn't have anything to offer, there was never any other conversation.

I remember at one book fair in New York he was with a woman and baby and introduced me to his wife. I was quite surprised someone would have married him. It was also at this book fair that I had a document for sale by Joseph Smith, the founder of the Mormon Church. It was in my exhibit case, priced $12,500. Hofmann had seen it when I wasn't there and left a note that he wanted to buy it. Just as I walked up to my booth and read Hofmann's note, another Mormon collector, Brent Ashworth, whom I liked very much, said he wanted to buy it. I clearly remember thinking that in fairness I should sell it to Hofmann, that I shouldn't hold it against him that he was so lacking in personality. Hofmann walked up a moment later, bought it, and then sold it to Ashworth on the spot.

In 1983 Hofmann approached me and asked that I examine the handwriting of a letter apparently written in 1830 by an associate of Joseph Smith's named Martin Harris. Hofmann said the contents of what became known as the "White Salamander" letter would rewrite Mormon history if it were genuine. I told him I didn't want to be in another situation likely to receive wide media attention. The Hitler diaries story was just beginning to fade, and the thought of becoming involved in a

Mark Hofmann.

similar, even if less intense, story was not appealing. I was, however, persuaded to change my mind by a high official of the Mormon Church who telephoned asking that I reconsider. Remarks that I had made, to the effect that the Hitler diaries story would never have gone so far if the proper experts had been asked to authenticate them, were quoted back to me. The potential importance of the White Salamander letter to Mormon history was emphasized, and the attitude of genuine concern on the part of the Church convinced me that it was a worthwhile project.

I made it clear to everyone that I did not want to know any of the theological issues raised by the content of the letter and would only consider the content from a forensic standpoint—for example, checking specific facts mentioned that might be inconsistent with the dating of the letter. I thought it was important that I had no opinion of the theology involved.

Hofmann showing documents to leaders of the Mormon church.

There was no known handwriting of Martin Harris. With nothing to compare, an examination of the handwriting for indications of forgery would be based on deviations that forgers frequently make from normal handwriting. The paper and ink would be forensically examined, as would other issues such as postmarks that might prove inaccurate. I emphasized with everyone that I could not prove the letter genuine without any handwriting known to be genuine, but I could eliminate indications of forgery in the various areas of examination. I contacted Tony Cantu, Ph.D., the FBI's forensic expert, and asked him who would be the best ink and paper experts, and I sent examples to the two people he recommended. I examined the letter under high-power ultraviolet, and it showed no signs inconsistent with its being genuine. Every provable fact in the letter was checked through detailed historical records and all were accurate, including the postal schedule in Palmyra, New York, on October 29, 1830, the date of the letter.

The White Salamander letter.

133

The provenance of the letter seemed logical and reasonable. Hofmann said he bought it from Lynn Jacobs, a fellow Mormon and dealer in stampless covers, and Jacobs had bought it from a small dealer in New Hampshire who sold stampless covers. Collectors of stampless covers are not interested in the letters but only in the envelope, or in this case the folded address leaf, and they would not normally read the letters. (They are called *stampless* because they pre-date postage stamps.) I contacted the dealer in New Hampshire, who told me that he had owned the papers of "W.W. Phelps," the person the White Salamander letter was addressed to, and that he sold the covers individually. He confirmed he had sold this letter without having opened it, pricing it solely on the basis of the postmarked address sheet. Everything about this story made sense. Lynn Jacobs told me that after he bought it, he opened the folded address leaf out of curiosity and discovered its importance to the founding of the Mormon religion. He sold it to Hofmann, who sold it to Steve Christensen, who was giving it to the Mormon Church.

I wrote a report to Hofmann on March 20, 1985, saying that I could find no evidence that the letter was forged, which was not to say it was genuine, but nothing was inconsistent with the date. Both the paper and ink specialists wrote similar reports and, as I learned later, the FBI laboratory also wrote an almost identical report.

Only then did I fully read the letter and understand its implications to the Mormon Church; it cast doubt on the credibility of the Church founder, Joseph Smith. According to the Church, Smith was led by an angel of God to a hidden cache of golden plates, which contained a third volume of Scripture forming a companion to the Old and New Testaments. This third volume is the *Book of Mormon*, the basis of the Mormon religion.

The White Salamander letter presents a different version: Martin Harris quotes Smith as saying that he was led to the plates by a spirit, which transfigured itself into a white salamander and struck him. The salamander is a familiar folk-magic symbol, and the implication was that Smith was a dabbler in folk magic and the occult.

In the ten days after Hofmann's car was blown up the Salt Lake City police had rapidly begun to suspect that Hofmann was both the bomber and possibly involved in fraudulent documents. The homicide detectives later told me that Hofmann told them that when he opened his car door, a bomb fell out and exploded. When the federal ATF investigator called to the scene was told what Hofmann said, he said that while he knew nothing about the case, Hofmann must be the bomber because his account could not be true. The bomb had not fallen out—it exploded in the passenger side on the floor. Hofmann had had considerable publicity in Utah with the Mormon documents he had discovered, especially the Anthon Transcript, which was supposedly Joseph Smith's transcription of the characters that appeared on the golden plates. He had given this document to the Church, along with one in which Joseph Smith promised his son the right of succession, which implied that Brigham Young's succession was illegitimate. Together with the White Salamander letter, which he hadn't discovered but owned, Hofmann was involved with highly important and controversial Mormon documents. The police had found a large section of an Egyptian *Book of the Dead*, encased in Plexiglas, in his car, and within days they had connected this to a collection Hofmann was offering for sale.

The Egyptian *Book of the Dead*, secretly acquired from me, with damage from the bombing of Hofmann's car.

A letter, purported to be from Brigham Young, that was forged by Hofmann.

135

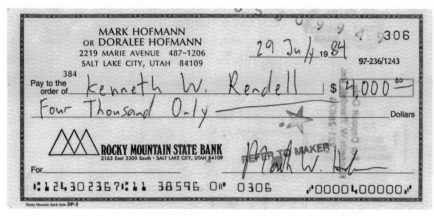

Hofmann's genuine handwriting.

Newsweek's issue of October 28 reported these developments, while the Associated Press newswire of the same day focused more specifically on the Egyptian papyrus and the fact it had come from me and Hofmann may have been misrepresenting it as an integral part of the founding of the Mormon Church. A second piece of papyrus, a fragment from another large piece, had been found in the safety deposit box of Steve Christensen. On November 6 the *New York Times* published an overview of the situation, focusing on the Mormon Church's interest in its own history, its extensive dealings with Mark Hofmann, and its refusal to release any information about the more than 40 documents it had acquired from him. The newspaper also reported initial information about the McLellin papers. William McLellin was an early leader in the Mormon Church and his archive concerned the founding of the Church. Hofmann had evidently sold the archive to multiple people based on my two Egyptian manuscripts. The *New York Times* article pointed out the Church's contradictory statements about their involvement with the McLellin papers.

When Ken Farnsworth, the Salt Lake City homicide detective in charge, and Gerry d'Elia, a prosecutor, came to my office on November 7, they focused on my relationship with Hofmann but then wanted to talk about the two pieces of Egyptian papyrus I had sent to Hofmann on consignment on September 16. Hofmann had called my office in August saying he had a client who was interested in an Egyptian *Book of the Dead* from the first to second century A.D., written in hieratic script (cursive writing). I was puzzled because this is the least desirable period of time, and most people associate hieroglyphics (pictorial writing) with Egypt. However, I had two *Books of the Dead* that precisely matched what he was looking for. I quoted him $10,500 for the pair.

Time magazine covered Hofmann's "newly discovered" documents on May 20, 1985. *Newsweek* reported on the Mormon forgeries and murders, October 28, 1985.

The significance of the papyrus manuscripts had to do with the McLellin papers. It was believed to contain papyrus fragments that were translated by Joseph Smith into the Book of Abraham. There had been no trace of the McLellin papers, and Hofmann's claim to have discovered them, complete with the original Egyptian manuscripts, created an enormous interest among Mormons.

The ATF officers in charge of bombings told the police that the remnants of all three bombs matched each other. Various people had witnessed a man delivering the first two bombs, and the descriptions matched Hofmann. The police were convinced they had their man, but they didn't have a motive.

I went to Salt Lake City shortly afterwards to see my longtime client Brent Ashworth, who had been a major client of Mark Hofmann's. Brent showed me some of the pieces he purchased from him. All were written on paper appropriate for their dates, but the handwriting and ink varied greatly. A Betsy Ross letter didn't resemble her handwriting and had a postmark not used until decades later. Documents of Daniel Boone and Paul Revere, while on old paper, were written in an ink not used until decades later, and there was a very unusual fuzziness to the appearance on both documents. The other letters that Ashworth had were written in ink that appeared contemporary, with none of the fuzziness and lack of line quality in the handwriting that was seen in the Boone and Revere pieces. We both assumed Hofmann may have bought forgeries from someone. There seemed no question that there were two forgers; there were stark differences in the forgeries.

When I met again with the police and prosecutors, they had concluded that Hofmann was the murderer and that the motivation was an elaborate fraud he had committed about the existence of the McLellin collection. They established that Hofmann had sold percentages of interest in the collection to many different people and had sold the entire collection to several other people, including a transaction financed by the Mormon Church. Hofmann had raised hundreds of thousands of dollars in the several months before the bombings and many of the buyers had been pressing him to deliver the collection, or at least prove that he had it. Several were asking for their money back since he could not show them the collection. Obtaining the two Egyptian *Books of the Dead* from me enabled him to show them "proof" that the nonexistent collection existed. The small piece cut from one of my papyri, mounted in Plexiglas, had markings on the reverse that were the same as those of Joseph Smith on the pieces Hofmann claimed were his inspiration. This piece was in Christensen's safety deposit box. Christensen had learned of Hofmann's multiple sales of the collection and told him he was going to press criminal charges.

A section cut from the second *Book of the Dead*, which was secretly acquired from me.

On January 31, 1986, I was visited by the principal investigators and the prosecutor, who brought with them the major pieces Hofmann had sold. After examining the 25 pieces for half an hour, I told them I thought all were forgeries. This was based upon easily observable facts: shaky handwriting and the color and feel of the ink and paper, which indicated they had been artificially aged. A few minutes of fairly routine examination with a high-powered ultraviolet light revealed that nearly all of the pieces had been coated with a chemical that turned the paper bright blue. Not only were paintbrush strokes visible but you could also see where clips had been applied in the corners to hang the pieces up to dry. One document that was genuine had a forged section added to it, and UV only showed blue in this area. This chemical was the agent that had prevented the feathering of the ink into the paper, a characteristic that would normally occur when ink is added to old paper. Additionally, there were discernible common characteristics in the handwriting of many of the letters and documents supposedly written by different people. This is a common mistake of forgers; they focus completely on the signature and are betrayed by mistakes in the general handwriting. Many of the Hofmann pieces were in a handwriting not otherwise known and therefore couldn't be compared to anything genuine, but when this group was laid out side by side, there were too many similarities among them.

They had also brought the White Salamander letter, and I laid it out with all the other clearly forged pieces. Under UV light, the White Salamander letter was the same color as a genuine letter of the same date, not blue like the other forgeries. This didn't mean that the White Salamander letter was genuine, but it did mean that it had not been treated with the same chemical used on most of these other pieces. For the first time the investigators told me the FBI laboratory had examined the White Salamander letter and reached the same determination that I had: there was no forensic evidence of forgery, which is not to say it is genuine.

I stressed again that there were two very different levels of line quality and ink composition, which strongly indicated at least two different forgers. The investigators, however, were focused on murder and motive. The only question, they said, was whether he would want to be hung or shot, the choices in Utah for a convicted murderer (there was a betting pool in the homicide division).

Three days later Hofmann was formally charged with two counts of first-degree murder and 13 counts of forgeries. His trial was scheduled for April, and for the next two months the media blitz in Utah continued.

Before the trial I went to Salt Lake City to discuss my role. I was adamant that I would not testify as an expert witness on the authenticity of any of the pieces; there was significant evidence that Hofmann would have tried to kill me if he could have gotten my home address. If I were the defense lawyer, I would have tried to discredit me as being justifiably prejudiced. Additionally, a local questioned-document examiner, used by the Salt Lake City Police Department in forged checks and contracts cases, was already going to be used in court. He stated he had replicated putting new ink on old paper, with the same undetectable characteristics of the White Salamander letter. I wanted to see how he had done this. The prosecutor, d'Elia, the homicide detective, Farnsworth, and I, with the White Salamander letter, went to George Throckmorton's house and down into his basement laboratory, where we found out he could not replicate this effect. I stated that if the White Salamander letter was a forgery, which seemed likely but unprovable, then there had to be two forgers, which Throckmorton agreed with. (Throckmorton, a fervent Mormon, later recanted the statement.)

The initial testimony in court concerned the identification of Hofmann as the person who bought the components for the bombs, and witnesses who identified him as the person delivering the packages. The paper and ink specialists the FBI had recommended I hire also testified about their examination of the White Salamander letter. I believed my testimony would be about my relationship with Hofmann and his very specific request for Egyptian papyri, a request he wanted kept strictly secret. The history of the pieces would also be a subject of testimony. I was told by the prosecutors that Hofmann's defense lawyers were the best in Utah: Ron Yengich and Brad Rich. I wasn't concerned about my testimony. It was all very factual. The courtroom was very small, and I was concerned Hofmann might stage a photo of the two of us during a recess.

Holding the Salamander Letter, testifying at the Mormon murder trial.

An article of the *New York Times* reporting on November 6, 1985.
The *Times* continued its coverage of Hofmann's trial into the new
year, as seen in another article from February 5, 1986.

Witnesses in this small courtroom entered from a door behind the witness stand—and were suddenly facing a courtroom full of lawyers, the defendant, the spouses of those killed, photographers, and the general public, which had also overflowed into an adjoining courtroom connected by closed-circuit television. His lawyer immediately launched into an attack as if I were an expert witness:

"I assume you have a questioned-document examiners certificate?"

"No."

"Isn't it customary for someone in your business to have one?"

"No."

"Are you aware of where there are such courses in forgery detection?"

"Yes."

"Will you tell the court where, in your opinion, the best one is?"

"Columbia University in New York."

I almost held my breath, waiting for the next question. I had deliberately been hesitant, almost stumbling, in my answers, trying to signal that this was a weak area and encouraging his line of questioning.

He asked it: "Can you tell the court why you have never taken this course at Columbia University?"

"I teach it."

I had testified many times in court but had never had a lawyer pursue a line of questioning when he didn't know where it was headed. A tenet of cross-examination is to never ask a question you don't know the answer to.

He moved on to the authenticity of the White Salamander letter, inaccurately claiming I had authenticated it. I quoted again and again my final conclusion that there was no evidence of forgery, which was not to say it was genuine.

He kept insisting that it had to be one or the other, and I kept insisting that there was insufficient evidence to conclusively reach a determination based on forensic evidence. Finally, as his frustration reached the boiling point, I turned to the judge and said that if someone would ask me the key question, they would get an answer.

The judge asked me what that question was, and I replied, "In light of the testimony that Hofmann asked Jacobs to say he had originally found it, and the inconclusiveness of the forensic tests, would I buy this letter?"

The judge replied, "Would you?" and I replied, "Absolutely not."

I was on the witness stand for two days and was not able to avoid commenting on the authenticity of the group of papers that the prosecutors had brought to Boston, nor the printing plates that I was shown by the prosecutors. I repeatedly said I was not testifying as an expert witness, but both on direct testimony and cross-examination I was treated as such. The headline of the *Salt Lake Tribune* read "Expert lauds quality of alleged forgeries / Hofmann papers better than Hitler diaries."

Overwhelming evidence continued to come together about this incredibly complex case of bombings, the fraudulent sales of a nonexistent collection, and the creation of fake Mormon currency, letters, and documents challenging the official history of the Mormon Church and a copy of "The Oath of a Freeman" purporting to be the first printing in America. Forensic tests were unable to determine it was a forgery. It was nearly sold to the Library of Congress for $1.5 million and the American Antiquarian Society offered Hofmann $250,000 for it. (In 2021 I purchased it at auction for inclusion in my Forgery Collection at the Grolier Club in New York.)

Absent from the trial was testimony from the Mormon Church about their dealings with Hofmann. When the police had asked the Church if they had the missing part of my Egyptian *Book of the Dead*, they said that they didn't want to discuss it, and that answer was accepted by the Mormon-dominated police department and prosecutor's office.

Despite all the overwhelming evidence, the Mormon lead prosecutor and defense team agreed on a plea bargain for Hofmann that would spare the Church any further embarrassment. Hofmann pleaded guilty to second-degree murder (unpremeditated—amazing when bombs were used) instead of first-degree premeditated murder and to forging the White Salamander letter, though he could not explain how he did it without the telltale signs of forgery in other letters. The prosecutor issued a statement that the public was served with this plea bargain, though news accounts said that the public did not agree with the deal. Hofmann agreed to answer all questions put to him by the prosecutors in exchange for not being executed, but his so-called confession is riddled with his attorney saying that he didn't want to answer the questions being asked, and the lead prosecutor accepting this dramatic violation of the plea agreement. Hofmann, in fact, benefited from the so-called confession because it allowed him to make numerous false statements that went unchallenged and portrayed him as a far more prolific and successful forger outside of the Salt Lake area than the evidence indicated. What was not brought out in the trial, because the forgeries and frauds were seen only as the basis of the murders, was what I considered to be very convincing forensic evidence that Hofmann was not the actual forger of the most accomplished forgeries. There were clearly two forgers of the letters and documents, but this evidence only complicated what the police and prosecutors considered a clear murder case. In fact, after going through Hofmann's own financial files, I pointed to evidence that would identify the other forger (he died several years later). But the group in the homicide section said there was only one issue and that was murder. After further parole hearings Hofmann's preliminary sentence from his original plea bargain was changed to life in prison.

Mormon Document Dealer Pleads Guilty of Murdering Two in 1985

By ROBERT LINDSEY
Special to The New York Times

SALT LAKE CITY, Jan. 23 — Spurning his father's appeal that he submit to execution to atone for two 1985 murders, a former Mormon missionary chose instead today to plead guilty to the crimes in return for a sentence of life imprisonment.

By pleading guilty to two counts of second-degree murder, Mark W. Hofmann, 32 years old, brought to a close what has been called the largest investigation in Utah history, a case that sent repercussions through the highest levels of the Church of Jesus Christ of Latter-day Saints, the Mormons.

Mr. Hofmann had been charged with first-degree murder, which carries the death penalty, in the separate bombing deaths of a man and a woman. According to family members, the plea arrangement in recent weeks spared his life was delayed in return by the intervention of his father, a Mormon, and other family members who said they believed that if the younger Mr. Hofmann was guilty of the murders he should be executed.

Doctrine of 'Blood Atonement'

This belief is rooted in the Mormon doctrine of "blood atonement," which holds that some crimes are so grievous that the crucifixion of Jesus had not redeemed their sins. The crimes that fall under the doctrine, promulgated principally by Brigham Young, who led members of the persecuted Mormon Church to Utah in 1847, include murder and adultery.

Mr. Hoffman, who admitted his guilt today for the first time, pleaded guilty to two counts of second-degree murder as well as to forging two documents about Mormon history, including the "white salamander letter," which had

Mark W. Hofmann
Associated Press

Iranian Tells of

By ROBE
Special to The

TEHERAN, Iran, Jan. 23 — The President of Iran said today that the Foreign Ministry had rebuffed a final effort by the Reagan Administration to

Finally, Hofmann's guilty plea brought an end to the scandal.

Chapter 12

Developing New Collectors

By the end of the 1980s I didn't know how my business could expand further. Thanks to Shirley becoming my business partner, she did know. In 1989 she brought up with me that we deserved to be in the most important antique shows in the country, most specifically the Winter Antiques Show in New York City. I told her, many times, that the waiting list was 20 to 25 years and that antique dealers had to demonstrate through participating in other shows that they would attract people to the Winter Antiques Show. There was almost no turnover of exhibitors. I appreciated how strongly she believed that we should be at that level to start with, but it was a hopeless dream, not a realistic goal. She went ahead and made a presentation to them.

In mid-December 1989 we were shocked to receive a call from the head of the show, legendary interior designer Mario Buatta, saying they suddenly had an opening for the show a month later, and could we be ready? Of course we said yes. We sat in our library at home that night wondering how in the world we could do this in a month, with Christmas in the middle. Most booths were custom built, with their own individual walls, as ours would be later, but what could we do in a few weeks? Our own library walls were covered in a green, felt-like fabric and Shirley learned she could get this in time, and we would use our own personal antique furniture.

The new partnership.

The Winter Antiques Show at that time was the most important society event for people interested in art and antiques. Opening night, with tickets costing in the thousands of dollars, attracted both collectors and potential collectors. We suddenly had access to people we never could have met otherwise, and they had access to being able to own original letters and documents of people that interested them but they had never realized could be obtained. We sold everything from a Mozart violin concerto manuscript to a Beatles record album signed by the Fab Four. Business was, literally and descriptively, "off the wall." Every day we had to bring more framed pieces from our Madison Avenue gallery to replace what had been sold.

Our first Winter Antiques Show booth.

Our booth was so busy that we not only generated publicity but, a year later, were moved to the front of the show. *Town & Country* magazine published a comprehensive feature story, not about me so much as about what we sold and who our clients were. The reporter had to have the names of some prominent clients, something I never discussed, but I came up with half a dozen people I knew wouldn't mind: Malcolm Forbes, who especially loved publicity; the industrialist Armand Hammer; Queen Elizabeth II; Ross Perot; and a few others. There was a predictable focus on prices in the article, and numerous specific letters and documents I had sold. The article

Our daughter Julia's first Winter Antiques Show. She later worked in our booth.

was the most focused advertisement we could have dreamed of.

Invitations started to flood in from other important antiques shows and in the coming years we experimented with Maastricht (The Netherlands), Chicago, Dallas, Houston, Basel, Los Angeles, Palm Beach, San Francisco, and others, but we had been spoiled by New York.

During the early 1990s I felt like business had developed into a high-speed train going on a new track. Thanks to our new gallery in a prestigious, ground-level location on Madison Avenue, publicity was focusing more on what we were selling and the excitement of connecting with interesting people in the past, and less on me personally. We changed our windows every day to coincide with historical references in the news that day or to mark a noteworthy or interesting historical event, so we could showcase our related material. We ran ads on NPR quoting from letters. We also discovered that we could submit ads to the *New York Times* on a standby basis; when the layout of the next day's edition was short a page, they put in our ready-made ad at a discounted rate. The first time we did this, we held our breath because the cost was still very high, but the result was terrific. We were selling 30 to 35 percent of the ad. Gallery traffic increased dramatically. Our annual sales, which I remembered being very proud of when they passed $1 million, were now consistently over $10 million.

A staged photograph by *Town & Country* in our library.

New clients were coming to the New York gallery all the time, and the feature stories in major magazines were a factor as well as our location. *Business Week*, *Connoisseur*, *Robb Report*, *Vanity Fair*, *Esquire*, Japanese and Chinese magazines, American and German *Vogue*, and many others focused mostly on the business.

But one new client will always stand out, not only from the 1990s but my entire career. I received a telephone call from the employee in our small gallery at the Place des Antiquaries that a man wearing a bright green Celtics T-shirt, gym shorts, and broken-down running shoes had just come in and bought $115,000 of important American Revolutionary War letters. We didn't know him, so we held the material until the check cleared. I was very impressed with what he had bought and called his office to invite him to lunch. In checking his address, I found that a favorite French restaurant was across the street.

Nothing could have prepared me for walking into the offices of Victor Niederhoffer. I was told I had to take off my shoes, which I said I would not do.

The receptionist came back and told me that it would be okay since I was wearing running shoes. I entered a large room with many TV screens and computer terminals and carnival-type music. Things were scattered all over the floor. My first thought was that I was in a marketing research office, where children would be brought in and observed as to how they reacted to different types of toys and clothing laying all over the place. Standing at a table was, I had to presume, Victor Niederhoffer, since he was wearing a bright green Celtics T-shirt and gym shorts. I reiterated that I was impressed with what he had purchased and wanted to have lunch with him to talk about his interests. He told me he wasn't hungry but pointed to a paper plate on the table with a cheese sandwich on it and a small bottle of water and said it was for me. I was immediately impressed by the conversation, if not the lunch. He told me why he selected the pieces. It was a brilliant analysis of each piece.

A musical composition by Wolfgang Amadeus Mozart.

An official document of Queen Elizabeth I.

The Madison Avenue gallery in 1992.

Victor Niederhoffer's book,
The Education of a Speculator.

Victor Niederhoffer gives my son
Jason a squash lesson.

Victor Niederhoffer was born in Brooklyn to a New York City cop and a teacher (his father later became a professor of sociology at Columbia's College of Criminal Justice). Victor had a scholarship to Harvard, where he studied statistics and economics, and later was a professor at Berkeley. He went into finance as a commodities speculator, where he was both spectacularly success-ful (ranked as the number one hedge-fund manager in the world in 1996) and called "The Blow-up Artist" by the *New Yorker* the following year, after he crashed and lost everything. He would make another fortune, lose that, and make it back again. Among the many things he collected were paintings of the *Titanic*, which hung throughout his offices as constant reminders that disaster was always one bad decision away.

But from my standpoint Victor Niederhoffer was one of the most all-around knowledgeable clients I ever had. He knew the most significant people in almost every area of human endeavor, from every age and nearly every country. He appreciated the importance of the content of letters without my having to tell him. While his eccentric ways could be very challenging, I always had great satisfaction in my role in building his collection.

In previous decades selling to institutional libraries had been a clear situation of whether or not I had something that would enhance their research capabilities. There was no personal side to it, except for acquiring the material. In the 1980s institutions faded in importance, in large part because I had gone after the sources of archives, and they were exhausted. Writing and publishing catalogs was now being done by Shirley, I was buying material, and we were jointly managing the galleries. In the 1990s my focus changed to a few major collectors with whom I would regularly meet personally and be intimately involved in building their collections.

I was also developing my personal interest in collecting World War II archives and artifacts as a counterbalance to the intensity, and stress, of my business life. My collection initially focused on how Britain, and Churchill specifically, motivated the British people to fight against Germany's overwhelming forces. The people never faltered in responding to Churchill's leadership, and together they saved the world from Nazi domination. My collection was not just intellectual—it was emotional as well. I was born during World War II, and no one my age was unaffected by the war. It was the principal subject of conversation when I was growing up. My collection gained direction when I was examining props at Paramount Studios, assessing whether I could create a special exhibit about the studio's history for them. I opened rolls of posters from the Battle of Britain and became immediately fascinated with the propaganda. It was financially inexpensive but extremely time-consuming to find the posters, leaflets, and other British propaganda I was looking for. There were no dealers, no internet, no eBay nor auction houses, and they could only be found at local flea markets outside of London, but this research was very rewarding in all senses. The normal cost of filling a shopping bag full of printed leaflets was about $10. It was a remarkable antidote to the stressful intensity of my business. In the early 1990s I organized an exhibition from my collection, titled *With Weapons and Wits—Psychological Warfare in*

World War II, at the Grolier Club in New York. It was very successful, personally and professionally. At that time there were no museums anywhere that were collecting World War II outside of very nationalistic viewpoints. I became the major collector of the overall subject of the causes and consequences of World War II, the home fronts, and how they were influenced.

As the only major collector, I quickly had many opportunities to meet prominent wartime figures and historians. Steve Ambrose, the popular World War II historian, and I became particularly good friends and

A typed letter signed by Winston Churchill, from September 1961.

together developed his ideas for a museum in New Orleans. None of us, not even with our optimism, had any idea of just how popular that museum would become. Initially called the D-Day Museum, a later marketing-oriented director renamed it the National Museum of World War II.

One of the people Steve introduced me to was Bill Colby, a World War II undercover operative and former head of the CIA, who I became personally very friendly with, especially after I sent him my book on forgery detection, and he wrote me a long-handwritten letter: "I congratulate you for your expertise and only wonder how we missed incorporating you in our profession—you have all the talents and we could have used you." My collection, which will be the subject of a later chapter, was a great escape into another world.

At the other end of the intellectual spectrum from my usual collectors, in 1993 our Beverly Hills gallery was visited by a producer of a television game show, *Wheel of Fortune*. They wanted to have various framed documents that would be prizes, and would pay us full price for anything a contestant won. The

Bill Colby, former CIA director, at a Washington dinner.

value of the pieces kept rising and a significant number would regularly be won. *Wheel of Fortune* became a good client. The producer wanted to create themed show locations where we would provide the ultimate prize. In New Orleans the show opened with historical footage of a Mississippi River boat coming down the river and a picture of a framed Mark Twain letter that would be the big prize. Many of the pieces they selected were $25,000 and $30,000, so the show, from our business standpoint, passed from amusing to lucrative. I was on the set one night during filming to talk to them about a show from Atlanta, developing a theme around *Gone with the Wind*. I mentioned to the show's host that I personally owned Clark Gable's jacket from *Gone with the Wind* and offered to loan it to him for the show. He told me he thought that was a tacky idea.

During this period, what started out as an ordinary but exciting tax appraisal became the source of a very personal and warm friendship, with remarkable insights into World War II, and a very successful business outcome. John Eisenhower, the only child of Dwight and Mamie, inherited a series of letters handwritten from his father to his mother during World War II, the only handwritten letters he wrote during the war. John had sent them to the Eisenhower Library as a donation. The library contacted me to do the tax appraisal, and I contacted John because I needed to figure out how to structure the donation for the best tax advantage. Ordinarily with an archive, the total is worth more than the sum of its parts, but in unusual circumstances the opposite is true, and this was an unusual situation. He thought this planning unnecessary because the letters couldn't be worth very much. John thought $50,000. I told him I could sell the letters for at least $2 million. He said he couldn't afford to give anything that valuable away and he would give copies to the Eisenhower Library, and I would sell the originals.

Eisenhower's letters to his wife showed a very private and otherwise-unknown personal side of him. Almost every one of the 319 letters had something interesting to say. He censored his own letters, and he only obliquely referred to major events ("You may have read in the papers that I am rather busy right now"—written during the Battle of the Bulge surprise attack by the Germans). But he

Dwight and Mamie Eisenhower.

wrote extensively about his personal feelings and goings-on. His four-page letter of February 15, 1943, is the most revealing insight of a commander-in-chief in wartime:

> I am human enough to want the official approval of my past action that such an unusual advancement implies [promotion to four-star general]—but anyone worthy of high command is so concerned with the enormity of the tasks, for which his own faculty so frequently seem so pitifully inadequate, that what the world calls success, or promotion, does not loom up as particularly important. I do not often write to you of my responsibilities, but it comes down to something like this. Most jobs in the world are such that the responsible man always has at his shoulders, a higher authority to whom a particularly serious decision can be referred. A few jobs are such that this can scarcely ever be done. My technical boss is a combined body of men [8] that is divided into two parts by the Atlantic Ocean. Moreover, an active theater of war must be commanded on the spot. So, the boss in that one has only one real confidant—his pillow, and only the underside of that! Loneliness is the inescapable lot of a man holding such a job. Subordinates can advise, urge, help and pray—but only one man, in his own mind and heart, can decide 'do we, or do we not?' The stakes are always highest, and the penalties are expressed in terms of loss of life or major or minor disasters to the nation. No man can always be right. So the struggle is to do one's best; to keep the brain and conscience clear; never to be swayed by unworthy motives or inconsequential reasons, but to strive to understand the basic factors involved and then do one's duty. It is not always easy—in fact the strain comes from not being sure that the analysis has been carefully and accurately made. And when it is clear that the only logical answer is certain to bring criticism, even possible official misunderstanding by superiors, then is when such things as popularity, favorable press, possible promotion etc. etc. must be completely disregarded—I'm simply trying to say that in a job like this so many things are so big that even a fourth star fails to cause any great internal excitement. I appreciate the confidence of my superiors—and feel damn humble in the face of it but I do not feel that my major job is finished. I have just begun and though the prospect is, in some phases, appalling, I can do my duty only if I steel myself to the requirements and meet them to the best of my ability. . . . I want always to do my duty to the extreme limit of my ability. . . .

The day before writing this letter, Eisenhower was at the frontline and his position was attacked and overwhelmed only hours after he left.

John and I became great friends and remained so until he died at 91. I spent many weekends at his home on Chesapeake Bay in Trappe, Maryland. I would fly to National Airport in Washington, where he would pick me up in his airplane. He was between marriages, so it was just the two of us for three-day weekends and we talked about every conceivable subject, especially how he survived being the son of a highly respected leader. John had a great understanding of how he had coped and managed to be his own person,

John Eisenhower.

and he talked openly about the conflicts in his own life dealing with a tremendously popular father. He told me many stories that were personal and have been left out of biographies. (When his father was particularly frustrated as president, he would pound his fist on the desk in the Oval Office and shout, "God dammit I won the war—that's enough.")

John had inherited a George Washington letter from his father that was as "appropriately personal" as his father's letters. It was written one week after Washington assumed the presidency.

> . . . This great sacrifice which I consider myself as having made for the good of my Country . . . I . . . judged . . . that it was my duty to embark again on the tempestuous & uncertain Ocean of public life, I gave up all expectations of private happiness in this world. . . . Nothing but a conviction of duty could have induced me to depart from my resolution of remaining in retirement; yet I greatly apprehend that my Countrymen will expect too much from me. . . . The extravagant (and I may say undue) praises which they are heaping upon me. . . . So much is expected, so many untoward circumstances may intervene, in such a new and critical situation, that I feel an insuperable diffidence in my own abilities. . . .

Eisenhower had it mounted with his own typewritten statement on White House stationery, dated August 5, 1954:

> Although I did not *know* of the existence of this letter, the words I used to many of my friends when I finally agreed in the spring of 1952 to . . . stand for the Republican nomination for the Presidency, were identical in meaning with those of President Washington's letter and in many cases identical in terminology.

I sold the letter for John to someone who has been put on a pedestal by many people in the world and will always be prominent in recent history. It eventually will be in a public collection, where it justifiably will inspire people in the humility of these great leaders.

In 1994 the publication of *Forging History: The Detection of Fake Letters and Documents* was the culmination of years of research. My goal was to demystify the authentication process, just as I had quantified the analysis of fair market value in the Otto Kerner tax court case 20 years earlier (the full story of the Kerner case is in chapter 18). Autograph dealers always said they just "knew" whether something was real or not. I knew the "feeling" that something was a forgery, or genuine, had to be based on observable facts, on instant mental comparisons of normal, genuine handwriting of a period and of a particular individual. Dealers weren't aware of all the factors they were instantly seeing and considering. In view of all the highly publicized forgery cases, I thought it important that collectors see for themselves how handwriting is proven genuine or false. There had never been a detailed, heavily illustrated book on the subject, and my book, published by the University of Oklahoma Press with more than 200 illustrations, has been the standard reference ever since.

It begins with the "general characteristics of forged writing," showing in 68 illustrations, many through a microscope, the general differences between normal and forged writing. The second chapter, "The Materials: paper, ink, and writing instruments," includes basic information in identifying the age of ink and paper, and when different kinds of pens

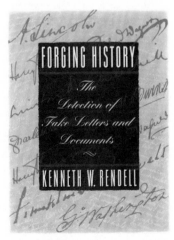

My 1994 book, *Forging History.*

were used. Comparing suspect handwriting with a known genuine example is illustrated with the examples used in the Hitler diary case. Typewriters were individual before the invention of electric ones made the alignment and impression of individual letters uniform, another useful diagnostic.

The historical letter and document field has been "haunted" by the forgeries of Shakespeare, Lord Byron, Walter Scott, George Washington, Abraham Lincoln, Benjamin Franklin, Robert Frost, and many others. *Forging History* takes classic examples of these forgers and analyzes them using the different methods discussed previously, with most of the photographs being taken through my microscope.

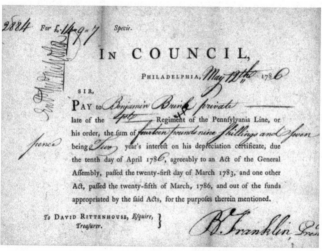

A genuine document signed by Benjamin Franklin.

Just as much of a problem as these forgeries were, are the "authorized" forgeries: secretarial signatures of everyone from Marie Antoinette to John F. Kennedy, intended to be deceptive and make the recipient believe they were genuinely signed. Many American presidents authorized secretaries to sign documents, President of the Confederate States of America Jefferson Davis authorized his wife to sign for him, Napoleon had secretaries signing, Walt Disney rarely signed any pieces as souvenirs, and with the invention of the autopen, in heavy use since 1960, even important letters by presidents have been signed by this mechanical machine.

In the spring of 1994 a personal event had a far greater impact on me that I ever imagined. My first son, Jeffrey, had been born in 1971; I will never forget his eyes opening the first time and the unbelievable thrill I felt. I saw in him a great adventure together, and because of an already deteriorating first marriage, it was, for too long, a very rocky adventure. My second son, Jason, was born 11 years later during a misguided attempt at reconciliation. By the time I was able to establish a more normal family structure with my marriage to Shirley and the court awarding me sole custody of my two sons, the three of us, particularly Jeffrey, had been through very difficult times.

When Shirley wanted to adopt a baby girl I was not enthusiastic, but she had done so much for my two sons in creating a stable, loving home for them that I went along with what she wanted. That attitude changed at the adoption agency in Atlanta in 1994, when I first held Julia and was electrified by the smile on her week-old face. Shirley and I were both 51 years old and having a new daughter at this time in

Our son Jason leaving the front door of the White House after a meeting about the new library, during the Clinton administration.

life was a very different kind of adventure. Like most people, I think, I believed there would be a difference with an adopted child, but there never has been—to my amazement, it made no difference at all. Jeffrey, Julia, and Shirley continue to be the great joys of my life.

"When Ken keeps your papers, you know you are famous." Jason and me with Ted Kennedy.

On the Carousel in the Tuileries in Paris.

My interest in World War II was continuing to grow during this time and be a counterbalance to the intensity of my business. Through the same types of networking I had used in business, I attended veterans' reunions and the very few conferences that were held. Shirley and I had gone to Normandy a number of times and planned to be there for the 50th anniversary in 1994. The night of June 6 we had a dinner at the Château d'Audrieu with John Eisenhower, Steve Ambrose, and Omar Bradley's chief of staff, Chet Hansen. Chet described in almost unbelievable detail the chaos on Omaha Beach, with the American troops pinned down by murderous German fire. Radio contact with the ships had been lost and he went in and out in his speedboat, through the landing craft blown apart or stuck on beach obstacles, repeatedly landing to assess the military situation and returning to the command ship to give Bradley the information to decide whether or not to try to pull the American troops off Omaha Beach.

A day later, what was being heralded as the largest military flea market ever was held in a farmer's field in heavy rain. It was accessed by an unpaved one-and-a-half–lane road. As I pulled up behind other cars, our car slowly slid down the embankment. There were no cell phones in 1994, and we were far from town. Shirley was adamant—this was an important opportunity to buy artifacts for my D-Day collection, and she would figure out what to do.

Later, as I was working my way through the dealers who had their artifacts laid out on tarps, we all felt the ground rumbling and looked up to see a giant tractor with an enclosed driver's cabin coming across the field. As it got closer, I saw Shirley sitting in the cab beside the driver. She had gone to the farmhouse and told them that 50 years ago the Americans came to save the French and today two Americans needed the French to come and save them. We celebrated everything I had found that day, including a crate containing the only known group—12—of the fake paratroopers dropped the night before D-Day. The crate had been found in a storage shed at a British airfield, where it had been left behind on June 5, 1944. I kept two of the fake paratroopers and gave ten to various military museums throughout the U.S. and England. If Shirley had not enabled me to roam the flea market and buy that crate, 11 museums would not have a genuine example of one of the most notable deceptions of the Normandy invasion.

Our car slid down an embankment at a D-Day flea market in Normandy.

Shirley comes to the rescue in a borrowed tractor.

In 1995 the second book that I had spent several years working on, *History Comes to Life: Collecting Historical Letters and Documents*, was published. I wanted each chapter to discuss the many questions collectors brought up with me: why people collect, what you can collect, who collects, where manuscripts are found, the detection of forgeries, how values are determined, and how to keep and preserve a collection. I also discussed 25 different areas of collecting, illustrating the signatures of the leading personalities. My second book, along with the first, received excellent reviews and sales.

During the administrations of Lyndon Johnson and Richard Nixon I provided many gifts to be presented by the president to heads of state on visits. Most of the time my suggestions were obvious, though their modest budgets were an issue. For Harold Wilson, the British prime minister, a framed document signed by Churchill; for the president of Mexico, a Benito Juarez letter in a leather folder; for the president of France, a French Resistance newspaper. At the same time Clem Conger, the curator of the White House, bought a number of pieces from me for the diplomatic reception rooms at the State Department. When Hillary Clinton moved into the White House and saw the sorry state of the library, I was asked to develop a plan to replace the mishmash of accumulated books with a more thought-out selection. This was a prestigious project that interested me, and I put a lot of thought into what the theme should be and what books would be included. The library, on the ground floor, is relatively small, and since it is used primarily for intimate receptions, each of the books needed to be carefully considered.

I selected 100 books representing the development of American society in the nineteenth century and 125 books representing the twentieth century. The number was not arbitrary—with a few multivolume works, it was what the shelves could hold. I enormously enjoyed the time I spent deciding on the books.

I was pretty blasé by this point about publicity. There had been feature stories in every major magazine about me, and numerous newspaper features. I hadn't done television appearances in some time because of their fleeting nature, but I was thrilled and honored when the *New York Times Magazine* wanted to include me in a cover story they were doing about collectors who pursued their own ideas. They wanted to write about my collection of 20,000 pamphlets, posters, and general propaganda concerning how ordinary people coped with the horrors of World War II. The "stars" of the article would be Dorothy and Herbert Vogel, a postal clerk and a librarian who 30 years earlier had begun collecting minimalist and conceptual works by little-known artists. They bought what they liked on their very limited incomes, and to them their collection was their own work of art, their form of self-expression. Even though my

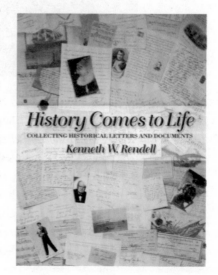

business was driven by selling expensive pieces (with my cost of doing business, it was impossible for me to sell inexpensive documents), my World War II collection of psychological warfare had cost relatively little. I had great respect for collectors who did not follow the crowd but followed their own instincts, regardless of whether other people were supportive of their tastes.

The Vogels had become legends for discovering artists that were completely unknown but later became important in mainstream museum collections. Their apartment had become so crowded they could barely live in it, and, at the instigation of the National Gallery of Art in Washington, they gave more than 2,500 works of art to the museum. In the words of Dorothy Vogel, "It's . . . our legacy to the country."

As the '90s were closing out, I was asked to be the keynote speaker at the 50th annual meeting of the Antiquarian Booksellers Association of America. My talk was entitled "The Future of the Manuscript and Rare Book Business." Rare-book dealers were always reminiscing about the "good old days," and I quickly defined my talk as not about nostalgia, nor that "in general, the whole field has gone to hell." I know I must have horrified quite a few of them by saying that "I enjoy this business more today than I have at any other time during the past 40 years. The collectors we deal with today are more apprecia-tive, responsive, and interested than any previous generation." I wanted the rare-book dealers to understand why my business was successful. To start with, most of them were appallingly condescending, even with me, and most were bibliographical snobs, telling collectors how they had to collect, acting as intel-lectual elitists, and presuming that anyone interested in a rare book would already know everything about it. I was honest in telling them how much these attitudes benefited my approach, which was to respect prospective collectors and know what pieces they could be interested in if the descriptions were writ-ten for intelligent people who did not have an advanced degree in the subject. Chances are these prospective collectors were highly intelligent and successful in professions that were mainstream in society and would be very put off by the self-created snobbism of the rare-book world.

Today's prospective rare-book collectors most likely have graduate degrees—in business, not liberal arts—and their approach to collecting is with excitement at gaining a closer relationship to a subject that they enjoy and have a good personal knowledge of. Twenty years later, as the rare-book dealers continue to talk about how everything has "gone to hell," very few have embraced the collectors of today. If I was asked to deliver another talk on the future, I could just dust off the one from 20 years ago.

Chapter 13

The Jack the Ripper
Diary Hoax

The discovery of Jack the Ripper's purported diary was first reported in 1992. My only reaction was curiosity as to what examinations had been done to determine its authenticity. After the Hitler diaries scandal of nearly a decade earlier, I assumed the English publisher, Robert Smith, would be extremely thorough. My personal interest in Jack the Ripper was non-existent, and I did not give the subject any further thought until I received a call from Carol Ross, general counsel at Time Warner Books, in the first week of August 1993. She was reacting to a story in the *Washington Post* about Warner's impending publication of the diary. The article quoted both Warner Books and the English publisher stating that elaborate authenticity procedures had been taken to ensure that this wasn't another "Hitler Diaries." She was calling me, she said, out of an abundance of caution. She wanted to know if they could hire me to review everything to make sure that the authentication was rock solid. I met with the editorial team involved with the Jack the Ripper diary at their New York headquarters. They were certain there could be no problem and, reminiscent of the situation at *Newsweek* on my first day, told me they had advance orders for 200,000 copies of the book, and that it was reviewer-proof—no matter what reviewers said about the book, it was an automatic bestseller because of the advance orders. The publication date was October 7, to coincide with editions being published in England, Canada, Australia, Germany, France, the Netherlands, Spain, Italy, and Japan. They gave me galley proofs of the book, and we agreed to meet again the next day after I had reviewed them. They also gave me the dramatic brochure by the British publisher advertising the book with the headline "7 October 1993—the day the world's greatest murder mystery will be solved."

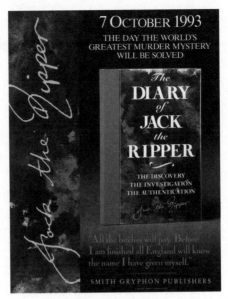

Publicity material for *The Diary of Jack the Ripper.*

A full page of the brochure was devoted to "Where is the Proof?" After mentioning the Hitler diaries, the publisher, Robert Smith, quoted from the various experts who examined the diary, and in reading these quotes one would certainly believe a thorough job of examination had been done to prove it was authentic. However, as I read through the page proofs of the 235-page book, I was overwhelmed by the similarities to the Hitler diaries: numerous instances of conclusions not based on the facts presented, and an unknown history of the diary—the original discoverer was dead, and if genuine, it took over 100 years for it to be found despite its author (supposedly Jack the Ripper) writing, "I place this now in a place where it shall be found." The text of the book, I thought, proved that it very likely was a hoax, but it didn't seem possible that it had gotten this far and no one else had picked up on these inconsistences.

As I read the history of the diary, following a series of somewhat-logical points building to a conclusion, suddenly—with a great leap—the author was at the conclusion, while I was still looking for the explanation of how she got there. The story crossed a chasm, propelled by enthusiasm, leaving me on the other side. The author expressed such an attitude of "positive thinking" in the book, I was concerned about her objectivity.

At a meeting at Warner Books the following day, Chief Executive Officer Laurence J. Kirshbaum and Editor-in-Chief Joann Davis made it absolutely clear that Warner Books would delay publication if necessary and cancel it if I determined the diary was a forgery. In view of the statements concerning authenticity made by the English publisher, it was possible, I told them, that I could neither prove nor demonstrate a definitive conclusion. If there were questions of authenticity but not proof of forgery, Warner would publish the book with my report as a foreword. I was concerned when I asked everyone around the table, who had been the fact checkers, somewhat rhetorically, "Don't tell me—the book was too good to fact check?" There was an ominous silence.

Other than knowing the catchiness of the name Jack the Ripper, I knew little about the case, only that it involved serial killings and was apparently unsolved. I had no idea why the subject was a major publishing event, and I had absolutely no idea why anyone was fascinated with a serial killer. Having to familiarize myself with the case was a very unpleasant education, though necessary to intelligently consider the text.

The major difference with the Hitler diaries was that they could quickly be proven genuine or false because of the amount of genuine handwriting of Hitler. With Jack the Ripper, the situation was more complicated because there was no known positively genuine handwriting of the killer (nor was his or her true identity established). Of the person purported in the book to be Jack the Ripper, James Maybrick, it was indicated that there was only one genuine signature known. (It was not until later that a sufficiently lengthy document, entirely in Maybrick's hand, surfaced.) Since time was a major factor, rather than examine the diary from what I judged to be its most vulnerable

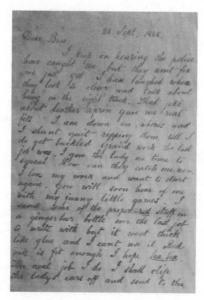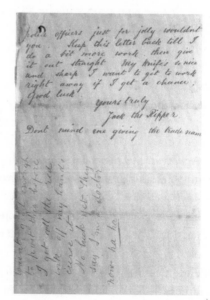

The first use of the name Jack the Ripper, in the 1888-dated "Dear Boss" letter.

point—paper and ink analysis, which frequently, when forgery was evident, made other examinations unnecessary—I put together a team of experts to examine all elements simultaneously. Robert Smith, the English publisher, refused to send the diary to America for examination, claiming that the author, Shirley Harrison, needed the original to complete work in England. The paper and ink analysis would, therefore, have to wait until we had the original diary, and the text would be my first line of investigation.

The book describes the alleged discovery of the Jack the Ripper diary by Tony Devereux, who gave the diary to a friend, Mike Barrett. According to Barrett, Devereux refused to explain where it came from. (Devereux was now dead; he never mentioned an obviously very valuable diary to his family.) Barrett claimed to have researched the diary's contents and determined that the text was written by James Maybrick, a Liverpool cotton merchant. Maybrick had been addicted to arsenic and strychnine, and his young American wife was charged with murdering him after years of marital problems. The author, Shirley Harrison, detailed Maybrick's life, presumably based on accounts written about Maybrick after his murder in 1889. Having claimed that the diary's author was Maybrick and that he had to be Jack the Ripper, Harrison included the full text of the diary with an analysis by David Forshaw, a psychiatric consultant in addictions. Dr. Forshaw concluded that the diary did indeed reveal the mind of Jack the Ripper. The book ended with a discussion of the authentication process.

The first expert I brought in was Joe Nickell, most noted for his work and book concerning the Shroud of Turin and the most skeptical person I knew (when I introduced him as such, he always followed by saying he doubted it). Dr. Nickell and I discussed the text of the book at length, and we were both concerned that the author approached the diary with little skepticism and that too many assumptions were presented as facts. A number of "facts" were incorrect, while several were actually contradicted in other parts of the book. We both believed that simply on the evidence presented in the book, we could only conclude the diary was a forgery.

An example of a conclusion being reached without any stated basis was the diarist's use of the term "one off." The earliest known use of this phrase in America is 1925, and 1934 in England, according to the Oxford English Dictionary. Yet after quoting both Oxford and Webster's by name, Harrison wrote, "I have also learned of oral uses of the expression in late Victorian times that have not yet found their way into the dictionaries." No sources nor explanations were given for this statement, yet a factor in questioning the authenticity of the diary text was summarily dismissed. This was only one of many examples of important statements with no apparent foundation. (It was also quite clear to anyone familiar with Victorian prose that many other phrases and uses of words in the diary were not in use in the 1880s.)

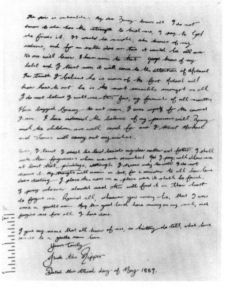

A genuine example of James Maybrick's handwriting.

A page from the diary claimed to have been written by Maybrick.

One of the most important pieces of evidence described in the book proved, if one were to accept the "facts" as stated, that the diary was a hoax. A letter was sent on September 25, 1888, to "The Boss, Central News Office, London." This letter, genuinely written in 1888 and widely publicized then, was signed "Jack the Ripper," the first use of this name. The letter may or may not have been written by the murderer, but either way the diary directly reflected the unique language found in it. This unique language in the "Dear Boss" letter was cited to prove the diary's authenticity. Much later in the book Harrison reported that the documents expert consulted by the English publisher "does not link the handwriting of the diary with that of the 'Dear Boss' letter." There can be only one conclusion: The diary, which copies the letter's language but does not match its handwriting, must be forged.

I was especially interested to see the full, original reports submitted to the author by the experts hired to prove its authenticity. It is my standard practice to insist upon seeing the complete files and reports because I may interpret an expert's report differently. This was never truer than in this case. Surprisingly,

Smith provided the files, after invoking secrecy agreements signed by all of his experts to prevent me from speaking with them.

Dr. Nicholas Eastaugh had been engaged to do a forensic examination of the ink, and his test was very competently carried out. His finding—that there are no elements in the ink that are inconsistent with a date of 1888—is correct, but what was not published was that he stressed that other major tests needed to be done as well. In June 1993 he wrote to the publisher, "I think it would be very dangerous to quote [me] . . . saying I say the ink is Victorian, when I don't—merely that it could be."

Dr. David Forshaw's 59-page report was quoted extensively throughout the book, providing the basis for asserting that, from a psychiatric standpoint, this was the diary of a person who shows the personality of a serial killer. (When I inquired about Dr. Forshaw's experience and qualifications as a specialist in serial killers, I was told that his work was confidential and could not be discussed.) The report he submitted to the author and publisher contained two statements that were startling. In the opening of his lengthy report Dr. Forshaw wrote, "Starting from the assumption that the journal is genuine, the aim of this contribution is to come to an understanding of James Maybrick the man, and of the state of mind of Jack the Ripper."

People who have not been involved in major literary forgeries are unaware of the resourcefulness of the perpetrators of such hoaxes. In the Ripper case many persons stated that it was too elaborate to be a hoax; they were not aware that virtually everyone also said that no one could possibly forge nearly 60 Hitler diaries, nor could anyone create Howard Hughes's autobiography nor Benito Mussolini's diaries, nor could someone in Salt Lake City forge letters and manuscripts whose content would shake the Mormon Church. If investigators assume that something is too complex to be a fraud, then they are likely to be deceived, and forgers are not always motivated by money or fame; their goal can be the simple satisfaction of fooling the experts.

The original diary was finally brought to Chicago by publisher Robert Smith in August 1993 for the examination of the handwriting, ink, and paper. I met him at the laboratory of Maureen Casey Owens, former president of the American Society of Questioned Document Examiners, along with Joe Nickell and Robert L. Kuranz, a research ink chemist.

All of us had the immediate reaction that the diary was written much more recently than the late 1880s. I was also struck by the uniformity of the writing and ink—highly unusual in a diary—a uniformity that immediately reminded me of my first glimpse of the Hitler diaries. It was clearly written at a few sittings, not over time.

I was also surprised that the diary was written in a scrapbook, not a normal diary book. Scrapbooks, larger in format and made of very absorbent heavy paper, were used for mounting postcards, photographs, valentines, and other greeting cards, and I had not previously encountered one used as a diary.

We were all very suspicious of the fact that approximately 20 pages at the beginning of the book had been torn out. There was no logical explanation for the purported author, Maybrick, a man of means, to have torn them out himself. If for some reason he wanted to use a scrapbook for a diary, he would have bought a new one. An ultraviolet examination showed that there had been postcards on the first, now torn out, page. The images were offset on the inside front cover.

Our examination had to be able to answer everyone's questions—Warner Books was going to lose a lot of money in sales, as well as the expenses they had already incurred, if we convinced the British publisher not to issue the book. Therefore, every type of forensic test was undertaken, though none were actually necessary once we saw the original diary.

I was quoted, accurately, in the *Washington Post* saying that if I wrote a book about the Jack the Ripper fraud, one of the chapters would be entitled "Yes, But. . ." and it would detail the innumerable times I told Robert Smith facts and he ignored what I said, responding, "Yes, but. . . ." When I sat down with him to tell him that there was not a shred of evidence it was genuine, and overwhelming proof it was a hoax, he continued to argue. We were in the cocktail lounge of the Drake Hotel in Chicago, and I kept hoping his ordering "executive-size" martinis would make him mellow, not more belligerent. Finally, he said to me, very sadly, "You don't understand—Jack the Ripper is my winning lottery ticket in life."

Warner Books immediately issued a press statement announcing that they were canceling publication. I had suggested their going forward with the book as fiction and that I would write a section about how it was uncovered, but CEO Kirshbaum believed that Warner should distance itself from the hoax. Robert Smith went ahead with his publication in England, changing the dust jacket to indicate that the authenticity was controversial and that readers could decide for themselves.

Quite unexpectedly, the Walt Disney publishing subsidiary Hyperion decided to publish the book in the United States, with the statement "includes the full text of the diary and the arguments for and against its authenticity" on the dust jacket. It seemed appropriate that Walt Disney, a company based on fantasy, decided to publish this fantasy, fully aware that everyone Smith claimed

The revelation that the Jack the Ripper diary was a forgery
made headlines both in the United States and in England.

had authenticated the diary had now publicly said it was a hoax. Disney did
publish my detailed report to Warner Books and Smith's nonsensical rebuttal.

I met once with Shirley Harrison, the author of the book. She was a kindly,
grandmotherly type, who responded to my demonstration of the handwriting
comparisons proving the diary was forged by incomprehensibly taking out an
antique pocket watch she said proved that the diary was genuine. I wondered
if she had studied under a magician. She asked me to read a metallurgical report
on the watch. She made no sense. I told her that unless she could wave the
watch over the diary and change the handwriting, it was irrelevant.

A week after Warner's press release that they were canceling publication, I
was in New York when the *Larry King* show tracked me down and asked me to
appear on the show that night in Washington. The author, Shirley Harrison,
would be on the program, and they wanted me to refute what she would say.
When I mentioned to my wife that I had turned down *Larry King*, she told me
I had to do the show and defend my position. I was concerned that I would be
seen as tearing apart this nice, old, grandmotherly woman, but I called them
back and went to Washington. I had been on the *Larry King* show several times,
especially with the Hitler diaries. Unlike other shows, Larry King did not come
out and talk with guests before airtime, and I was sure, having met him several
times, that he was unlikely to remember me. But I wanted him to have me in

context, so in the few seconds I had between his walking onto the set and going on air, I reminded him about our talking about the Hitler diaries. It was all I needed for him to introduce me at the opening of the show by saying, "All of you will remember Ken Rendell, who has appeared on the show previously in other journalistic fraud cases." It set the stage that this was another fraud.

I had brought with me a Victorian-era scrapbook to illustrate the kind of scrapbook the diary was written in. I kept it on my knees under the table, but as we came to the first commercial break, I had a different idea. I pulled it out but didn't open it. When Larry King asked what it was, I said it was the next fraud I was working on, Sherlock Holmes's diary. It took a few seconds before he said, "Wasn't Sherlock Holmes fictional?" I replied that the forger hadn't realized it and forged the diary of someone who didn't exist. As we went back on the air, King was laughing and set an appropriate atmosphere when he asked Shirley Harrison why she believed the Jack the Ripper diary was genuine. She replied that she had believed it for six years, giving me the opening to comment that I had believed in Santa Claus for six years, but that was no reason to continue to do so. Larry King let her continue on with irrelevant reasons as to why it was genuine, and I was spared a sparring contest.

I understood her maintaining her belief—like the publisher Robert Smith, it was her winning lottery ticket as well. It was the biggest story she would ever have. What I have never understood is that the Ripperologists—this very strange group of people who know every minutia of each of these grisly murders and regularly visit the scenes of them—embraced the diary as proof that the identity of Jack the Ripper was known. I would have thought they would continue to thrive on the speculation that it was Queen Victoria's son, not in the belief that it was an unimportant cotton merchant. More books came out after the Smith/Harrison one, defending the diary as genuine and attacking me as an enemy of the "Ripperologists." *Jack the Ripper: The Final Chapter* begins, "Incredibly, not one person has been able, or even attempted, to explain how it was forged or by whom. Why not? Because it is genuine." The logic was straight from *The Diary of Jack the Ripper*.

The whole thing was so crazy I thought it needed a celebratory event to bring it to an end, at least for the rational people involved. I arranged a luncheon at Brown's Hotel in London, whose dining room is straight out of the era of Jack the Ripper, for all the British experts who had been so misused by Smith. In the spirit of the disgruntled Ripperologists, lunch consisted only of foods mentioned in the fake diary. They were a good group of people, who were experts at what they did but naïve when it came to knowing how their reports could be misrepresented under the secrecy agreements they had signed.

Chapter 14

Appraising Richard Nixon's White House Papers and Watergate Tapes

The federal government confiscated Richard Nixon's White House papers and Watergate tapes in 1974 to make sure that nothing was destroyed. Nixon's lawyers sued the federal government in 1980 for the monetary value, on the same basis that someone would sue for the value of land taken in eminent domain proceedings. They maintained these were his personal property, as presidents had traditionally owned their White House papers. In 1991 the federal district court in Washington, D.C., ruled that they were not his personal property. The following year the appellate court in Washington ruled 3-0 that presidents had always owned their White House papers and Nixon was no exception. (In 1978 the Presidential Records Act changed this.) The case was sent back to the district court to determine how much Nixon was entitled to be paid.

At this point Nixon's law firm, Miller Cassidy, began a search for an appraiser and interviewed possible experts to represent them. When they contacted me, I said I could only consider spending a maximum of two weeks, and I would give them a plan as to how they should proceed. My obligations in my own business were such that, no matter what I was charging, I could not afford to spend any more time. Included in the two weeks would be a meeting with the Justice Department to explain and answer questions about how I arrived at my value. I knew they could not find an appraiser with my track record of being upheld on my appraised values. I reiterated my appraisal would be realistic and fair, which is the reason I was very successful. If I could not reach an agreement with the government, I would introduce them to someone who could spend the time going to court. As long as Nixon's evaluation was well presented, it should be accepted to avoid a costly trial the government was unlikely to win.

I never considered whether my personal opinion of Nixon would have any bearing on my impartiality. Some years earlier I had handled a correspondence of Richard Nixon during his Senate campaign in 1950 against Helen Gahagan Douglas. In those letters he viciously plotted attacks against her, based on almost no factual information, insinuating that she was a communist. Nixon defeated her and gained the nickname "Tricky Dick."

I followed the events of Watergate with as much frustration and fury as anyone, but I also knew Nixon had ended the Vietnam War, which Lyndon Johnson couldn't do, and opened relations with China, something no one thought would happen with a Republican president. My evaluation would be impersonal and based on an unbiased assessment of the market.

His lawyers agreed to my proposal for the two weeks. I knew they had contacted other appraisers, and I don't think anyone else presented them with such a reasonable and realistic approach. My consulting fee staggered them. They kept saying that they wanted to hire me, they just could not pay me what I wanted. I told them that my fee was not negotiable and that they were making the mistake of focusing on what this came to on a daily basis, rather than what the value of my report would be. I also told them to consider my fee compared to their own and how much time my work would save them. At that time I did not realize this was not a good sales point. We agreed to a meeting at their offices, at my daily fee of $5,000.

I met in their Georgetown offices in Washington. Seven or eight of Nixon's lawyers were on three sides of a conference table. I was on the other. They asked where the rest of my team was, and I said they were working in Boston and there was no reason for any of them to be attending the meeting. I stressed that I was very un-bureaucratic and, looking at so many lawyers on their side,

I knew we did not share that philosophy. They agreed that I would go through Nixon's papers, listen to the Watergate tapes, and determine the fair market value. I would then present my report. If they agreed, I would meet with the Department of Justice lawyers to see if we could agree to a settlement without any further expenses.

Nixon's papers were in storage at a nondescript National Archives facility in Virginia. They estimated there were 44 million pieces and 4,500 hours of Watergate tapes. In any appraisal, but especially one of this size, I needed to determine what was created on paper versus discussed on the telephone, the quality and the importance of what was created, and the policy or attitude concerning what was saved. If important policies were mainly created in meetings or on the telephone, without memos memorializing them, the value to future historians and researchers of the papers would be considerably less.

Everyone's papers from the Nixon administration were there, with the exception of Henry Kissinger, who had transferred them to the Library of Congress before the government confiscated the others. The rest appeared to be complete; their importance varied from person to person, but they gave a seemingly complete picture of the White House activity supporting Nixon. Haldeman's and Ehrlichman's papers were not all that interesting because they reflected the carrying out of decisions made in meetings. Decisions were not discussed, nor policy created, in their papers.

Nixon's own papers were amazingly important. He would go to the Executive Office Building at night and write out ideas and thoughts on yellow legal pads. This huge quantity of legal pads concerned the most important decisions and policies of the Nixon White House. They were at the heart of the positive part of the Nixon presidency. I was especially impressed with the pages of his notes on the pros and cons of opening relations with China. As Nixon's evening progressed, you could see in his handwriting the effects of his drinking as his pen strokes became slurred, but still very legible. His ideas were serious, and they were well thought out. These writings, hundreds of pages, would tell researchers and historians more about the reality of the Nixon White House than anything else. During the George W. Bush administration I visited the Oval Office with my family and, as we were leaving, the Secret Service invited us over to the renamed Eisenhower Office Building. The agent who accompanied us took us to the room where Nixon had his private office and wrote all of these manuscripts. He said they thought I would like to see the room since I was so familiar with what Nixon did there. I was surprised that he knew about my knowledge of Nixon's habits, though I knew that everyone coming to the

Oval Office is researched by security. He was the agent who regularly helped Nixon get back to the White House after nights of heavy thinking and drinking.

I was told I was one of the first people listening to the Watergate tapes, and I found the experience unnerving. I had not anticipated the poor quality of the recordings and had the sense that I was hiding under the desk eavesdropping on someone's private conversations—which I was. There was a noticeable difference in Nixon's conversations depending upon whom he was meeting with. With Haldeman and Ehrlichman I had the impression that he was trying to be "one of the boys," which he definitely was not. There was a lot of posturing because of his social awkwardness.

My time at the National Archives left me very impressed with the importance and quality of Nixon's White House papers. It was impossible to know how important the Watergate tapes were beyond the evidence about the break-in; they were difficult to understand, and it would take as long to listen to them as it did to create them: 4,500 hours.

Having established the quality and importance of Nixon's papers, I had to determine what the market was and how much I could have sold them for. I would never consider something like this in terms of what it would be worth to collectors. The White House papers of a president would create their own market. On the open market numerous institutions would want the prestige of having a presidential archive, and Nixon's importance and notoriety would add significantly to the value. $27,500,000 had been raised privately to build the Nixon Library, and I thought that was the best place to begin my research. I wanted to meet with Maurice Stans, who had been finance chairman of the Committee for the Re-Election of the President, raising record sums for his campaign and later raising the money for the Nixon Library. A meeting was set in Pasadena, and I immediately went to California.

Stans greeted me in his large and impressive apartment. He was pleasant and cooperative but told me that raising the money for the library had exhausted him and he couldn't possibly raise more. He was 85 years old, and after Watergate, during which he was accused of a lack of record keeping for not knowing where the cash went that ended up with the burglars, he did seem worn out. I asked him for a list of who had contributed the $27,500,000, which he confidentially showed to me. He gave me permission to call the donors I personally knew. Among them were Helen Copley, the owner of Copley newspapers, Walter Annenberg, the publisher, and Bill Simon, the financier. On average, each of them agreed they would have given double their donation, and the next morning this information persuaded Stans that it was likely the rest of the donors would have done so also.

I went back to Washington, feeling very proud that I had established what I considered a rock-solid value. I laid out the details to Stan Mortenson and the other two lawyers who were most actively involved in the case, Marty Minsker and Scott Nelson. My proposal concerning the Watergate tapes was that we should give them to the government as part of a negotiated settlement at $30 million. I didn't think any judge, especially one who had already ruled he didn't think Nixon should be paid anything, would give Nixon the total amount he wanted. The judge needed to be able to say that he had gotten the Watergate tapes for nothing while agreeing to $30 million for the papers.

The lawyers pressed me as to why I hadn't arrived at a value for the tapes, and I told them that I had only been able to come up with one way to sell them. I noted the legal definition of fair-market value doesn't include good taste. The highest value would be obtained by cutting up the tapes and mounting strips in Lucite blocks, with the specific words underneath and "Richard Nixon's Watergate Tapes" printed above. They could be sold through a mail-order company. A word like "the" would be priced at $49.95, and various expletives running from $249.95 for one word to $499.95 for an expletive-laden phrase. Nixon's personal lawyer erupted, "You are talking about the former president of the United States." I responded, "I am talking about the unindicted co-conspirator in the Watergate break-ins." My chemistry with Mortenson had never been good, and it wasn't improving.

013911

DATE	DESCRIPTION	AMOUNT
1/25/93	Two Days Consultation in Reference to the Nixon Papers & Expenses Plus preparation of proposal	$11,826.14

Nixon's lawyers were appalled at my consulting fee. I saved one of their check stubs for a Washington meeting.

He wanted me to raise my appraisal of the papers to $45 million, and I said I did not negotiate appraised values. He then said he didn't want an appraisal of one amount for the entire archive, even though I kept arguing that this was the only way to get the highest price. He thought that every piece should be evaluated individually and we continued to argue, with my stressing that if that was done, and the values were based on the collector market, it would come to a lot less than $30 million. It would also be very expensive and could take a year to do. It did not occur to me that a major difference between my approach, which I believed would convince the Justice Department was fair, and his was the amount of the legal costs. The meeting ended poorly. In a letter to Mortenson's law partner, Marty Minsker, I wrote, "I am no longer interested in working on the Richard Nixon case. I cannot see how there is any reason for me to spend more time on the subject. My talents are in my ability to market manuscript collections. This was the perfect type of collection for me to market. . . . It was graphically clear to me in our meeting that Stan was interested in my talents only as an employee who would do what he was told. He had the wrong guy."

I did, however, follow through with someone who might be interested in taking on a long-term appraisal of the individual pieces. I was in Austin, Texas, for a meeting at the University of Texas and was socially meeting with a former librarian there, John Payne. He drove me to see a piece of land he and his wife had bought, and as we sat on this idyllic site, he said he didn't know when they could afford to build a house on it. I told him I had a project that could take him a long way toward paying for a house, provided he was willing to spend many months in Virginia, plus additional time in court, and would most likely lose the case. He was just starting in the appraisal field, and it was an opportunity that made great sense for him. It would also make great sense for Nixon's lawyers, as he had the time and was willing to evaluate all of the Nixon papers individually. They would find out that Payne was not going to be dictated to about the total value they wanted.

It took years to prepare for trial, which began in February 1999 and lasted for five months. The Beverly Hills agent/dealer Chuck Sachs was the government's expert witness and testified that the Nixon White House papers and Watergate tapes had a maximum value of $1.5 million. In initial cross-examination Scott Nelson, the bearded, friendly-appearing but superb cross examiner on the Nixon team, asked Sachs about his conversations with the Nixon lawyers when they interviewed him as a possible expert. Nelson asked Sachs to repeat what he told them he thought the minimum value of the papers would be, and he said, "I don't remember." Nelson reminded him it was over $37 million and that the Watergate tapes would be worth a minimum of $2.5 million and likely far more. Asked if this refreshed his memory, Sachs said it did not. When asked what fee he quoted for the appraisal, he again said he didn't remember; Nelson said it was $6 million. The government objected to this way of getting the information into testimony, and Nelson said that their lawyers would testify, if necessary, that these were the amounts. There were several pages of Sachs's testimony in which he repeatedly failed to recall conversations based on that meeting, but during many days of subsequent testimony he remembered the most obscure details.

News coverage of the payment
for Nixon's papers and tapes.

The transcript of Sachs's lengthy testimony shows that he mentioned me hundreds of times. When he first brought up my name and the Justice Department's lawyer responded by asking him to identify me, Sachs told the court that I was the most important dealer and appraiser, and he had hoped the government would hire me but could not because the Nixon legal team had already. Sachs quoted extensively from articles I had written and appraisals he had been able to get copies of, including an appraisal of George Gershwin's papers done for Warner Bros.' donation to the Library of Congress. Sachs speculated innumerable times on how he thought I would have evaluated the Nixon papers.

The trial went on, seemingly forever, with Chuck Sachs, the government's expert, and John Payne, the Nixon team's expert, citing hundreds, perhaps even thousands, of Nixon papers and the specific values that they had assigned to each of them. It must have been painful for the judge listening to this repetitive testimony.

In June 2000 an out-of-court settlement was announced: The government offered to pay $18 million for Nixon's White House papers and Watergate tapes. The Nixon Library received $6 million. Federal estate and other taxes amounted to $3.7 million. The Nixon family received less than $90,000. Nixon's law firm received $7,385,000.

Chapter 15

Bill Gates and the Quintessential Library Project

In late 1995 I was a guest on NBC's *Today Show*, talking about an extraordinary collection of letters written by each of the U.S. presidents, which we had for sale. Watching the show that morning was the architect and interior designer of the new home that Bill and Melinda Gates were building on Lake Washington, across from Seattle. Thierry Despont's path had crossed mine socially and hearing me talk about the presidential collection gave him the idea that it might interest Bill Gates.

The collection did interest Gates, and Gates invited me to come to Seattle and meet with him and Melinda about building a library in their new house. Gates's secretary gave me a date in January, noting that it was the only date the couple had available all winter. I've always had the policy to arrive well in advance of important meetings. I don't risk bad weather or canceled flights. Usually, half a day is sufficient, but with potential snowstorms in Boston and

New York I decided to go three days ahead. (Two days before our meeting the Boston and New York airports closed.)

With extra time, I got to know the Seattle Art Museum and continued to study my comprehensive notes on the history of mathematics and computer and software development.

I had studied everything I could about Bill Gates. This is always my approach with any potentially important client. It is critical to understand clients personally and be able to suggest historical subjects or people who might be of interest. In the case of Bill Gates, there were many books about him, all discussing his business career. There was almost nothing about his personal life. Everyone who had worked with Gates at Microsoft, which he co-founded with Paul Allen in 1975, described him as a brilliant, driven, impatient multitasker who is frequently confrontational and combative.

I would be well prepared in the subjects, specifically math and computers, that I assumed would interest him. I knew the major figures in the history of mathematics. I had handled letters of Leibniz, Descartes, Newton, and, of course, Einstein. There were many other important people, and I learned about the contributions they made to mathematics, the books they wrote, and the rarity and availability of their first editions. Fermat, Pascal, Gauss, Euler, Gödel, Boole, and many others were on my study sheets.

In the field of computers the only major figures I knew well were Alan Turing and Charles Babbage, both credited with being inventors in the early stages of development. I was familiar with Turing because of his work breaking the Enigma code in World War II. I learned about innovators such as John von Neumann, Claude Shannon, Norbert Wiener, and Grace Hopper, a trailblazer in the design and implementation of programming languages.

I was as prepared as I could possibly be but was anxious because of Gates's notorious impatience. At 6:30 on a January night a car, arranged by Gates's office at Microsoft, picked me up in Seattle and took me to an "experimental" house built out of materials that the Gates were considering to construct their new home. This experimental house sat on a cliff, above the building site on Lake Washington. As we pulled up to the front door the driver told me to go right in. The door was unlocked.

There was no one else there. I walked down a corridor to a living room and took a seat on a sofa in front of a large picture window that apparently looked out onto Lake Washington. I could see nothing but blackness and the reflection of the room.

Finally, I heard a door open and footsteps down the corridor.

"Hi, I'm Bill Gates and this is my wife, Melinda," the man said.

I thought, "No kidding. If you aren't, I'm in the wrong house!"

He was nothing like the man I expected. Both Bill and Melinda were very friendly. They congratulated me for having the foresight to arrive in Seattle before storms paralyzed the East Coast. As the three of us moved into the dining room and began to talk about what they had in mind for their new home, they listened and attentively discussed my questions. None of Bill's legendary impatience was on display. He and Melinda didn't know what they wanted to do for a library, and they were surprisingly open, modest, and respectful of my knowledge and my suggestions on how to proceed.

Our conversation shifted easily to the specifics of their personal interests and passions. Bill and Melinda each had their own favorite authors. Bill's favorites were F. Scott Fitzgerald (*The Great Gatsby*), J.D. Salinger (*Catcher in the Rye*), and John Knowles (*A Separate Peace*). Melinda had a long list of favorites.

As we discussed Bill's interest in the history and development of mathematics, I suggested that I get original editions of all the major mathematicians. He asked me what we could get of Carl Friedrich Gauss, who, prior to my preparation for this meeting, I knew little about. I talked knowledgably about the importance and availability of Gauss's doctoral dissertation on the fundamental theorem of algebra.

Both Bill and Melinda were interested in acquiring books in areas that they wanted to learn more about. Several times, Bill modestly pointed out to me that he had dropped out of Harvard. At one point I asked him to close his eyes and imagine coming home and walking into his library after a tough day at Microsoft.

"Imagine reaching for a book that your mind would be absorbed in," I said to him. "What is that book about?'

Bill answered instantly: "development of technology." This was the spark I needed.

I told them about other collections I had built and other libraries I had put together for collectors. I offered to send them a large book with inventories of these collections, so they could write their reactions to the subjects, authors, and books listed. The subjects covered everything that I had worked on, from colonial America to the American West, to music and literature, to the White House Library on culture, and many other subjects as well.

They wanted me to come to their current home, also on Lake Washington, to look at the books they already owned. This, they said, would give me a better idea of their personal lives and interests. It was not only a very satisfying business evening but a surprisingly personal pleasure as well.

The next morning I had some questions related to our conversation the night before and called Bill at his office. His executive assistant told me that she would put the call through because she was aware of our meeting, but going forward I should know that Bill always wants results, not questions, after a meeting. If I thought it necessary to speak with him again, having just met with him, she said, the chances were high that it would negatively impact our relationship. I was now intruding into his business world and had been lulled by my experiences in his personal world the night before. My questions could wait until my next scheduled meeting.

When I arrived at my next meeting with Bill and Melinda Gates, I found myself in a relatively modest house further down the coast of Lake Washington. Melinda, who was in the last stages of pregnancy with their first child, had been confined to bed. She came to the head of the stairs, wearing her pajamas and bathrobe, to greet me and explain her situation. This warm gesture continued the couple's unpretentiousness—and the obvious difference between their existence in their Microsoft world and more simple private life. In later years, when I had meetings at Microsoft with Chief Technology Officer Nathan Myhrvold down the hall from Gates, I was wary of crossing paths with "the Microsoft Bill Gates." At home, in the evening, and on weekends, Bill was a completely different person.

In March 1996, three months after our initial meeting, the Gateses sent my nearly three-inch-thick book back to me, heavily annotated by both of them. We next met in April, shortly after the birth of their first child, to work out the details of what they wanted and how we would proceed. The library, we agreed, would contain books about subjects that interested them, not books meant to impress others. Their collection would span three types of collecting: (1) reading copies of their favorite books, and other books for reference; (2) first editions of select books in various subjects of interest; and (3) special collections of historical letters, documents, and manuscripts that they would consider acquiring as I presented them. We agreed on a budget that would enable me to acquire everything that was of importance to them. Both Bill and Melinda were very excited about the project and thrilled about what I told them I could do.

This was a refreshing change from so many book collectors who appear blasé and are simply checking off titles.

They set a timetable: I would have 12 months to complete the library. As personable as Bill and Melinda were toward me, I knew this was an absolute deadline, just as the budget was absolute.

Shirley and I agreed we had to look at this project like a military operation, organizing many different aspects of it to move forward simultaneously. While Shirley said she knew that I had organized enormous projects in the past, she had no idea how all this could be accomplished in the next 12 months. I reassured her that I had no idea either, but we would do it.

 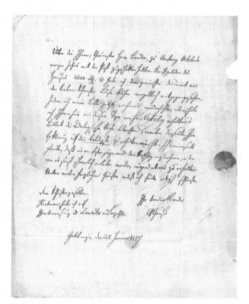

**My selections for the Gates library included works by
Leonardo da Vinci and Carl Friedrich Gauss.**

Thierry Despont, the Gateses' designer and architect, gave me the architectural designs and drawings for the three-room library pavilion so I would know the available shelf space. As for the books that would go on the shelves, there was no internet to find books in 1996. In order to locate the approximately 10,000 volumes of reading and reference books, we hired a woman familiar with the book business to travel around the country to antiquarian book dealers. While she was on her odyssey, we rented a warehouse to process and catalog the 10,000 books. Using Despont's architectural plans, we replicated the bookcases for the three rooms to design the layout in reality, not on paper. Meanwhile, our head of research began to assemble a staff of six people to catalog more than 1,000 books each month.

While all this was underway, I set out to acquire the rare books. Though they were not necessarily expensive, I was buying on such a scale that I was pouring millions of dollars into the rare-book market. This caused widespread rumors about who my client was. Two years earlier Gates had publicly bought

Leonardo da Vinci's Codex for just over $30 million, and the 72-page manuscript, handwritten by Leonardo, traveled extensively on exhibit throughout the world. Nearly everyone assumed Bill Gates was my client.

I was far and away the largest dealer in historical manuscripts, and it was logical that Gates would come to me. I never acknowledge who I am working with, and everything about my relationship with Gates was highly confidential. Within my business we always used a codename for him, even as we talked among ourselves. One time, during a meeting with me, Bill picked up a folder marked "Admiral" and asked who Admiral was. "That's our codename for you," I replied. He was impressed with our security.

Until Bill talked about his library and my role collecting the manuscripts and books for him and Melinda—in a January 1997 *Time* cover story titled "The Private World of Bill Gates"—I never confirmed whose library we were forming.

During the first year I was also locating important manuscript collections for the Gates. In monthly meetings Bill would quickly assess my offerings and make instant decisions. At one point he told me that he must be my ideal client because he gave me decisions on the spot and paid for the collections the next day. I told him that he wasn't; my ideal client was in his 90s and didn't intend to leave his collection to an institution, so I would get a chance to buy it back and sell it again. Since Bill is 12 years younger than I am, that did not seem likely.

Shirley took on the project of designing and creating special binders for key manuscripts, which we called the Creativity Collection because most of them dealt with creativity. She had been listening carefully when Melinda said she wished there was some way to share their collection of letters and documents with friends, family, and colleagues without damaging them. Shirley's ideas went over well but required literally thousands of hours for our team of binders to complete. At one point, when we were dangerously low on leather, she wondered if it

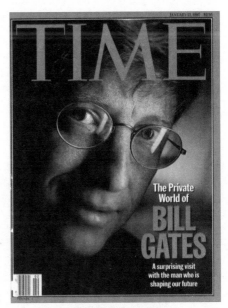

The January 1997 issue of *Time*.

would be easier, and cheaper, to just buy a goat herd. That was a Microsoft way of thinking.

The building of the Gates library pavilion was progressing more quickly than the rest of their house. At more than 60,000 square feet, the home under construction was highly customized with the most advanced technology, which made the project all the more complex. One day Neil Crawford, the Gateses' general manager of construction, put his arm around Shirley's shoulder and pointed across Lake Washington to the tallest skyscraper in Seattle. He had built it in less time and for less money than Bill and Melinda Gates were spending on their new home.

As we approached the move-in date in April I imagined it as our own

No rare-book library had ever before arrived by crane.

D-Day invasion. The Gateses' house was being built into a steep hillside, and the library pavilion was on the second level. Unloading on the lake level was impossible because there was only a small courtyard. We would be able to use a large crane to load pallets of boxed books from our two trucks parked above the library down to an area outside the library doors. But we only had use of the crane for 45 minutes, commencing at 7 a.m. sharp. Our trucks could not arrive before 6:45 a.m.

Efficiency was critical in unpacking and shelving three library rooms in a day.

Because it rained all of the time, quite literally, from September through May, everything would be shrink-wrapped, and we would have to be able to move all of the boxes into the library rapidly because there was no space in the construction chaos to safely leave them outside.

We had been shelving the now nearly 13,000 books in the library built in the warehouse in Boston as we would in Seattle. The shelving matched exactly, so every bay and each shelf was numbered, every shelf photographed, and the books put in boxes and onto pallets in the exact order we wanted to unpack and shelve them. The day before the books arrived we put large bay and shelf numbers, as well as photographs of the books, on the shelves in the Gates library.

Jason, Rosalie Fawcett, and me.

With our full Gates library team—researchers and administrative people from Boston and conservation specialists from San Francisco—we rehearsed everything that could possibly go wrong. Or we thought we did. We had determined how long it was going to take to unload the books from the trucks and how long it would take to attach, lift, and land each pallet in front of the library doors. I imagined our crew being like the team that services cars in a race: the car pulls in, everything gets done simultaneously, and the car is back on the racetrack in moments.

The day turned out to be even more stressful than we had imagined. Even for Seattle, the rain was a downpour. My manager in charge of unloading the pallets became flustered with how quickly they were arriving at the library level. I had to take over her role and ordered our staff inside the library to go outside to help unload the pallets faster. The construction staff started calling me "General Patton."

Because of the security that was required for the books being brought into the library, and our having such a large team there, it made sense to move the manuscript special collections on the same day. These came from Boston in a chartered plane, which was met by armored cars at the Seattle airport.

By the end of the day everything was properly shelved, and there were no mishaps. In keeping with the D-Day analogy and the famous movie, I will always think of that day at Bill and Melinda Gates's house as my "Longest Day."

Six months later, on Saturday, October 4, 1997, Bill and Melinda held an open house for more than 150 people. They welcomed guests in their vast reception hall on the lake level of the house—a floor designed for large-scale entertainment. On one wall twenty-four 40-inch video screens projected photographs. Also on this level was the family's screening room, a spectacular swimming pool, a gym, an arcade, and Bill's high-ceilinged trampoline room.

I was quickly dubbed "General Patton" by the construction team.

Guests could walk up the grand staircase to the halls outside the library pavilion. The library itself was roped off, but people could peer inside to read inscribed in large letters around the rotunda: "HE HAD COME A LONG WAY TO THIS BLUE LAWN, AND HIS DREAM MUST HAVE SEEMED SO CLOSE THAT HE COULD HARDLY FAIL TO GRASP IT." This was Bill's favorite line from *The Great Gatsby*. On the dock in front of the house Bill also paid homage to Fitzgerald's book: he had a green beacon, the same beacon as on Daisy Buchanan's dock.

Six months after we assembled the library, we had the opportunity to share it with guests at Bill and Melinda Gates's open house.

Bill caught sight of Shirley and me and apologized for the chaos of the big crowd and promised that dinner, which he had planned for the following night, would be very different and personal. When Shirley and I arrived back at the Gates home the next evening, the atmosphere was completely changed. Bill and Melinda welcomed a small group of people in a now nearly empty reception hall. Guests were encouraged to roam around the library. For most, it was the first opportunity to see the Leonardo da Vinci Codex. The Gateses displayed the magnificent manuscript in glass exhibit cases set into a massive table. Shirley and I loved watching Bill and Melinda as they took letters and manuscripts, in the special bindings Shirley created, off the shelves to show to their friends. They asked both Shirley and me to give tours through the collection.

For us, this was an honor and a thrill. It was our first exposure to the Gates family's social world.

Seeing the library that Bill and Melinda created based on their personal passions and interests prompted quite a few other people to think of doing something similar. Jeff Bezos, who was part of the small dinner group that evening, told me that he was enormously impressed by the collection and asked if I could build a library for him. Back then, in 1997, Bezos was only three years into building Amazon, and the company's future was in doubt because of the enormous debt he had piled up. Obviously, he overcame his early financial challenges, but the material did not exist for me to build the library he wanted.

That same Sunday night I started talking with another friendly fellow who, when I asked him what he did for a living, said that he sold coffee. Sometime later, as Starbucks became a household name, I realized I had been talking to Howard Schultz.

Dinner that evening was at round tables in the Gateses' dining room, and I was seated between Paul Allen's mother, Faye, and Bill's sister, who lived in Spokane. Melinda welcomed everyone, and then she paid Shirley and me a great tribute by saying that despite all the frustrations in building their still-unfinished new house, they would always remember meeting us and working with us to build the library.

Melinda also publicly posed a question to me: If she were going to put something in the cornerstone of their new house—to be opened in the future—what did I think it should be? I said it should be something that would tell people what she and Bill are really like personally, not just how they're described from a business point of view.

Neither Shirley nor I really had any idea where this was headed, but with the completion of the fundamental library and this spectacular introduction to their Seattle friends, we flourished in their world. We moved on to acquiring for the Gateses important manuscript collections in their areas of interest. By now it was broadly known that we were working with them, and collectors and dealers came to us with letters, manuscripts and collections that might interest them. In their specific fields of interest, I went to collectors I had known for many years and told them that they had an opportunity to sell their collections at a favorable price but that it might not be there in the future. Many took advantage of the opportunity, and Bill and Melinda Gates formed an important collection in the span of only a few years.

Our work with the Gateses created a new archive in our own collection: dozens of handwritten letters from them to us. With wonderful enthusiasm, Melinda wrote notes to Shirley about their daughter Jennifer and our daughter

Julia. Bill and Melinda both thanked us for everything we were doing for them. It was notable that their wonderful excitement was expressed in handwritten letters—not emails.

The spirit of creativity and discovery in Seattle felt light years ahead of New York. Microsoft thought in terms of challenging the idea of what is possible. At Microsoft, they were going beyond the horizon every day. I was reminded of the adage, "Pessimists see difficulty in every opportunity, while optimists see opportunity in every difficulty." This seemed to be the motto of everyone we were meeting.

Bill and Melinda Gates both expressed their
appreciation to us for creating their library.

Many of the upper-level Microsoft executives had broad cultural interests, just as Bill and Melinda did. At the Gateses' first dinner I had hit it off with Paul Allen's mother, Faye, and she invited me on many occasions to her home for lunch. Her house, which was part of her son's compound on Mercer Island, was basically a large library with spectacular twentieth-century impressionist paintings. The architecture of the buildings was much more conservative than the Gateses' house, and the furnishings and paintings were in keeping with Paul Allen's quiet, introverted personality. One of Paul's major interests, music, resulted in his building a futuristic museum called Experience Music Project (today known as the Museum of Pop Culture), in Seattle.

At one of my lunches with Faye, she told me that Paul's music museum was almost finished, and she was going to see it for the first time that afternoon. She invited me to come with her. I was fascinated as I watched Faye, a former librarian, take in her brilliant son's futuristic museum—the exhibition of his deepest passions and musical dreams. That night I had dinner with Paul, and I told him I had gone to his new museum with his mother. Just like any son, he was anxious to know what her reaction was.

Paul Allen was a dreamer, and we discussed turning one dream of his into reality. He thought of buying large ships and converting each into a museum specializing in a different subject: science, history, art, music, and so on. These ships, staffed with teachers, would travel to coastal cities around the world and stay for a period of time so that school groups could come and learn about things they otherwise wouldn't be exposed to.

I thought Paul's idea was terrific, and not just because I would be acquiring the artifacts for the museums. I met with the directors of several museums where Paul had proposed other ideas, and I learned that he typically delegated the execution of his ideas—and in this case, execution could be a nightmare. Allen's museum ships never came to be.

Bill Gates told us that he was planning a Microsoft Summit for CEOs, and on the last night he would bring everyone to his house for a reception and visit to the library. Bill said he wanted Shirley and me to be there so we could talk with their guests about the library. We asked Bill's office to provide us with a guest list in advance so we could research each person and think of letters and manuscripts they would find of particular interest. I already knew some of the people scheduled to be at the first annual Microsoft Summit: Steve Forbes, Meg Whitman, Steve Wynn, and a few others. Our research on people I didn't know turned out to be invaluable in making the CEO attendees feel welcome at the Gates home.

Shirley and I continued to do this for several years at the CEO Summit, and eventually we created master lists of manuscripts and rare books that could be displayed for the guests depending upon their interests. The most memorable guest of the Gateses, who visited many times a year, was their close friend Warren Buffett. He came to know their library collection as well as anyone. Buffett would bring people into the library and start pulling letters and manuscripts off the shelves, telling them with great enthusiasm how fantastic each piece was. When I told Buffett that I could build a library for him in Omaha, he said that he already had one—Bill's—and there was no need to create another!

BUSINESS
@
THE SPEED
OF THOUGHT

Ken,
Thanks for building such a special library for us. Best wishes,
Bill Gates

Chapter 16

Surviving the Ultimate Challenge: The Death of Our Son

I n my early adult life I came to the belief that the ultimate failure would be to find out I had little time remaining in my life and I had left many things unsaid and undone with the most important people in my life. To me, ultimate failure would be dying with many regrets. I never realized my lifelong attitude of telling people what I wanted to say to them—and always doing the things I wanted to do with them—would save me from an all-too-common disaster in life.

Our son Jason, 18 years old, died suddenly in an accident in our home just after Christmas 1998. I was working at Bill Gates's house in Seattle when my wife called me. The first words I said to her were that our marriage would survive. I knew a tragically large number of people whose teenage sons had died in accidents, and their marriages were destroyed. Many developed drinking and drug abuse problems. Losing a child is the ultimate disaster for a parent. It is unexpected. It is incomprehensible. And whatever the cause, it makes no sense.

As neuroscience developed, I read various articles on why so many teenage boys die in accidents. The part of their brain that recognizes risks is not as developed as the parts that encourage risky behavior. Jason was a risk taker. He and I had done a lot of mountain climbing—rock, snow, and ice—and I always had a guide with us because I was concerned he would ignore my warnings. He did pay a lot more attention to the guides, but when we would get to the top I always had to worry that he assumed he was safe because the dangerous part of the climb was over. It was difficult to get Jason to realize that this was actually when he was most vulnerable to carelessness.

Jason and I shared many adventures together.

Our family went through hell after he died. No one can understand it unless it has happened to them. No one else can understand that how you deal with the loss of a child is very personal and individual, and whatever works for you is the correct thing to do. Also, well-meaning people do not understand that rationalizing the loss of a child with their own religious beliefs is upsetting and infuriating. I doubt that many of these people would, if they lost their child, be comforted by the same religious rationalizations. For me, those were the most maddening condolences.

It is a disaster, and there is nothing comforting that anyone can say. The only comfort you can feel is in knowing that people are thinking of you at a tragic time. I also came to realize quickly that every parent is so struck by the possibility that they look to the bereaved to assure them that it is survivable. They don't mean to be selfish, but the thought is so frightening that I felt people were panicking in desperation.

Over time—a long time—there started to be slight breaks in the black clouds that overpowered our lives, and very gradually these breaks became bigger and lasted longer. But for me, the horror of the loss has never gone away. People who talk about bringing closure have never been through it, or they would know there is no closure. Survival, not closure, is the goal.

It was also important for me to come to grips with the question, "Why me?" I realized that the answer is, "Why *not* me?" It seems unnatural to think that disaster might happen to you. But bad things do happen to good people, and life is random. I

Climbing in the Tetons in Wyoming.

STEVE FORBES
133S BURNT MILLS ROAD
BEDMINSTER, N.J. 0792I

Dear Ken:

All of us were shocked and immensely saddened by the news about Jason. There cannot be a more devastating blow in life for a parent than this. Our hearts go out to you. I remember Jason as he was beginning to learn to walk when Bob and I visited your house in the late 1970s, a memory which makes this terribly untimely loss even more stunning. One desperately wishes there were ways to lessen the pain and sense of loss. May you at least be comforted by warm memories in the months and years ahead. You are in our prayers.

As ever,

Steve

Jan. 10, 1998

Ken + Shirley,

We are so sorry to hear of your son's death. As parents, we can only begin to imagine how terrible Jason's loss must feel. We hope you find comfort in one another, in the eyes of your young daughter + in your special memories of times with Jason.

You are in our thoughts + prayers. Warmly,

Bill + Melinda

know exactly where I was—walking on a beach—when I asked myself that question for maybe the thousandth time, and the answer suddenly became clear. No one is immune to the tragedies of life.

Shirley and I also realized that when one of us was being overcome with grief, the other could not help and would be pulled into the abyss if they tried. We each had to handle these very frequently overwhelming senses of grief individually, but constantly talk about them with each other, in a general sense, very personally and with sensitivity. There is a desperate wanting to turn the clock back, thinking that it is a nightmare, and you are going to wake up.

The most important factor in my surviving Jason's death is that I had left nothing unsaid. I didn't need to turn the clock back to say things to my son that I always wished I had said. And there was nothing I had wanted to do with him that I hadn't done. I had no regrets. After an extremely protracted and difficult divorce the court gave me sole custody of my two sons; I had not asked for this, but it was the decision of the court that this would be best for them. Shirley and I made a very secure and loving home life for both of them. My wife raised Jason with all of the care, affection, and stability that he hadn't had.

We had no regrets, and that is what ultimately saved us. You can't live your life in fear of tragedies, and you shouldn't live your life putting off expressing affection, caring, and attention.

Chapter 17

Is Nothing Sacred? Forging Elvis Presley Manuscripts

I n 2000, for the first time, I was confronted with a collection that I thought could be a fraud but I personally wanted to be genuine. Three reputable autograph dealers and one prominent rare-book dealer individually offered me several manuscripts that they represented as written and signed by Elvis Presley. They evidently came from the same source. The manuscripts included the lyrics of "Love Me Tender," "Hound Dog," "Blue Suede Shoes," and "Don't Be Cruel."

I was a teenager when Elvis Presley came on the scene in the 1950s, and he dominated music when I was growing up. These were the songs of my teenage years, and I really wanted the manuscripts to be genuine.

All three dealers were convinced that the manuscripts were authentic because their history was clear all the way back to when Elvis supposedly wrote the songs, and they said the manuscripts had been authenticated by a number of Elvis Presley experts. Additionally, Christie's and Bonhams auction houses had each sold at auction a manuscript from this original group.

I agreed to buy everything I was offered if I was satisfied with the manuscripts' authenticity. I had seen those Elvis manuscripts in the Christie's and Bonhams auction catalogs, and I thought it suspicious that both manuscripts were stained in the same way. People normally don't write on stained paper, though the manuscripts could have been stained in a later event.

In their catalogs each auction house gave the same detailed history of the provenance. Christie's and Bonhams wrote: "Andy Schroer, author of *Private Elvis: Elvis in Germany—the Missing Years* obtained these lyrics from Frau Pieper, Elvis Presley's landlady in Germany, who rented her house to Presley ... in 1959, during his Army service. These lyrics, like the only other examples of lyrics in Presley's hand to have been offered at auction and sold through these rooms in 1996 and 1997, came from Presley's personal notebook. Elvis had left this behind with his landlady in Germany when he returned to the states in 1960. Elvis apparently used to rehearse in the living room of the house he rented from Frau Pieper using a piano he hired for the purpose. . . ."

While the damage to the two manuscripts sold by Christie's and Bonhams was suspicious, I assumed that the auction houses had checked these details about the provenance.

I personally knew all three dealers who were offering me the Elvis Presley manuscripts. I had sent each of them a copy of my book on forgery detection,

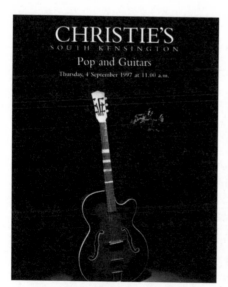

The catalog cover for Christie's sale that included the purported Elvis Presley manuscripts.

A page from the auction catalog describing the history of the manuscripts.

so they were aware of the thorough authentication examinations that uncovered many forgeries.

When I asked each of these dealers for the proof of authenticity that had convinced them, I was given two- or three-line statements with no forensic references as to why the dealers believed they were genuine. They said that dozens of experts had authenticated the manuscripts, but they didn't have any copies of authentication reports.

The source for one dealer had given him two very ornate letters of authenticity and a certificate of authenticity, complete with embossed and wax seals. These did not say one word about how they were authenticated—only that they were, and they were signed by an unknown "expert." No one questioned the authenticity. The reasonable explanation was that they were all driven by how much money they could make from them. I had agreed to pay $250,000 for the three manuscripts I personally wanted: "Love Me Tender," "Hound Dog," and "Blue Suede Shoes."

I soon realized that I was dealing with an outer ring of reputable dealers and a series of inner rings of questionable people who operated around the core of where the purported Elvis Presley manuscripts originated. Dealers I had either never heard of or was barely aware of started to flood me with emails telling me that the manuscripts were genuine, but none of these emails presented evidence of authenticity, such as comparisons with known genuine examples of Elvis's writing. Everything was anecdotal: The person had spoken with someone who once knew someone who was related to a musician who once played with Presley . . . and they were sure that the manuscripts were genuine.

The statements in these emails were that ridiculous.

Eventually, the rare-book dealer got the London autograph dealer who had sold it to him to provide information about the authentication. The London dealer also presented ornate certificates of authenticity, complete with seals (always a suspicious sign!):

I, J.M. Bakker, from JMB Records Collectibles of the Netherlands, is stating that the following Elvis Presley memorabilia, is in fact authentic. Elvis Presley's handwritten sheet with the famous song lyric of the song *Don't Be Cruel* which has been written in Germany and was used to send to Elvis' company 'Hill and Range' for the copyrights. This handwritten song lyric of the song *Don't Be Cruel* was originally obtained by Mr. Jurgen Keilwert from Mrs. Pieper, Elvis' landlord during the time Elvis was serving in the U.S. Army in Germany from 1958 until 1960. I purchased this Elvis Presley handwritten piece of memorabilia from Mr. Jurgen Keilwert, which himself purchased it from Mrs. Pieper from the place she lived, and Elvis rented in Bad Nauheim from 1958–60.

The elaborate certificate bore a signature but no address and I told the dealer I had to have the address. I thought it suspicious that there wasn't one on such an elaborate certificate, and it could be an attempt to divert attention from the person who wrote it to the elaborateness of the authentication, which in fact was simply a statement of where the manuscript came from and had nothing to do with verifying the handwriting. Also, since Presley didn't write the lyrics, he couldn't have copyrighted them.

Meanwhile, the barrage of emails and irrelevant statements and arguments from self-declared experts and directors of unknown Presley museums continued. The dealer with the most elaborate letters and certificates of authenticity pointed to the fact that a third auction house had authenticated and offered one of the manuscripts from this source. I called the auctioneer and asked how he had authenticated the manuscript. He told me that his consignor had guaranteed authenticity. Turns out, his consignor was the dealer who told me that the auctioneer had authenticated it! This was just plain fraudulent.

I pursued two lines of investigation: the provenance of the Elvis manuscripts and the handwriting. While Elvis Presley's signature is common, his handwriting is very rare. In my 62 years of experience I have seen only one or possibly two letters written by him. I contacted the archives at Presley's home and museum, Graceland, and thought a visit to Memphis would provide genuine examples to make comparisons. I was shocked that Graceland had nothing in its archives other than one manuscript, written near the end of Presley's life, about karate. (The manuscript notes written very late in his life from the Las Vegas Hilton Hotel were at a time when his handwriting was considerably altered by drugs and his physical condition, and therefore not helpful.)

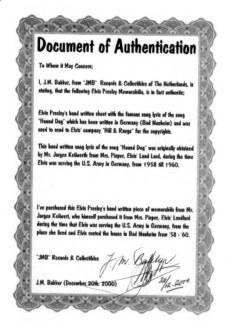

Document of Authentication

To Whom It May Concern;

I, J.M. Bakker, from "JMB" Records & Collectibles of The Netherlands, is stating, that the following Elvis Presley Memorabilia, is in fact authentic;

Elvis Presley's hand written sheet with the famous song lyric of the song "Hound Dog" which has been written in Germany (Bad Nauheim) and was used to send to Elvis' company "Hill & Range" for the copyrights.

This hand written song lyric of the song "Hound Dog" was originally obtained by Mr. Jurgen Keilwerth from Mrs. Pieper, Elvis' Land Lord, during the time Elvis was serving the U.S. Army in Germany, from 1958 till 1960.

I've purchased this Elvis Presley's hand written piece of memorabilia from Mr. Jurgen Keilwert, who himself purchased it from Mrs. Pieper, Elvis' Landlord during the time that Elvis was serving the U.S. Army in Germany, from the place she lived and Elvis rented the house in Bad Nauheim from '58 - '60.

"JMB" Records & Collectibles

J.M. Bakker (December 20th, 2000)

The forged Elvis Presley manuscript of "Hound Dog."

Genuine Presley handwriting.

There were no handwritten letters to his wife, Priscilla, nor to his manager, Tom Parker. The Graceland archivist told me that there were fewer than ten letters known to have been handwritten by Presley. With all my research I discovered only four. Presley himself commented on the rarity of his letters: "For the first time in 100 years I am writing a letter. You can see why I don't like to write. The reason being I can't write. . . ."

I ended up comparing three pages of lyrics, each from a different song, with three handwritten letters that were known to be genuine.

The first thing I noticed was the consistency of the writing in the lyrics. In the unquestioned genuine letters written by Presley, his handwriting varies considerably even within the body of the same letter. The pages of lyrics picked up on many of Presley's writing habits, but not on the apparent slowness of his writing—he practically drew each letter, like an artist (or a forger), and his formations of particular letters of the alphabet were inconsistent.

Based on handwriting analysis alone, it was clear to me the manuscript lyrics were forgeries. I could have brought an end to all this then and there, but I was so appalled by the arrogance and stupidity of the dealers that I wanted to discover who was the originator of the fake manuscripts. The torrent of emails arguing that the manuscripts were genuine galled me. So did all the letters about their authenticity—none giving one word of evidence. A common statement was that the members of Elvis's "mafia," who were with him in Germany, would authenticate the manuscripts. Two men, Red West and Rex Mansfield, were frequently put forward as having seen Elvis write these lyrics. Graceland put me in touch with them, and they told me that Elvis would never have written lyrics out.

Several European experts referenced Presley's secretary, Elisabeth Stefaniak. More than one manuscript included the direction, "Liz, get this one typed" in his purported handwriting. I found Elisabeth in Tennessee, and she told me that Presley never called her Liz—and she never saw anything like this written by him.

Finally, my disgust with the behavior of these dealers became too much, and I decided to bring this sick farce to a halt. I understood how the Hitler diaries had happened: the fault lay in the intense competition between media businesses that were run by people who knew nothing about forgeries or frauds and believed that they were hiring good experts. I also understood how the diary of Jack the Ripper had gone as far as it did, as authenticity would have been like a winning lottery ticket for the British publisher. I will never understand, however, why so many mainstream autograph dealers continued to argue and deceitfully evade obvious questions about the Elvis Presley manuscripts.

Chapter 18
Pricing the Priceless: Appraising Major Archives

I have always thought of pricing historical letters and documents as an equation in which assigning values to a series of variables is important in arriving at an accurate price. If it is a document of a common type that comes onto the market with any frequency, then you have to price it competitively with what other opportunities collectors have. The only way you could ask a higher price is if you add a value that others have not—an elaborate frame, a person who can answer questions and discuss the piece with the collector, a location where the originals can be seen in person, or some unusual research background that has been discovered. Otherwise, an Abraham Lincoln–signed military appointment in fine condition has to be priced competitively with the others that are likely to be on the market at the same time.

It is a very different situation with a letter with important content. The importance in history of the person who wrote the letter, and the importance of that person to their field of endeavor, are two basic factors. In most cases, the creator of a major idea is of more importance than the developer of that idea. The composer is almost always more important than the performer, the inventor more important than the developer. Demand and interest on the part of collectors and institutions is nearly as important. Mozart, for example, is as important as a person can be to collectors all over the world. There is no national language barrier in music. By contrast, there are many important historical figures, such as British prime ministers, with few interested collectors, and the value of their letters is not in keeping with their roles in British history.

Financial value is also affected by the importance to collectors of the individual's field of endeavor. The manuscripts of an important person in the field of science tend to be much more valuable in monetary terms than those of the most important person in the field of theater history.

The importance of the content of the letter is the variable that causes the greatest fluctuation of prices of the same person. Not everyone will agree on the degree of importance of a particular letter; different content affects different people differently. Also, the relative scarcity: a witty and amusing letter of George Bernard Shaw is common, while a similar letter of T.E. Lawrence is quite unusual. The subject matter of the letter is also important in another way. Generally, the most valuable content relates directly to what the writer is best known for. Arthur Conan Doyle is a popular figure with collectors. He wrote many interesting letters about spiritualism, the subject that most interested him in the later decades of his life. However, that is not what interests collectors who know him in the context of Sherlock Holmes.

Rarity is a major factor, but only one of many. Generally, rarity is determined by the following factors: the length of a person's life; involvement in activities that either did or did not result in the individual writing many letters and signing documents; whether the individual was well known during and after his of her lifetime, causing people to save their letters, or became well known decades after their death, by which time most of the material would have been discarded. Active collecting in earlier decades may have made their letters and documents, which were once common, rare. (Mozart is a good example.) Many institutions, and some private collectors, have collected so aggressively that they have virtually everything a particular person has written.

Evaluating collections of one person's papers, or an archive relating to one subject or person, employs many of these considerations, but there is also the very important factor of opportunity. In the decades that I evaluated archives, this was of major importance because many institutions were interested in acquiring collections and while they would not have bought a few letters, if they could acquire an important correspondence the value was worth far more than the sum of the individual pieces in the archive.

I started in the business of appraising archives for tax donation purposes because it was a good business opportunity and because the people who were doing appraisals were notoriously unreliable in getting work done on time. After listening to a number of my institutional clients complain about them over several years, I decided to get into the field in the late 1960s. One of the major benefits of working on appraisals is learning about subjects you don't initially know much about. For example, I knew nothing about science-fiction literature when I began doing appraisals of donations to Syracuse University's science-fiction collection. I educated myself, and while science fiction never became a personal interest of mine, I became sufficiently knowledgeable to judge the importance and research value of manuscripts.

Over the decades I did the appraisals of thousands of collections and archives. Most were evaluations of the fair market value for tax purposes, but in many other cases I was determining the fair amount that an institution should offer to pay for a collection or for an owner to ask. There were also a number of cases that required negotiations with different entities that had ended up in adversarial positions. Understanding the parties involved, what they really wanted, and how they had ended up in confrontational circumstances was just as important as understanding the financial value of the collections involved.

While always intense work, there were numerous pleasurable discoveries and experiences. When I worked on someone's papers I had the most intimate insights into their thinking, and usually into their feelings as well. One exception were the letters of John Foster Dulles, Dwight Eisenhower's secretary of state, to his son. They were as devoid of emotion as Dulles's public personality would indicate. In contrast, the papers of Chief Justice Fred Vinson wonderfully revealed the personalities of both Vinson and Harry Truman, who appointed him secretary of the Treasury before nominating him to the Supreme Court. In a humorous letter from Truman, typewritten on two pages of White House stationery, the president expressed "alarming concern" about his own judgment in appointing Vinson to be in charge of the country's finances. On the second page Truman continued that he based his concern on his disappointment in the tips Vinson gave him for the past weekend's horse races. The Vinson papers were also full of IOUs from Truman's poker games. It was the kind of personal view that could be fully appreciated only by seeing and holding those documents in your hands.

Many appraisals took me on adventures to fascinating worlds I otherwise would never have seen. When the Academy of Motion Picture Arts and Sciences asked me to visit the legendary director George Cukor, I found myself on a trip back into the Golden Age of Hollywood. Cukor had the kind of grand

Hollywood estate that you would imagine the director of *Gone with the Wind* would have. Servants brought food and drinks, and Cukor was extremely entertaining. He told me that he didn't want to donate his papers to the Academy. He wanted the Academy to buy his collection because, he said, he was broke. So broke, he added, that he needed to sell his dog, and how much would I offer?

As I went through his papers, he told me marvelous stories about many of the people whose annotated scripts were there. Before leaving I asked him for the name of his lawyer and permission to speak with him. I knew the Academy had no intention of buying his papers—they expected them as a gift—but there was no point in their paying me to do an appraisal if he couldn't use the tax deduction. His lawyer told me that Cukor had an immense income and could use any amount of tax deduction.

Not all appraisals worked out the way I expected them to. The New York Public Library wanted to acquire the papers of the author and film maker George Plimpton. The sense of adventure that Plimpton applied in his writing and films—and the roles he took on as a quarterback in a National Football League game, a goalie in the National Hockey League, a pitcher for the Yankees, a catcher in a circus trapeze act—fascinated me. The New York Public Library had a very small budget, but I agreed to do the appraisal and the negotiations with Plimpton because I wanted to meet the man and learn more about him.

As it turned out, this was, among all the appraisals I ever did, one of my biggest disappointments. Plimpton sat in the living room of his East 72nd Street townhouse, and no matter what I asked him, he said he didn't know. I don't think he was deliberately being difficult. He was a writer and an entertainer on a public stage, but in a private, one-on-one situation he had little to say.

When Mark Twain's private papers were given to Vassar College, I thought I might be similarly disappointed in seeing the private side of that entertaining author. I was not. In his hundreds of personal letters Samuel Clemens was just as amusing as Mark Twain was in his books and quips. Clemens's public writings as Twain seemed to be an extension of his true personality, not something that he worked on as many authors do.

Occasionally, a conflict has come up with the institution. The University of Kentucky asked me to come to Lexington each year to evaluate donated collections. One year there was a small box of manuscript material about Daniel Boone. The curator told me he didn't think it was worth much and he had shared his belief with the owner. Based on this assessment, the owner donated the manuscripts to the university and signed a donation form. I immediately recognized that the manuscripts about Boone had been written by John James

Audubon, the legendary naturalist, and could be sold on the market for about $100,000.

The curator agreed the person would not have donated them if he had known they were worth $100,000. But the manuscripts now belonged to the university, and it was too late to change that. My view was that the donation had been made on the basis of erroneous information, and the university had to explain the situation, share my appraisal, and see what the donor wanted to do. The curator was hesitant to do this, but the director of libraries agreed with me. A fair compromise was reached: the university would pay the donor $50,000. Everyone was satisfied. It was a proper outcome in a situation that I encountered more often than I thought I should have.

I found myself, throughout the decades that I did appraisals, constantly fascinated and occasionally flabbergasted. Before a reform in the Internal Revenue Service's regulations, institutions were able to appraise donations themselves, and there were many abuses. Institutions feared that if people knew the true value, they would not make the donation. This was particularly true of the Library of Congress. After the change in the IRS regulations, I regularly did the appraisals there. One day, in the Music Division, a curator brought in a book truck containing boxes of George Gershwin's manuscripts. I thought there was some mistake, as it had nothing to do with the Gershwin appraisal I was there to do. He said they had been donated a few years before and had been evaluated by the Library of Congress. He thought their value was far below the market value and the tax deduction given to the Gershwin family was only a fraction of what it should have been. I did a new appraisal and the family filed amended tax returns and received the tax deduction they were entitled to.

The negotiations to acquire the papers of Will and Ariel Durant, who synthesized much of human history and thought in their works *The Story of Civilization* and *The Story of Philosophy*, on behalf of Boston University started off much like the Plimpton appraisal had, with Will Durant saying literally nothing. In contrast, his wife and writing partner answered every question I posed dur-

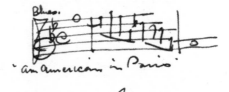

Notes by George Gershwin.

ing our first day. At the end of the day Will asked me to go for a long walk with him in the Hollywood Hills, and there he never stopped talking. I thought I was making good progress with the Durants until I explained how I arrived at my appraisal values: by making comparisons with literary and historical figures in the same field. Ariel told me that there was only one person I could compare her husband to: "Jesus Christ."

The fair market value that I arrived at was unacceptable to the Durants. I don't believe any amount would have satisfied Ariel. Tragically, when she and her husband died a few years later, within two weeks of one another, their papers were sold in batches at a yard sale. The papers were scattered among many people who simply wanted to buy souvenirs. Will Durant's extensive research files, which I thought had significant value, disappeared.

Music is a great source of personal enjoyment for me, and the archives of major composers were wonderfully exciting to work on. I saw some of my favorite music in original drafts—and got the chance to see how the composers developed their final versions. The most unexpected collection turned up with a Dutch couple who had retired to Cape Cod. After they moved from New York City they opened a trunk that had belonged to the woman's father in Holland. It was full of musical manuscripts, and she had no idea what they were. We identified the manuscripts as those of Johannes Brahms. There were dozens of compositions, worth hundreds of thousands of dollars. When I gave the couple a rough idea of how much the collection was likely to be sold for, they responded, "Really? Do you think people like us would need that kind of money?"

Johannes Brahms.

This couple wanted to donate the Brahms collection, and the likely candidate was the Morgan Library & Museum. They had attended many exhibitions there and the Morgan had a great music collection, so it was a logical fit. I met with Charles Ryskamp, the Morgan Library's director, and told him that the anonymous donors were originally from Holland. Coincidentally, he said, Queen Wilhelmina would soon be coming to dinner at the Morgan Library. He offered to invite the couple. I relayed that information, and they told me that they appreciated the offer but would not make the trip to New York, since Queen Wilhelmina would be staying with them on Cape Cod.

Jerome Kern.

Later that year, at a family Christmas gathering in Holland, the woman who had committed to making this donation told her siblings what she had found in their father's trunk. Her siblings were stunned that they were donating the manuscripts to the Morgan Library. The siblings, who did need "that kind of money," ended up blocking the couple's gift. I ended up arranging the sale of the collection in Europe.

Winning the IRS Case Against Governor Otto Kerner

In 1973 the Internal Revenue Service asked if they could hire me to appraise the archives of Otto Kerner Jr. Kerner had been a governor of Illinois, a Federal Appeals Court judge, and chairman of President Lyndon Johnson's Advisory Commission on Civil Disorders. The IRS counsel said I would need to appear in Federal Tax Court to testify if the amount of my appraisal was less than the amount claimed by Kerner's appraiser.

The prospect of appearing in Tax Court for the first time didn't concern me. All the appraisals I had done for taxpayers, which at that point totaled more than 300, had been accepted by the IRS. Unlike other appraisers, I spoke from the standpoint of a dealer. I talked about a collection as if I were going to buy it and offer it for sale. I always provided a detailed narrative to assure that anyone reading my appraisal understood my logic and reasoning. I knew it would be different in court—I would be cross-examined and challenged—but I felt confident that a reasonable judge would agree with what I came up with.

Kerner's appraiser was Ralph Newman, a dealer/appraiser I knew fairly well. Newman was much older than me and operated the Abraham Lincoln Book Shop in Chicago. I had visited him many times, seeking historical letters and documents to buy. Newman didn't have much of an inventory in my field. What he did have was an ego on a grand scale. I've always judged people like Newman as being fundamentally insecure and needing to believe in their own PR—which tends to be, for them, a fatal mistake. Visits to Newman's bookshop always took much longer than needed, as I listened to his stories about the great things he was doing with the long list of impressive people he knew intimately. Newman told the same stories year after year.

I imagined that any appraisal Newman did would be full of the boasting and bluster that were hallmarks of the façade he put up in business, and once you punctured the façade you would find out there wasn't much behind it.

I went to Springfield, Illinois, to evaluate the Kerner Archive in the State Library. I expected to find many letters from John F. Kennedy and Lyndon Johnson, particularly since LBJ had appointed Kerner to chair the National Advisory Commission on Civil Disorders after race riots killed 43 people in Detroit in 1967. But I couldn't find a single letter from either Kennedy or Johnson. When I checked the carbon copies of outgoing letters that Kerner had written to Kennedy and Johnson, I found many references thanking them for the letters they had sent to Kerner.

Given what I couldn't find, it was obvious that valuable letters had been removed from the collection.

As I researched the archive I started categorizing sections on a point scale, from one to five, ranking them in terms of historical importance and interpreting that into the potential commercial market. That analysis was fairly straightforward. The Illinois State Library had raised $25,000 to purchase a very good archive of a Civil War–era governor of Illinois. I also considered that if Illinois declined to purchase the archives, Brown University, Kerner's alma mater, would be a potential buyer. The sum I came up with was one-third the amount of Newman's appraisal.

I told the Internal Revenue Service I was prepared to proceed if Kerner did not settle. He didn't and a date was set with the Tax Court.

In several meetings in Chicago the IRS lawyers stressed that the problem with expert testimony was they typically emphasize their experience and proclaim that they just "know" what the value is. I told the IRS that as a dealer, I had to understand and frequently explain to a collector how I arrived at a value. The IRS lawyers were visibly relieved.

Entering the courtroom that winter day in Chicago, I felt like a fine-tuned athlete ready to do battle. Otto Kerner sat with his Washington, D.C., attorneys at their table to the left, and his distinguished-looking, white-haired appraiser was in the first row. The Internal Revenue Service presented its case first. Responding to the IRS lawyers' questions, I explained my appraisal report in detail. Then it was Kerner's high-priced lawyers' turn. I envisioned myself entering a fencing match.

★★★★ Chicago Tribune, Wednesday, November 13, 1974   Section 1   5

Otto Kerner, some 20 pounds lighter since October 1973, with his daughter, Helena, at the Federal Building Tuesday.

Kerner's gubernatorial papers being examined

FORMER Gov. Otto Kerner's gubernatorial papers are being combed by federal agencies for ... disputing a claim by the Internal Revenue Service that he owes $19,000 in income taxes ... the Kerner papers apparently have been researched in an attempt to find possible evi-

And that is what it turned out to be. Kerner's attorney immediately bore in on my credentials, first asking if I was an historian. I asked him to define "historian." A basic tenet of cross examination is to ask only questions that you know the answer to, and as Kerner's lawyer gingerly asked about my education, he clearly wanted to prevent me from giving him answers he didn't want. I knew his game. After we dueled about my education, he turned to the appraisal itself.

His next question was as anticipated as an opening move in a chess match: "How long did you spend examining the archive?"

This is always a trick question. If the answer doesn't seem like a long time, the lawyer's comment would be: "You mean to tell this court that you arrived at your appraisal after spending so little time on the examination?" If the timeframe seems long, the attorney's comment would be: "You mean to tell this court that someone as experienced as you had to take so long to arrive at an opinion? You must have been very unsure."

I told the court that I took the appropriate amount of time, given the volume and complexity of the material. Kerner's attorney couldn't budge me from my stance. My cross-examination ended with me feeling a great sense of satisfaction. I admired Governor Kerner and all he had done in the public good, and what I had told the court was rock solid and based on impartial and well-thought-out reasoning. As I left the witness stand and walked past the defense table, my satisfaction was ruined by Kerner's words to me. "You son of a bitch!" he muttered.

The government's case rested, and I looked forward to dueling with Kerner's appraiser during cross-examination. Ralph Newman's testimony was as pompous and arrogant as I had expected and hoped for—all the better for cross-examination. Asked about being expelled from the Antiquarian Booksellers of America, Newman brushed off the matter by claiming that there was jealousy because he was so successful and important. Newman projected an attitude that he was above it all and too important to be involved in details, no matter that they were at the heart of his evaluation of the Kerner material.

The Tax Court judge ruled that the value of Kerner's archives was exactly what I had said—one-third the amount of Newman's bloated estimate. The judge quoted from my analytical report, detailing how I had analyzed the collection and arrived at my value. The IRS subsequently adopted my analytical appraisal methods as their standard, and the Society of American Archivists published my analysis and endorsed my methods. For me, this was a tremendous validation of my dealer-based method of valuation, especially my consideration of the potential market as a major determining factor. This was the reality in a dealer's world, but it had not been applied in the appraisal field.

One year later Ralph Newman, who had boasted in the trial that he had appraised Lyndon Johnson's presidential papers and Richard Nixon's gubernatorial papers, was convicted of preparing a false affidavit to enable Nixon to secure a tax write-off for a donation of his gubernatorial papers.

Paramount Pictures' 75th-Anniversary Exhibition

One of my most interesting projects was in 1989 when Barry Diller, the president of Gulf & Western Industries, wanted to create a traveling exhibit to celebrate the 75th anniversary of its subsidiary, Paramount Pictures. The timeline was tight and the budget was small, but the project interested me. I agreed, for a flat fee, to review the movie studio's props, archives, and costumes and determine what I could create for an exhibition.

I stipulated that I had to have access to all areas of the studio and a New York City facility. I was given a letter, with Diller's name on it, stating that everything was to be open to me and everyone was to give me full cooperation.

I walked from the executive suite in the Gulf and Western building, on New York's Columbus Circle, to the Paramount warehouse, where I was met by a stone-faced staffer who would not let me in. I showed him my letter and he asked, "Who the hell is Barry Diller?" A call to Diller's office straightened out his attitude. Within the next few days I moved on to Los Angeles and the Paramount Studio lot.

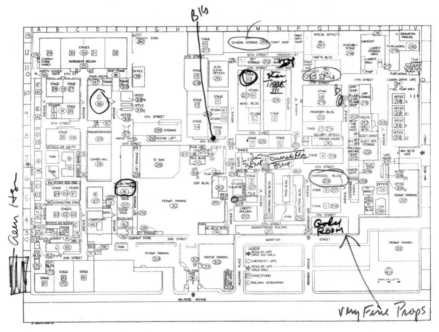

A map of the Paramount Studios lot.

Driving down Melrose Avenue and through the iconic gates onto the Paramount lot was impressive, but my first meeting at Paramount quickly brought me down to earth. The man in charge of the actual studio facility told me that his job was to get the maximum amount of money out of the facility, and that meant renting offices to producers and other people who wanted the prestige of being on the studio lot. He remodeled older buildings when he needed new offices. When he heard that I was coming to go through all the prop storage areas for the proposed exhibition, he decided to throw out all the older props. He wanted the buildings empty so he could remodel them for potential rental income. He was worried I would declare the older prop-storage areas necessary to save for my project. He had zero concern for my project, and the people he reported to, he told me, had nothing to do with Barry Diller's interest in the 75th anniversary exhibition.

The Paramount wardrobe department was barren for a different reason. Costumes were cannibalized—taken apart and the materials reused to make costumes for other movies. Paramount had saved only a few pieces, including Rudolph Valentino's costumes and Grace Kelly's gown from *To Catch a Thief*, which was rotted along the hem. In the costume department the only interesting information I learned was that many versions of a star's costume were made for various positions in which he or she would be filmed. I saw on one rack ten or twelve versions of the same suit for Sylvester Stallone, depending on whether he was standing, walking, or sitting in the shot.

The staff people on the studio lot were generally friendly and eager to help me, but they couldn't identify specific props from modern movies. Most of the props that hadn't been disposed of were generic—related to periods of history such as World War II, ancient Rome, or the 1970s—and they were used over and over again. This area was very large and not under the control of the facility manager.

I spent nearly two weeks climbing under soundstages, poring through long-neglected archives, and listening to staff lament executives' lack of interest in the studio's remarkable history. I did learn about how movies are made—including studios' notoriously detailed accounting (I had to use my project budget number to take a shower).

I finished my assignment at Paramount with a sense of frustration that it wasn't possible for me to create an exhibit. I did gain some appreciation of the magic behind how movies get made. I was particularly impressed with the lot where I parked every day. The lot was five feet lower than the road, and when needed for a Paramount movie it became the floor of a giant water tank for ocean scenes. Behind this parking lot was an enormous blank wall that, via the magic of moviemaking, became the sky and the horizon. Though it didn't work out, Paramount Pictures, in true Hollywood fashion, was entertaining.

The Greatest Landscape Designer in America: Frederick Law Olmsted

When the National Park Service called to ask me if I could appraise the fair market value of the archives of Frederick Law Olmsted, I was excited. I knew how important Olmsted was to the field of landscape architecture and was aware of some of his most famous projects, but I would need a more detailed knowledge. The National Park Service wanted to buy the archives, and because of internal budgetary deadlines, they had a limited time to make the purchase.

This was a contentious situation. The Richardson family that owned the Olmsted landscape architectural business, including all the archives of his designs, had reasonably hired Childs Gallery, one of the most prestigious in Boston, to appraise them. Childs had focused on Olmsted's designs for the campus of Stanford University, one of his most outstanding university designs, and determined what they thought either Stanford or an alumnus would pay for them. Then, according to the National Park Service, they had multiplied that dollar amount by the number of plans and designs of other universities, plus private residences, that Olmsted had designed. That calculation led the Richardson family to be told a value of nearly $3 million.

Olmsted's design for Central Park in New York City.

The National Park Service knew this methodology was flawed, since Olmsted's designs for Stanford were clearly among the most complete and therefore the most valuable. Stanford is an atypically wealthy university, and you cannot extrapolate to other schools the value to its universe of alumni.

Concerned about the faulty methodology, the National Park Service hired Goodspeed's Book Shop in Boston to appraise the archives. According to the Richardson family, a representative of Goodspeed's viewed the collection, part of which was stored in a barn, only from a distance. Apparently to avoid getting dirty, the Goodspeed's representative did not actually look at any plans and designs. Based on that superficial assessment, Goodspeed's arrived at a fair market value of $150,000.

The two flawed methodologies resulted in two widely disparate estimates: $3 million and $150,000. There were hardened positions on both sides. The Richardson family, understandably upset, would not accept less than $2.5 million for the Olmsted archives. The Park Service was just as rigid: It would not pay more than $150,000.

I immersed myself in the world of Frederick Law Olmsted. I did not know that I had been enjoying so many of his innovative landscaping creations for much of my life. Outdoor settings that I thought were natural had been created by Olmsted. The legendary landscape designer actually did move mountains. New York's Central Park, a paradise in the middle of a booming city, was designed by Olmsted. Prospect Park in New York was also his creation. In Boston he designed the famed Emerald Necklace around the city, as well as Franklin Park.

As I researched Olmsted's papers, I could hardly believe the scope of his work. In designing the area around Biltmore in North Carolina for George Vanderbilt, Olmsted planted thousands of full-size trees and tens of thousands of bushes, creating a complete environment that extended as far as you could see from the Vanderbilt house. Olmsted made the entire landscape look as if it had always been there. His landscaping was the epitome of what the Gilded Age could do with money.

For two weeks my research team and I went through all of Olmsted's layouts and designs—approximately 100,000—and categorized them by type of project. While most were for private residences, it seemed that all the major public parks in the Northeast were also designed by him. When I presented my appraisal (Childs and Goodspeed's declined to attend, both saying they were "out of their league") and detailed how I arrived at my number, which was $525,000, the Richardson family was very upset. My valuation was $2 million less than what they were counting on. The Park Service was equally upset, which was difficult to understand. The National Park Service's mandate was to determine the fair market value, and they had hired me specifically to arrive at a realistic amount. As long as my number was a fair assessment of value—and I felt confident that it was—the National Parks Service had done its job of spending public money carefully.

It took hours of angst-ridden discussion to get the parties to accept my valuation. Finally, around midnight, we all agreed that nobody was happy with my evaluation—and no one could find fault with how I arrived at it. The Richardson family agreed to sell the archive for $525,000, my appraised value, and the National Park Service reluctantly agreed to pay that price.

Winston Churchill wrote that you never look at a tree again in the same way if you try to paint it. You see the different reflections of light off the leaves, the different textures, and many different shades of color. I felt that same way after working on the Olmsted collection. Central Park is my favorite area in New York City, and on the way to meetings in the city I frequently take long walks through Olmsted's spectacular wonderland. Knowing that all the hills and waterways were created by Olmsted has given me an even greater appreciation of his genius and the extraordinary impact he continues to have on people's lives.

The Settlement of Northwest America: 12 Million Uncataloged Documents

I wasn't surprised when the Internal Revenue Service challenged the Burlington Northern Railroad's tax deduction for the donation of its archives of the Northern Pacific Railroad, the first transcontinental railroad across the northern part of the country. The IRS based its challenge on the Kerner decision. When the tax lawyer from Burlington Northern called, he told me it was already scheduled for Tax Court, and they wanted a proposal from me to do a new appraisal. The archive was in a warehouse in St. Paul, Minnesota.

My interest in doing this appraisal went well beyond business. When I was a kid, growing up in an overcrowded house in a stifling neighborhood, there were railroad tracks about 100 yards behind our house. Every steam-engine locomotive that went by represented traveling out of the neighborhood. The trains symbolized another world somewhere out there—the dream of a different place. Lying in bed at night, I would hear the locomotive's whistle beckoning me to come, to discover a bigger world. Trains represented mobility and adventure—the adventure of new places, new opportunities.

Of more interest to me as an adult was the settling of the country. The Northern Pacific Railroad brought immigrants to settle on the land and create farms. The railroad was also the means to ship their produce to market. The Northern Pacific Railroad had offices all over Europe, especially throughout Germany, recruiting immigrant families. The opportunity to work in the archives of the settlement of the northern plains was very exciting to me.

My grandparents immigrated to the United States from Eastern Canada to better their lives, and I have always felt a connection with people who are willing to emigrate for a new life.

The IRS valuation was ridiculously low, and from a business standpoint the idea of winning a second Tax Court decision, this time for the taxpayer, was very appealing.

The challenge for me was how I could mentally organize, comprehend, and analyze 12 million uncataloged, and possibly unorganized, pieces and meet the Tax Court schedule. I spent more than two weeks walking in the woods, focusing on how I could organize this enormous project.

The lead tax lawyer for Burlington Northern came to Boston to meet with me about the case and how I would approach it. To Burlington Northern, it was purely business. They wanted to win because it was their duty to their shareholders to get the maximum tax benefit.

I knew the archives were in St. Paul, Minnesota, and we would be working on this in the winter. Having grown up in Boston, it never occurred to me that winters in St. Paul could be so much worse. It was a shock when I tried to go running my first morning there and thought my lungs would freeze in a matter of minutes. There were electric outlets at every parking space because if you didn't plug in the electric heater in your car engine, you would never get it started again. Buildings had heated walkways between them.

Preferred stock from the Northern Pacific Railroad.

Pat Bozeman, my principal assistant, and myself in the
Northern Pacific archives in Minnesota.

The Northern Pacific archives went on and on.

An advertisement for a tour on the Northern Pacific line.

The archive was in a warehouse but, having done hundreds of appraisals in warehouses, it never occurred to me that the storage area would have neither electricity nor lights. One person on my appraisal team was a Jane-of-all-trades, and it was her responsibility to deal with logistical issues. She quickly had lighting installed and moved on to the logistical problem of how the archives were stored. The shelving units were 14 feet high and archival boxes were on pallets. We rented forklifts to bring pallets down so that we could determine what was in the boxes. It quickly became apparent that this was going to take far too long, so we rented a number of hydraulic platforms so that instead of bringing the boxes down, we went up to where they were and worked at that level.

There were thousands of letters from all the important financiers. I needed to have a good idea of just how important they were, so I established criteria for judging the letters and had my staff read through them and score the quality of the contents from 1 through 5. Some of my catalogers, I'm sure, were frustrated at not being able to completely read long letters, judging just by the first few lines if they were important. Yet it was necessary to have the discipline of these criteria because we so easily could have drowned in 12 million pieces and not finished the appraisal in time.

I didn't have to go to Tax Court to win the case. The Internal Revenue Service agreed with my appraisal and the trial was canceled.

The Crime of the Century: Sacco-Vanzetti Defense Papers Unsealed After 75 Years

I never imagined that the Boston Public Library would be where I would appraise one of the twentieth century's most notorious collections. The library was the repository of the extensive archives of the Sacco-Vanzetti Defense Committee after the execution of the two men in 1927. The papers had been sealed for 50 years, and I was asked to appraise their fair market value for the son of the founder of the defense committee, who wanted a tax deduction.

My knowledge of Sacco and Vanzetti was superficial, so I read most of the books about the two men and their trials. In 1920 Nicola Sacco and Bartolomeo Vanzetti, Italian immigrants and anarchists, were charged with the murders of two people in a robbery. This was considered the crime and trial of the century, with worldwide public sentiment that the two men were being persecuted for their political views and their Italian immigrant status. In the archives were thousands and thousands of letters to the defense committee from workers' union groups, making relatively small contributions to pay for their defense.

The total came to over $300,000, a staggering amount of money for a legal defense in 1920. Their legal defense, despite these funds, was inept at best. Quickly, and on thin evidence, Sacco and Vanzetti were found guilty. In 1927, after all their appeals were denied, they were executed in the electric chair at Charlestown State Prison.

Vanzetti and Sacco.

In the archives I read dozens of manuscripts and letters written by Vanzetti, who came across as likable, philosophical, and not the type of man to kill people in a robbery. In "The Plutocratic Press and the Sacco Vanzetti Case," Vanzetti wrote about "the hatred, the prejudices . . . the sadistic hostility of the press" toward their case, adding, "Nothing can show, better than such a degradation, the immorality of our times and of our society of civil and religious . . . cannibals."

Sacco, in contrast to Vanzetti, wrote infrequently, and in the materials that I read, he came across as cold, emotionless, and accepting of his fate.

After the two men's execution, no one knew what happened to Sacco's body. Reviewing the archives, I solved the mystery. Among many boxes of letters and documents I found an unmarked and sealed tin can with, I could tell, something inside it. I found documents in the archive that Sacco had been cremated and realized that what was inside the tin can was Sacco.

I told the director of the library, and he quietly transferred Sacco's remains to the Italian Consul in Boston, who then sent them to Sacco's family in Italy.

While I was working on the Sacco-Vanzetti papers, I boarded a shuttle flight to New York and sat down next to someone I knew: John Coolidge, a prominent Bostonian whom I had dueled with on the Frederick Law Olmsted papers. Coolidge, who was a descendent of Thomas Jefferson, asked me what I was working on, and I said I was doing an appraisal of Sacco and Vanzetti's papers. Coolidge told me an amazing story. At the time of the famous trial, Coolidge was a young man living with his family next to William Thompson, the prominent establishment lawyer who handled Sacco and Vanzetti's appeal with the enormous amount of money donated. When Coolidge's father asked Thompson why he was representing the two convicted killers, Thompson replied: "To make sure these Reds don't get off."

After innumerable hours working in their archives, I agreed with the historians who speculated that Sacco was guilty and Vanzetti was not, though Vanzetti likely knew who the other murderer was.

Three Unfortunate Appraisals of the "Papers" of Martin Luther King Jr.

In 1987 Coretta Scott King filed suit against Boston University for the "return" of her deceased husband's papers. The school's president, John Silber, called and asked for my help. I believed the lawsuit was without merit. Boston University—where Martin Luther King Jr. had earned his doctorate in theology and where I had, two decades earlier, spent countless evenings in basement classrooms attending night school—had put great effort into acquiring the papers of Black leaders and activists. Howard Gotlieb, Boston University's head of Special Collections, was ahead of his time in appreciating the importance of America's civil rights movement.

While King's widow claimed that her husband's intention had been to deposit his papers temporarily with Boston University, this was undercut by legal documents and a video of King announcing the gift to the school.

Forced to shift strategies, Coretta Scott King's lawyers argued that Boston University had failed to honor its responsibility in cataloging and properly preserving the collection.

That brought me into the case as an expert to determine whether Boston University had cataloged and preserved the collection following accepted archival standards. The appraisal gave me the great experience of going through King's papers and reading the sermons that he delivered at various churches in Boston. I was reading and experiencing greatness as it was developing. The ideas being formulated by one of the most important social leaders of the century were in my hands. In my mind I imagined his voice speaking the words. It was one of my most incredible appraisal experiences.

Martin Luther King Jr.

Shirley and me with Howard Gotlieb.

I was afraid that the trial would be one of my worst experiences—the media had created a firestorm of false claims, and many people thought the papers should be given back to Coretta Scott King. The jury, however, considered the evidence and decided that King had deliberately and legally given the papers to Boston University. The jurors also found that the university was properly caring for King's papers and voted 10-2 that Boston University was the owner.

Some years later I was offered what was described as "Martin Luther King's Papers" by Sotheby's. The price was $30 million, and the auction house wanted me to ask one of my clients, specifically Bill Gates, if he would buy them and donate them to the King Center in Atlanta. When I went through the inventory, I decided that a realistic price would be $1.5 million. The value was in a few manuscripts of sermons that King had given. Another part of this collection was "the Martin Luther King Library," which consisted of many books inscribed to him. These books were unsolicited gifts to King—of little, if any, value.

Appalled by their proposed $30 million price, I asked who at Sotheby's had arrived at that value because I wanted to hear their reasoning. King's son Dexter, I was told, wanted $30 million and it wasn't Sotheby's opinion, though it certainly was represented as such.

I later learned there was lobbying by the Congressional Black Caucus to get the federal government to pay the $30 million to King's son and give the papers to the King Center. I was asked to testify as to my opinion of the value, but my lawyers advised me that I could be asked any questions the committee wanted to ask, and that the questions very specifically could involve sales of major pieces in high-profile collections that I had sold. This was private information that could only be released by my clients, so I had to decline testifying. Congress voted to buy the papers for $30 million: $20 million in cash and a $10 million tax deduction for Dexter King. Litigation between Dexter and his siblings over who owned the papers followed.

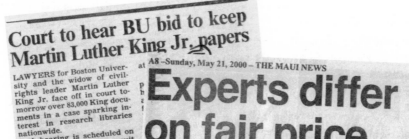

Court to hear BU bid to keep Martin Luther King Jr. papers

LAWYERS for Boston University and the widow of civil-rights leader Martin Luther King Jr. face off in court to-morrow over 83,000 King documents in a case sparking interest in research libraries nationwide.

A hearing is scheduled on BU's motion to dismiss a suit by the King estate, which seeks to reclaim the documents stored at BU and transfer them to the Martin Luther King Jr. Center for Non-violent Change in Atlanta.

Archivists are paying close

at A8 –Sunday, May 21, 2000 – THE MAUI NEWS

Experts differ on fair price for King papers

By JEFFREY McMURRAY
The Associated Press

WASHINGTON — Two experts advising Congress on whether to pay $20 million for Martin Luther King's post-1960 papers have reached conflicting conclusions, further clouding the issue for lawmakers.

An appraiser of historical docu-

documents at the King Center — almost randomly. But King's relatives have refused to make the SCLC papers part of any sale.

"It makes perfect sense for the Kings to want to get out of the historical archives business, but the King papers are not worth $20 million," Garrow said.

Included among the papers are that King's widow Coretta home.

By 2010, when I became involved with Martin Luther King's "papers" for the third time, I had retired from the appraisal field. I could no longer devote sufficient time to it. For decades I had been the IRS's expert on historical documents and archives, and I had agreed to continue to be an advisor. The IRS called to ask if I would review the estate appraisal of Coretta Scott King.

The Atlanta office was sure that the archive in Mrs. King's estate, appraised at $3 million, was vastly undervalued because of the $30 million value Dexter received. They had already set a date to challenge that amount in Tax Court. When I received the inventory, I was impressed with the cataloger's detail and read every line of the lengthy inventory. I thought the papers were worth $100,000 to $200,000. My estimate surprised the IRS, who cited the $30 million that Congress had agreed to. I explained that the pieces in Coretta Scott King's estate—Christmas cards addressed to Martin Luther King, fan mail, and books that had been sent to him, unsolicited—were of minimal interest and no research value.

I don't recall Mrs. King's estate containing anything actually written or signed by her late husband. The IRS dropped its challenge to her estate tax filing.

Jackie Kennedy and the Death of a President: Appraising a Box of Unknown Contents

On December 15, 1966, it was announced that Jackie Kennedy would seek an injunction to block publication of *The Death of a President*, William Manchester's authorized book about the assassination of John F. Kennedy. Mrs. Kennedy and Robert Kennedy had chosen Manchester to write the only book they would cooperate with. Manchester had met Jack Kennedy when they were both recovering from serious injuries in the Pacific during World War II and had written *Portrait of a President: John F. Kennedy in Profile* about JFK's first year in the White House. Manchester recorded 220 minutes of audio tape during four interviews with Mrs. Kennedy. He also interviewed Robert Kennedy for 93 minutes.

At this time I didn't know any of the parties involved, but my personal sympathies leaned toward Mrs. Kennedy. She pleaded that she had revealed too many personal details during the interviews with Manchester, and she wanted these details removed from the book.

News accounts indicated that it was Robert Kennedy who wanted his derogatory statements about Lyndon Johnson removed, presumably because they could hurt his plans to run for president in 1968. The Kennedys and Manchester reached a settlement requiring Manchester to remove certain text and turn over his original tapes of his interviews, along with typewritten transcripts, to the National Archives and eventually to the John F. Kennedy Presidential Library. All of this material would be sealed until 2067. No one other than the parties to the agreement would know what was in this material.

The Death of a President, published the following year, was spectacularly successful. The book sold more than 1 million copies, earned the John F. Kennedy Presidential Library more than $1 million, and garnered over $1 million in serialization rights and $300,000 in foreign sales.

Seven years later, in 1974, the IRS asked me to appraise the audiotapes and transcripts that now belonged to the Kennedy Presidential Library and were

sealed until 2067. I didn't know how I could appraise something that I could neither see nor listen to—nor even know what information the tapes and transcripts contained. I asked the IRS several times how they thought I could do such an appraisal? I was told to use my "best guess." I told them that I do not guess, and they would have to find someone else for the job.

The IRS did not find someone else, and I agreed to write an analysis of this challenging situation. I judged the value of the unknown recordings and transcripts to be $50,000. I told the IRS that I would not be willing to go to court unless the taxpayer, William Manchester, claimed more than three or four times that amount. My report discussed the potential research value and compared it to a sealed box concerning the wife of President James Garfield, who was assassinated in 1880, being opened today, and how much interest there would be in what it contained. Even if the contents of that theoretical box revealed that Garfield's widow had been behind his assassination, at most it would be a one-day news story. I thought the comparison was relevant. Kennedy's impact on America was based on his youth, the sense of change, his vibrancy, and the hope that his new ideas brought to the White House. He died before he could carry out many of these ideas, and I thought his reputation would fade when the people who experienced him as president were no longer living. Garfield was elected with a lot of promise, and he too was assassinated before being able to create a legacy of accomplishments. My report concluded that the only value in 1967 was the publicity and notoriety that an institution would receive by becoming the repository. I never heard anything further from the IRS, so I assume that whatever Manchester claimed as a tax deduction was not far off from my valuation.

Two years later, in 1976, at an antiquarian book fair, I was startled to see for sale the original galley proofs of *The Death of a President*. The proofs contained the sections of text that had been removed according to the legal settlement. I purchased the proofs for $1,200. I bought them because I didn't want to see sensationalized whatever it was that had caused Jackie Kennedy so much stress. I also personally didn't want to know what that text was. I have never read through those galley proofs.

Later Mrs. Kennedy and her children, Caroline and John, became regular clients at our Madison Avenue gallery. Dick Goodwin, Mrs. Kennedy's close advisor who acted as her personal lawyer in the Manchester case, became a dear friend of ours. Bill Manchester and I eventually became friendly over his book *Goodbye Darkness*, in which he described the lingering nightmares of his service in the Marines in the Pacific in World War II. *Goodbye Darkness* is one of the most insightful accounts of the struggle to survive the horrors of the war.

The Ultimate World War II Appraisal: General George S. Patton

Over the years I wrote a number of letters to George Patton's son explaining why I would like to see his father's collection, but I never received a response.

Then, one day in 1994, the intercom in my office announced, "General Patton is on the phone for you." When I answered, a gruff voice simply stated, "Johnny Eisenhower tells me you are the guy to straighten out my old man's affairs. Be here at 0800." I didn't hesitate in saying "No, general, I can't." I knew that if I took orders from him, I would never be able to establish a professional relationship, assuming there could be one.

When I arrived at his house two days later, I was shown into the "war room." Patton, who I took to referring to as George IV (his father was III), was a dynamic, fit, and brusque 71 years old. He handed me a yellow legal pad and told me to start with the swords. I handed it back to him and said we had a lot to discuss before we could agree to work together. He had no idea what I would charge, I had no idea what was involved, and so far we had only established that he was used to giving orders and viewed me as a subordinate.

The collection was immense. Patton, the World War II general, was in the 1912 Olympics for fencing, and not only were his dueling swords in a closet, but so were the many versions of his redesign of U.S. Army swords. He had saved his command flags; numerous Third Reich souvenirs that had been presented to him; Japanese swords he had purchased while stationed in Hawai'i; World War I German artifacts that he had brought home; his helmets; his childhood bow-and-arrow set; his walking stick, which was made from the first tree knocked down by an American tank in France; many personal artifacts; Civil War saddles, guns, and artifacts from his ancestors and his own McClellan saddle from 1910. He had owned a large number of pistols—dozens—and, most amazingly to me, the souvenirs he kept from the Mexican bandits he personally killed while stationed on the border before World War I. It was an amazing—and overwhelming—collection, far greater than anything I had anticipated.

His son wanted to give the artifacts to the Patton Museum at Fort Knox, Kentucky, and his father's library to West Point. The movie *Patton* had come out in 1970 and created a tremendous interest among collectors in anything he had signed or owned. Some of Patton's artifacts, books, and personal letters had left the family and been sold in recent years, establishing values. Besides his namesake son, Patton had two daughters, and when they died, personal and military artifacts and books filtered onto the market. There was also a trove of letters that came onto the market from Patton's grandson, Robert.

Lieutenant General George S. Patton confers with General Omar Bradley (center), his superior, and General Bernard Montgomery in France, July 1944.

The variety and quantity that was going to be given to the Patton Museum required extensive research into the value added when artifacts are owned by notable people. For example, the German Luger pistol which Eisenhower's chief of staff owned was sold for $14,000. The pistol and two Medals of Honor that belonged to the brother of George Custer were sold for $250,000; Clark Gable's pistol sold for $29,000, while a sword presented to him realized $39,500 and a rifle $12,500; J. Edgar Hoover's pistol presented to him sold for $75,000; Annie Oakley's rifle realized $185,000; and one of the uniforms worn by George C. Scott in the movie *Patton* sold for $9,350. The pistol Jack Ruby used to shoot Lee Harvey Oswald sold for $220,000.

As part of the appraisal process, I went to Fort Knox to negotiate the gift his son intended to make and walked into a firestorm of hostility and lack of cooperation. I invited the Patton Museum director to dinner and tried to impress on him that I was there to smoothly arrange the transfer of everything from Massachusetts. During dinner I listened to a tirade against George IV, who had been stationed at Fort Knox. It seemed that Patton visited the museum every day and complained about everything.

As part of my normal due diligence, I wanted to review the deeds of gift from the World War II general for what the museum already had. They couldn't provide them. Evidently, the museum had never legally been given the artifacts, and that included the most iconic ones of all: the ivory-handled pistols he famously wore. I also discovered that Patton had deposited, but not given, a large collection of American, German, and Italian machine guns. These would be worth a significant amount of money as guns alone, even without any Patton connection.

The most challenging evaluation were the Patton pistols. There were several dozen that belonged to him, including semi-automatics that he routinely carried in his waistband. But the most famous ones were the pair with ivory handles. One was a .45 caliber Colt single-action revolver, the other a .357 Magnum revolver. Patton had a custom-made, black leather holster belt and

Major General Hugh Gaffey and Lieutenant General Patton in Normandy, 1944.

throughout the war was pictured wearing his two ivory-handled pistols. I spent months considering what they could be sold for and finally arrived at a value I felt was fair.

The Internal Revenue Service agreed, and all of the appraisals I did of the George Patton artifacts and library were accepted without question.

Despite George IV's military demeanor and exterior, we developed an affectionate relationship until he died at 80 from complications from Parkinson's disease. He was born on Christmas Eve, and every other year his wife Joanne had a birthday party. I will always remember the crusty major general playing on the floor in front of his fireplace with our daughter when she was very young. He was someone who had to live up to his family heritage, to his name and the image of who he was expected to be. But behind that mantle he was a warm person. His wife Joanne, the daughter of a general, has ever since been a close friend of our family. In what she described as the ultimate irony, she brought her son Ben to a dinner at our museum, and he talked about helping veterans with PTSD through film. Her father-in-law, the World War II general, had epitomized the attitude and belief that "shell shock" was a character defect, and he was severely disciplined by Eisenhower for slapping a soldier in a hospital. Now his grandson was developing ways to treat what the general had viewed as weakness. Society, and the Patton family, had come a long way.

Chapter 19

The 2000s

Most people remember where they were December 31, 1999, the eve of the new millennium. I recall that night with great joy. My six-year-old daughter and I danced in the new millennium to music played by Microsoft co-founder Paul Allen and friends on the Big Island of Hawai'i.

As a family, we were still tortured by the loss of our son Jason. The depression and mourning were almost overwhelming. Black clouds hung over every day, and only very slowly were there any intervals of gray. An occasional blue clearing would quickly appear, only to disappear, yet as the months went by these clearings became more frequent and lasted longer. The only antidote to the gray was focusing on the good things in life and trying to maintain a sense of normalcy.

Our business was changing significantly. The rapid pace of building major collections had resulted in a depletion of important historical letters and manuscripts available for sale by private collectors. In many ways this was almost a relief to me. Business had been like a rocket flying through the 1990s, as we acquired tens of millions of dollars of historically important documents to create several major collections.

Our New York gallery continued to do well financially and to reward us personally. Part of the success was because we provided more than just rare and expensive documents. A factor in the success of our galleries was an observation that had occurred to me years before. I was listening to a group of dealers bemoaning the lack of "good material." This "good material" was defined as being signed by major figures, with interesting content, and bought at below-market prices. They were all reciting the worn-out refrain that the key element in the business was buying, but I thought there was another element. There was a lot of good material in the dealers' inventories that could have a broad appeal, but they were all focusing on rarity alone. Over decades, when I had opportunities, I bought large groups of documents: 200 documents signed by Queen Victoria, a group of 100 presidential documents signed by Ulysses S. Grant, more than 100 documents of King George III, and several hundred checks signed by Thomas Edison. Other caches included hundreds of original wanted posters for John Dillinger and Bonnie and Clyde and stock certificates signed by Cornelius Vanderbilt. Someone interested in Victorian England was thrilled to acquire an attractively framed and well-presented official document signed by Queen Victoria at a reasonable price. The same was true for someone who read about the Civil War—a Ulysses S. Grant signed document, framed with a portrait, for less than $500 was a great acquisition. Our attitude about having many pieces was not that they were too common but that we could offer them at reasonable prices. Focusing on what we could find, and not lamenting what we couldn't, was important to success.

I finally felt I had time to accept invitations from friends and organizations that interested me. One group was as far from my base as possible. In February 2000 I was staying with my friends Scott Cook and Signe Ostby, the founders of Intuit, in Woodside, California, when they hosted a dinner of Silicon Valley CEOs. I was included.

As a result, I was regularly invited to these CEO dinners in Silicon Valley. They were wonderful experiences in a world about which I knew

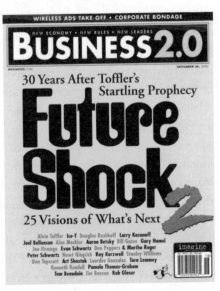

I thought the invitation to join the illustrious tech leaders was a mistake.

nothing except the end products. I found most interesting the discussions of what the general public's reaction to ideas would be. I received an email in mid-2000 from the magazine *Business 2.0* asking me to write an essay for the cover story, "Future Shock 2: 25 Visions of What's Next." I called the editor to explain that while I was a member of the CEO group, the invitation had been sent to me in error because I knew nothing about technology. He said it was not an error: he knew who I was, and he wanted me to write from my point of view. My name appeared on the cover, along with Bill Gates and 23 other leaders of the revolution in technology. It was an amazing tangent from my real world.

The new millennium also gave me more time to pursue my interest in collecting artifacts from World War II. Born in 1943, I had grown up very much affected by World War II. It was the greatest human drama of modern times, yet few people were collecting artifacts from the war. World War II had been horrible and terrifying, and people wanted to forget it. By the 1990s a half century had passed and there were still no museums devoted to World War II, except for national museums in Europe that focused on how their country won the war.

I had built a warm friendship with the renowned historian Steve Ambrose, who had turned his focus to World War II. Steve was teaching at the University of New Orleans and had the dream of creating a museum that would focus on D-Day and honor the designer of the boat that made possible the landings at Normandy.

I joined Steve as a founding trustee. The announcement of the plans for the D-Day Museum was set to take place at a spectacular dinner in New Orleans. At Steve's request I sent 25 mannequins in World War II uniforms to line the entrance to the ballroom and provided exhibition cases with iconic artifacts. That evening at the gala, a person who reacted with fascination to the spy artifacts was Bill Colby. He had been in the OSS, the World War II precursor to the CIA, and had parachuted into both France and Norway on sabotage missions. Colby, who later headed the CIA, told me he had not previously seen many of the espionage, sabotage, and assassination artifacts I displayed. During the war, agents were issued only what they needed for their particular missions.

When Colby asked me to be the speaker at the 50th reunion of the OSS, I was dumbfounded. How could I speak to these people who had courageously fought behind enemy lines to save the world? I told Colby that I felt like a groupie being asked to speak to a crowd of rock stars. He said they wanted me because I was keeping alive what they did. Colby asked me to bring some OSS sabotage and espionage artifacts and weapons.

I put a lot of thought into my talk. I decided to bring two sets of papers: one was what the OSS fought to discover and steal, and the other what the OSS fought to protect. The operational plans for the German V-1 rocket and the top-secret D-Day invasion plans, which included a section describing the OSS's missions, were my focus. In the following years Colby and I regularly had interesting lunches at the Cosmos Club in Washington.

June 15, 2000

Mr. Kenneth W. Rendell
Kenneth W. Rendell, Inc.
46 Eliot Street
South Natick, MA 01760

Dear Ken:

The number of people I have to thank is almost overwhelming, but I must start with you. And although I make my living with words, in your case they just fail me. Still I do want you to know that I am fully aware that we could not have done it without you. Your help, support, hard work, enthusiasm, judgment, contributions, and most of all your presence, were critical to the success of The National D-Day Museum's creation and grand opening.

George McGovern told me, after returning home, that he had just been through the best four days of his life. Each of the Medal of Honor recipients said the same to me as well. So did all the World War II veterans who were present, and already I'm hearing from those who couldn't make it but watched the proceedings on television.

I was so proud of everyone, from the Department of Defense team and the originators and creators of the event, through the veterans, the people who made the Museum, and most of all the people of New Orleans, who participated in making the whole event so marvelously grand. That was the best military parade I've ever seen. And the best was seeing, on the streets, the people of New Orleans, none of them drinking or being rowdy or calling out "Throw me something mister," but instead holding up signs that said "Thank you" to all the veterans.

There is more, much more, to be said, but first of all this: We could not have done it without you.

Sincerely,

Stephen F. Ambrose

A letter of appreciation for my assistance in
bringing the National D-Day Museum to life.

The famed Iwo Jima picture signed by three of the men who raised the flag.

The Marines landing on Iwo Jima for our visit. The only way onto the island was by an official Marine Corps visit.

Part of the Marine Corps Armada arriving on Iwo Jima.

Another remarkable OSS agent I came to know was Geoff Jones, who parachuted into France to organize resistance attacks and gain intelligence prior to D-Day. After Colby died in an apparent canoeing accident in 1996, Jones formed Veterans of OSS and included me in the group's reunions. Geoff and I met monthly for lunch at 21 in New York City. He always brushed off his war missions. His modest attitude was typical of the World War II veterans I came to know. The heroes were in the cemeteries, they said, noting that they got lucky and just did what they had to do.

At the top of Mt. Suribachi with Jack Lucas, the youngest recipient of the Medal of Honor.

In my business I was dealing with a different war. I was offered the most important letter Abraham Lincoln wrote about the Civil War. In a ten-page letter dated October 5, 1863, Lincoln presented his analysis of the country's situation. He was writing to the chairman of a group of 30 delegates from Missouri and Kansas.

We are in the Civil War. . . .
There always is a main question:
but in this case, that question is a
perplexing compound–Union and
Slavery. . . . It is easy to conceive
that all of the shades of opinion
. . . may be sincerely entertained
by honest and truthful men. . . .
Each will prefer a different way
of sustaining the Union. . . . Deception breeds and thrives. Confidence dies, and universal suspicion
reigns. Each man feels an impulse
to kill his neighbor, lest he be
killed by him. Revenge and retali-
ation follow. . . .

Abraham Lincoln.

President Lincoln writes about the Union fighting the Civil War.

Lincoln then discusses the problems in Missouri and Kansas:

A controversy rapidly grew into almost unmanageable proportions. One side ignored the necessity and magnified the evils of the system; while the other ignore the evils and magnify the necessity; and each bitterly assailed the motives of the other. . . . I exhausted my wits and very nearly my patience also, in efforts to convince both that the evils they charged on each other, were inherent in the case, and could not be cured by giving either party a victory over the other. . . .

Lincoln explained military decisions he has made concerning the problems between Kansas and Missouri and continued:

I do not feel justified to enter upon the broad field in regard to the political differences between radicals and conservatives. . . . The public knows it all. It obliges nobody to follow me and I trust obliges me to follow nobody. The radicals and conservatives each agree with me in some things, and disagree in others. . . . I do not question their right. I too, shall do what seems to be my duty. I hold whoever commands in Missouri or elsewhere responsible to me, and not to either radicals or conservatives. It is my duty to hear all; but at least, I must within my sphere, judge what to do and what to forbear.

The collector who owned it, whom I had known for decades, wanted a price that was eight times what Christie's auctions told him it was worth. I thought it was worth every penny of what he wanted. I unhesitatingly bought it, and immediately sold it to one of my major clients.

Shortly afterward I was offered another extraordinarily important Lincoln letter, written entirely in his own hand from Springfield in July 1859. This one was about his old adversary, Stephen A. Douglas:

Douglas (who is the most dangerous enemy of liberty, because the most insidious one) would have little support in the North, and by consequence, no capital to trade on in the South, if it were not for our friends magnifying him and his humbug. . . . Douglas' popular sovereignty, accepted by the public mind, as a just principal, nationalizes slavery, and revives the African slave trade inevitably. Taking slaves into new territories, and buying slaves in Africa, are identical things – identical rights or identical wrongs – and the argument which establishes one will establish the other.

Lincoln wrote about several possible candidates for president, concluding, "I must say I do not think myself fit for the presidency."

A letter written by Abraham Lincoln to General George McClellan in 1862.

Another aspect of the Civil War came to me at the request of Warner Books. Harvard professor Henry Louis Gates Jr. had bought at auction, for a very reasonable price, the diary of a fugitive slave woman. Gates believed that the manuscript had been written around 1875. Warner Books, his publisher, wanted me to forensically confirm this. The forensic evidence indicated to me that the manuscript was older than 1875. It was probably written just before the Civil War, which made the diary much more important—one of few accounts by a fugitive slave woman before the Civil War.

Our evolution into finding more time for a wider range of events and experiences took many turns. The founding of the J.P. Morgan Library in New York was celebrated at a dinner in his dining room. While Shirley was regaled by the conversation of Morgan's grandson, seated next to her, I was not as amused being seated next to a national television personality who was irrationally impressed with himself. Shirley and I both, however, appreciated the irony that we were having dinner in the dining room of the richest person in America at the turn of the twentieth century and later that same week we would be having dinner at the home of Bill and Melinda Gates, the richest people in America at the turn of the twenty-first century.

The New York Times

On Long-Lost Pages, a Female Slave's Voice

By DAVID D. KIRKPATRICK

In the spring of 1857, one of John Hill Wheeler's slaves slipped away from his North Carolina plantation and made her way north to New Jersey. There she promptly picked up a quill pen and began to write a novel, combining the story of her own life with elements of the many sentimental sagas she had evidently borrowed from Mr. Wheeler's shelf.

This is the origin of a 300-page manuscript called "The Bondswoman's Narrative," according to its new owner, Henry Louis Gates Jr., the chairman of the African-American studies department at Harvard University. He says that the manuscript, unpublished and unnoticed for more than 140 years, is the earliest known novel by a female African-American slave and probably the earliest known novel by a black woman anywhere. If so, it is one of only a handful of novels by African-American slaves.

Professor Gates was the only bidder for the manuscript at an auction at the Swann Galleries in New York this year, and he acquired it for less than $10,000. Two well-known experts on detecting literary forgeries, Kenneth Rendell and Joe Nickell, have verified its authenticity after an extensive investigation, assessing its

"The Bondswoman's Narrative" was recently authenticated.

Jared Leeds for The New York Times

contemporary historical references and the age of its ink and paper.

The novel, signed by Hannah Crafts, is a woman's melodramatic account of her life as a house slave to a number of owners and then as a teacher in the North.

In one episode, the narrator accidentally gives her owner's wife a cosmetic powder that somehow turns her face black. The humiliated wife later punishes the narrator for gossiping about the incident by trying to force her to marry a field hand whom she scorns as beneath her. Horrified at the prospect, she flees to New Jersey by taking advantage of her light skin and disguising herself as a white boy.

Replete with the heavy-handed moralizing and preposterous coincidences characteristic of the popular women's fiction of the time, the unedited novel is unlikely to attain the status of a literary masterpiece. But its existence suggests that

Continued on Page A20

The *New York Times'* coverage of the discovery of one of the few known manuscripts written by an enslaved woman before the Civil War.

The pace of my life, though changing, was continuing at high speed. My business partner, Shirley, was working more than full time publishing monthly catalogs, combining the new material that I was able to find and what we had in the gallery. Her decades of experience in investigating, organizing, writing, and producing news, feature stories, and documentaries was applied to our previously rather staid catalogs. She investigated new printing companies and methods and started to do full-color catalogs. The covers featured an historical scene and person, for example, Mark Twain and a Mississippi riverboat, Albert Einstein's portrait set against the universe, Thomas Edison's initials and the light bulb (an original light bulb was in the catalog), Dwight Eisenhower addressing the troops the night before D-Day, and numerous others. They were highly produced catalogs.

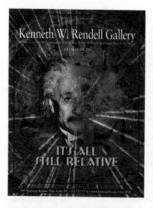
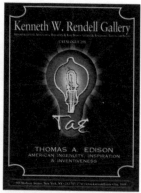

Our catalogs showcased pieces of importance and enabled us to give them a new home with an appreciative collector. In 2008 our Catalog No. 310 featured on the cover one of the most important Thomas Jefferson letters ever offered for sale. I had owned the letter for a few years and had hesitated to incorporate it in any of the large collections I had built. I didn't want the letter to be buried in a vast collection. Rather, I wanted it to be placed on a pedestal by an appreciative collector. But I didn't know who that collector would be.

In the letter Jefferson writes:

> No provision in our constitution ought to be dearer to man than that which protects the rights of conscience against the enterprizes [sic] of the civil authority. It has not left the religion of its citizens under the power of its public functionaries, were it possible that any of these should consider a conquest over the consciences of men either attainable, or applicable to any desirable purpose. To me, no information could be more welcome than that the minutes of the several religious societies should prove, of late, larger additions, than have been usual, to their several associations: and I trust that the whole course of my

life has proved me a sincere friend to religious, as well as civil liberty.

I thank you for your affectionate good wishes for my future happiness. Retirement is become essential to it: and one of the best consolations will be to witness the advancement of my country in all those pursuits & acquisitions which constitute the character of a wise & virtuous nation: and I offer sincere prayers to heaven that its benedictions may attend yourselves, our country, & all its sons.

A year earlier a well-known religious leader had come into the gallery and bought several relatively inexpensive documents. Shortly after Catalog No. 310 was published, he called, excited to talk about the Jefferson letter. The price was $1 million, I told him. I could not have been more shocked when he said he would buy it.

In many ways his purchase was indicative of the way our business changed from the old days of building large collections. In the new twenty-first century important individual pieces were selling very well, and we frequently couldn't predict who was going to buy them.

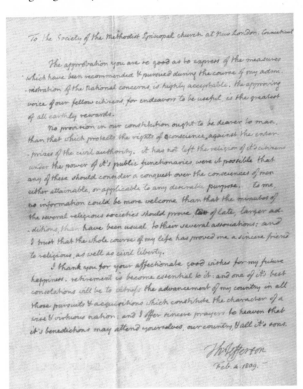

One of the most significant Thomas Jefferson letters ever written.

Of all the unusual things to happen at this time, I became involved with the subject of the Rosebud sled in Orson Welles's masterpiece *Citizen Kane*. An important client commented how much he regretted that Steven Spielberg had bought the Rosebud sled. I told him I had appraised the archives of RKO Pictures, who made the movie, and I could find out if there was more than one sled. I put together a detailed report that held out the possibility of another one that could be acquired. Three sleds were made of balsa wood for the final scene of the film, where the sled is thrown into a furnace. The scene was shot using only one sled, another was the one sold to Spielberg, and the third sled possibly survived. The idea of there being more than one sled led my client to lose interest.

By 2008 I had worked through many recessions over the past 50 years, and, like most people, I assumed that conservative financial policies would carry us through with only a blip. Our Madison Avenue gallery sales were strong until the end of 2009, when the Great Recession of 2008 finally caught up with the buying attitudes of people. Established collectors were unchanged, but the casual buyers definitely pulled back while the financial markets did not rebound as they had in normal, cyclical recessions.

Our gallery continued to be affected by our having sold so much material by the major figures in history that we could not find what was popular with visitors to the gallery. Our own success in selling was causing a concerning shortage of what was of interest to the general public.

Meanwhile, I was fully occupied with a new French client (described in the following chapter), who was buying large groups of important French and other European manuscripts. I was visiting him monthly, in addition to visiting collectors all over Europe to acquire the material I was selling to him.

The situation in New York City continued to change. Our section of Madison Avenue, on the upper East Side, began to change focus, with flagship designer stores beginning to rapidly replace individual galleries and stores that relied on actual sales. We faced the additional problem that the Carlyle Hotel, our landlord, had been sold to a Hong Kong Chinese businessman; he had paid a record price and needed to increase his revenue. Our lease was coming up and our rent would triple, which made it, regretfully, financially impossible for us to continue after 25 exciting and successful years. We had had the perfect location, and we couldn't see any other affordable location making sense. There was also the precipitous decline in the availability of documents from the most popular historical figures. Overall, the closing of our gallery had little financial effect given all our activity in Europe, but personally it was the end of an era of bringing the pleasure and meaningfulness of historical documents directly to so many people.

Chapter 20

The Billion-Dollar French Manuscript Scandal

For decades I have advised collectors to value opportunity. If you don't acquire a coveted manuscript when you have the chance, you may never have the opportunity again.

I have followed my own advice. Letters of Napoleon Bonaparte have always been underpriced. He was a micromanager and involved himself in seemingly every detail of his army, dictating and personally signing many letters every day. One long-established rare-book dealer in Paris always had letters for sale, mostly routine but occasionally more interesting in content. In the early 1990s I started to buy everything he showed me, until he started to run out of routine letters and increasingly showed me more interesting ones. A family owned the bookshop, and as I became more friendly with them, they mentioned a collection of Napoleon that their family personally owned and that they would consider selling.

Finally, I acquired everything they had. It was a great collection, with Napoleon's annotated military books from school, his earliest military plans from Italy, his letter to a first love (highly passionate and detailed), love letters to Josephine about his plans with her upon his return from Egypt, and hundreds of other letters about his military campaigns, his plan to invade Russia, the operations of the French government, the affairs of his brothers and sisters and mother, his plot in exile to return to France, and his memoirs written on St. Helena, which was his final island of exile.

I had collected, in total, more than 500 letters and manuscripts by Napoleon, plus artifacts such as his traveling briefcase, his personal silverware, his compass, and his maps. This was the finest privately owned Napoleon collection.

Part of the joy of collecting for me is finding someone who appreciates the material as much as or maybe even more than I do. In 2007 I decided to look for a buyer for my Napoleon collection. I came close to selling the vast collection to Viktor Baturin, a wealthy contractor and brother of Yelena Baturina, the richest woman in Russia, who was married to the mayor of Moscow. Baturin was well-known for staging full-scale Napoleonic battles with artillery and hundreds of men on horseback, dressed in Napoleonic uniforms. He was the kind of passionate eccentric I wanted to meet, and I was confident that my Napoleon collection would capture his interest.

My planned meeting with Baturin in Zurich—a neutral ground that I had suggested—fell through at the last minute. He had gotten into a spectacular breakup with his wife, had locked her out of his estate, and had her arrested when she climbed over the wall to see her children. He cancelled his trip to meet me. (Vladimir Putin later turned on him over building contracts and he went to prison.) Returning from Zurich, I stopped in Paris to have dinner with the Bodins, my close friends since the 1970s. After I explained the turn of events with Baturin, Thierry Bodin asked me to send him the description of the collection.

Napoleon letter signed.

A month later I received an "urgent" fax from Thierry: "I have just sold your Napoleon collection for $6.5 million. It will come back to France. If I could have confirmation by return, it would be great. I have dinner tomorrow night with my customer."

I was speechless. I had spent months working on the sale of the collection, at that same price, with a very difficult Russian and now, suddenly, the collection was sold. Moreover, my Napoleon collection would return to France, its true home. I never imagined that this was a possibility; the French were always minor collectors of their own history, which is why I was able to buy so much important French historical manuscript material over the decades.

Two weeks later I was back in Paris with Thierry to meet the buyer, Gérard Lhéritier, in his impressive offices overlooking the Champs-Élysées. Lhéritier, who spoke no English, had formed a company called Aristophil and was excited about acquiring my collection. I appreciated what Lhéritier told me about wanting to bring back to France historical letters and manuscripts that foreigners had bought during France's difficult decades after World War II. I applauded his initiative. I was also the major private owner of important French manuscripts.

I returned to Boston with two missions: to investigate Gérard Lhéritier and to organize my other European manuscripts that I could offer him.

Probing Lhéritier's background was essential. In several previous situations collectors had said they planned to collect on a large scale, but I found that they lacked the funds. Investigating Lhéritier, I learned he had accumulated his initial wealth in Monaco, selling commemorative postage stamps to the public as investments. He had gotten into a dispute with people affiliated with Prince Rainier of Monaco over their printing more stamps than agreed, was arrested, and then was cleared of all charges. As far as we could determine, Lhéritier was buying manuscripts with the money he had made in his Monaco postage stamp business.

Gérard Lhéritier.

Trusting Bodin's initial assessment of Lhéritier, I believed he was a potential buyer of much more. I assembled a spectacular collection that included letters and manuscripts of Bach, Beethoven, Mozart, Casanova, Churchill, Einstein, Freud, Monet, Nietzsche, Proust, Puccini, Rubens, Sartre, Seurat, Tchaikovsky, Verdi, and Wagner—plus a few Americans such as Edison, Fitzgerald, Hemingway, and Lindbergh. After several meetings with Lhéritier, where he reviewed all that I was offering, he told me that he would

The first sale to Aristophil.

buy these additional pieces for $5 million. He would need a few months to raise the money.

I also offered Lhéritier a French manuscript of great importance: King Louis XVI's farewell to the French nation. Ever since I had purchased this document in Paris years earlier, I had wanted to find a collector who would fully appreciate it. I felt that Lhéritier was that person. He was enormously excited to bring this great historical manuscript back to France. I was almost as excited as he was.

In the fall of 2008, over lunch at our usual restaurant, Laurent, adjacent to the Champs-Élysées, Lhéritier told me that the Napoleon collection would be exhibited "around Napoleon's tomb" in the Dôme des Invalides in Paris. I was stunned. I couldn't comprehend how a private person could secure such special exhibition space inside Les Invalides, France's national military museum. The opening of the exhibition would be December 8, 2008.

When Shirley and I arrived in Paris for this, countless newspapers were running stories about the Napoleon collection. The public excitement was very gratifying to us. And the gala evening at Les Invalides exceeded all expectations. An honor guard of 100 Napoleonic soldiers lined the entry walkway through the garden, as musicians clad in Napoleonic uniforms played French patriotic music. What a showman Lhéritier was! The exhibit inside the museum's gold-domed chapel, one of the most monumental spaces in Paris, was contained in a series of tall glass vitrines, and the red leather bindings that Shirley had designed focused attention on the extraordinary documents and manuscripts of Napoleon.

Lhéritier came over to greet us, and he told Shirley, who speaks fluent French, to make sure that I understood that he did not want anyone in the press hearing me speak English and identifying me as "the American collector." He wanted, and deserved, the attention to be on him. I was thrilled to see the collection that we had put together and labored over in this spectacular setting. Shirley and I went around the exhibit with our friends, the Bodins, who had made this possible.

The invitation to the exposition opening at Les Invalides.

Lhéritier's plans eventually were becoming clearer. He was forming investment funds for other people to invest their money in his efforts to return important French letters and manuscripts to their country. Meanwhile, Aristophil, Lhéritier's firm, was building a museum on the Boulevard Saint-Germain, one of Paris's expensive streets, to display the manuscripts. Lhéritier was also publishing a quarterly magazine, *Plume*, about the world of collecting historical documents.

With Thierry Bodin, Europe's leading manuscript dealer, at Aristophil's extravaganza opening exposition of The Napoleon Collection they sold him, 2008.

All this promotion was ambitious and impressive, but it concerned Thierry Bodin and me. Most major collectors acquire historical material as an intellectual or emotional investment, not a financial one. Collectors motivated by the desire for financial gains drive prices up, making it difficult for other collectors to acquire material, and destabilize markets when they have to sell in a downturn. Lhéritier was buying heavily at auction, creating an opportunity for many people to sell more than what otherwise would be on the market. It was important for him to create the atmosphere of a rising market, and I think consignors bidding him up certainly accomplished this.

Plume magazine's coverage of the Napoleon documents returning to France.

After selling him almost our entire inventory of European material, I realized that he was not buying from other dealers. He wanted to make large purchases only, not a few pieces here and there, and he only wanted to deal with people he was comfortable with. Dealers told me they couldn't get any response from him. I developed a regular routine of scouring the market for material, acquiring it, and cataloging the documents and manuscripts in the style that would appeal to him. While his main office and museum was in Paris, he lived in Nice on the Riviera. I went to his office in Nice monthly with a bag full of descriptions. His office was on the ground floor of a small office building where he had a private beach, almost next to the marina where he kept his boat for deep-sea fishing. He would go through what I brought, take out anything that didn't interest him (at most only one or two pieces), and I would give him a price for the group. Our meetings were always followed with an elaborate gourmet lunch. If I was headed to Paris, I would spend the afternoon on his private beach before taking the early evening flight. He didn't have to wait—he bought his own jet.

By 2012, while we continued to be invited and attend openings of exhibitions in Paris, I could no longer put together significant groups of material for him. If I could have, I would have been more wary than ever about his financial stability. He showed me the seventeenth-century mansion he bought near his now-finished museum. It was a palace rather than an office building, and he

then spent tens of millions of euros restoring it. How he could afford all of this defied financial sense to me, and I was very concerned that it had little to do with business and a lot to do with ego. I always referred to his office as the "throne room," which he thought was funny. I meant it as a commentary on his motivations. I told him his offices were worthy of Napoleon—but he had to remember what happened to Napoleon.

Aristophil created a custom-built museum.

By 2014 Lhéritier was regularly organizing elaborate conferences that included former presidents of France, journalists, luminaries in various fields, and television personalities. They hailed him as "The King of Manuscripts." These conferences gave seemingly endless awards, many including cash. As was later discovered, some of the celebrities were also being paid to attend. Aristophil had by that year acquired over 136,000 letters and manuscripts and more recently rare books, having raised approximately $1 billion from 18,000 investors. Many had bought shares in Aristophil's various funds, promoted by a network of 800 professional

financial advisors. It was also reported
that insurance companies were promoting his funds as well. He had vastly
more money than anyone could have
realistically invested.

In 2015 Lhéritier suddenly was pro-
claimed the "French Bernie Madoff" by
French media. He was charged with
fraud, deceptive marketing, and breach
of trust. Rare-book dealer Jean-Claude
Vrain, who did appraisals for Aristophil, was also charged. Articles in the

Dinner at Aristophil's office palace.

New York Times and other publications pointed to claims that Lhéritier was
buying manuscripts for his own account, having Vrain appraise them at much
higher figures, and selling them to the funds at the new appraised price. For
instance, Lhéritier was said to have paid $560,000 for an Albert Einstein man-
uscript at auction; Vrain reputedly appraised it at $13 million, and Lhéritier
allegedly charged the fund that amount. When this manuscript was sold again
at auction it brought about what the investors had paid for it, $13 million.

I was as shocked as Lhéritier's 18,000 investors. I had assumed that Lhéritier
was buying on behalf of the funds that
he created and charging a percentage
commission.

The French government seized
Aristophil's assets and released Lhéritier on a bail of more than $2 million.
The government decided to liquidate
all the manuscript material over a five-
year period. This liquidation was carried out via numerous auction sales
each year. Thierry Bodin cataloged the
material so investors had a chance of
recouping at least some of their money.

"The incredible history of
the French Madoff."

But the market was being flooded, and collectors knew that a staggering amount
of material would still become available. Only half of the auction material initially found buyers, at an average of about 15 percent of what the investors paid.

In France, unlike in the United States, people who are indicted for crimes
are not guaranteed a speedy trial. Nearly ten years after Lhéritier's arrest, no
trial has been scheduled.

Chapter 21

Forming the Most Comprehensive World War II Collection and Museum in the World

I was born during World War II. My earliest emotional memories of the war are of the photo from inside the landing craft on D-Day, with soldiers running out, many falling into the water dead or wounded, and my father's best friend describing the terrible time he had as a medical corpsman in the Pacific. That image, and those stories, terrified me.

In the years after the war, veterans needed to replace the horrors of the war with glory and heroism to enable them to move forward. By the time I began my collection, in the late 1950s, World War II was seen as America at its best (which it was); the reality of the personal tragedies, the losses, the terror, the complexities and the staggering effects on the world, were essentially left behind in 1945. People, psychologically, needed to forget the reality and focus on the genuine patriotism of our military.

The reality of World War II is unimaginable today—it was unimaginable at the time. Sixty million people were killed. (Twenty million soldiers and forty million civilians—a number that may actually be too low because records in China and the Soviet Union were not kept.)

The entire world was at war. Every nation was either desperately doing everything it could to conquer other countries, or desperately defending itself from destruction. When you consider all of the industrial might of the United States—in a total war, involving every person and every industry, and the nation still was not able to defeat Japan after three and a half years—it brings a startling sense of the reality of the war. In the limited recent wars the country has been involved in, there has always been a step the United States didn't take. In Korea we could have used atomic bombs against the Chinese; in Vietnam we could have obliterated Hanoi. Political and humanitarian considerations prevailed.

But in World War II there were no such considerations. It was all-out war. Hitler would have dropped atomic bombs if he'd had them first. He unleashed rockets on London late in the war with the intent of killing as many civilians as possible. The Japanese killed millions of Chinese for sport; the Germans killed millions of Russians to establish the rule of terror; and when the onslaught turned on Germany, the Russians killed and destroyed everything on the way to Berlin.

The entire populations of nearly all countries were committed; two-thirds of the national production of the major combatants went into the war. It was total war. It was a war unlike the "Great War" of the previous generation. It was World War II.

My collection began in 1960 with the long-range goal of preserving the reality of the war and the lives of not only the leaders, but also of ordinary soldiers and civilians. I wanted to capture the atmosphere of the home fronts, and the changing roles of women. I didn't see World War II from only an American perspective; I saw it as the worldwide cataclysm that it was. I wanted to under-stand—and to this end, I wanted to preserve—the archival records and artifacts of the social and economic movements that led to war. What happened in the 1920s and '30s to Germany, the country that provided more American emi-grants than any other, and how Imperial Japan became so violent in conquering China, were subjects that intrigued me.

While archives could provide insight for scholars, only artifacts and docu-ments could provide connections for students and adult museum visitors. My concept was to create a mosaic of information, influences, and experiences from 1919 through 1945. I didn't want a collection of guns, medals, and uniforms only; I wanted the stories of the people who used the guns, wore the uniforms, and earned the medals. I wanted the human story and I wanted to explore the lessons of human nature found in their experiences. A paramount lesson, I knew, was that good people are at a disadvantage in recognizing evil, because they cannot conceive that bad people can act the way they do. Nazi Germany and Imperial Japan both clearly telegraphed their intentions, and acted on them, in the decade before the outbreak of the war. Winston Churchill, alone, warned, in newspaper articles, of the terrible threat from Hitler's Germany. People didn't believe him; they didn't believe that anyone would want another European war. Churchill alone understood that Hitler and Nazi Germany *did* want another war. Churchill referred to the 1930s as his "wilderness years."

The only museums at that time were national ones that celebrated how their individual countries gloriously won the war, with scant mention of any other countries. The collection would be international—after all, it was a world war—and it would reflect that the allied countries could not have individually defeated Germany.

Above all, I wanted a collection that represented the reality of World War II. I knew that the one element I could not incorporate into a collection was the anxiety and fear. As other museums were built in the coming decades, I have been outraged when they tell visitors they will know what it was like to land on D-Day, or be in a submarine under attack. Everyone in combat knew that a certain percentage of the people around them would die, and they knew the reality that that included them. War is not entertainment, and it is a tragic betrayal of those who suffered and died to focus on visitor numbers and not on historical reality.

Combat veterans all say that the heroes are in the cemeteries. Until late in life, few veterans would speak about their experiences. I was never judgmental about how they psychologically survived, whether it was by never discussing what happened to them or needing to see it as gloriously patriotic. However they needed to survive the nightmare, was the right thing for them to do.

As the collection began to expand from the original concept of letters and documents to include posters, leaflets, brochures, and newspapers, I had a growing sense of the importance of preserving in one collection the "atmosphere" of wartime, the record of the actions of these people as seen against the background of their intellectual and psychological environment. Letters and manuscripts concerning the war have always been widely collected, as have many of the artifacts in the "relic" class—uniforms, equipment, guns, and decorations. The printed material—posters, leaflets, and brochures, as well as artifacts that were not saved as war relics or trophies—were not actively collected, and they were also very difficult to find. The papers and seemingly unimportant artifacts were discarded during or after the war, and it became increasingly apparent to me that my including them in the focus and range of my collection was unique.

As I mentally assembled all of this into a comprehensive collection according to subject, the artifacts were seen for the role they played in the events and atmosphere of the time, rather than, for example, a series of French Resistance newspapers seen only in the context of printing and news development. The reality of the heroism of these French Resistance printers is brought out much more sharply when their "last chance" weapons—a single-shot cigarette lighter–gun, or razor-sharp lapel knives—are seen together with their newspapers and the German posters promising death to those operating clandestine presses.

In a similar way I hoped to stimulate thinking about what it was like to be in London during the Blitz, to land in Normandy on D-Day, to fight an enemy in the Pacific who was as difficult to understand as he was to fight, and to risk one's life daily. Many media stories understood this well and would frequently quote at length from pamphlets distributed in England during the Blitz entitled, "What to do in a gas attack," "Hand to hand combat with German paratroopers," "How to build a bomb shelter in your garden," and "What to do if your house is bombed." World War II was perhaps the last time tens of thousands of individuals could so dramatically affect world history. It was a war of clear good versus evil, a time in which people did not and could not choose not to be involved. Nearly all of the countries in the world were engaged in the war, and virtually everyone was playing a role in the wartime effort.

British instructional materials to protect citizens in the midst of World War II.

The importance of individuals is immediately apparent when one looks into an area such as the Resistance movements in Nazi-occupied Europe, but the importance of the individual is not as readily apparent in large-scale military operations. When closely examined, however, many seemingly impossible military situations were overcome by hundreds of heroic acts. The Normandy landings are a good example. On some beaches aerial bombardment and naval gunfire destroyed much of the German defenses and the Allies' superiority in men and equipment secured the beachheads. At Omaha Beach, however, through miscalculations, bombs were dropped further inland than where they were critically needed and, as a result, the American troops were barely able to get beyond the water's edge. For all practical purposes, they were defeated and needed to be evacuated, but literally hundreds of soldiers rallied their compatriots, and in hundreds of small actions finally carried the day. Every one of the American Rangers who climbed the hundred-foot cliffs of Pointe du Hoc overlooking Omaha and Utah Beaches, with enemy machine-gun fire pouring straight down on them, succeeded through their own individual efforts to make it to the top (135 of the 225 Rangers were killed or wounded). In a much larger context, many military historians have attributed the significantly greater success of some army groups to their commanders' attitude of rewarding individual initiative and thinking. Other army groups, led by commanders who insisted on doing everything "by the book," did not encourage or reward individual thinking, and were much less successful than they could have been.

The morale of individuals as well as entire armies and populations was vitally important in wartime. The Axis countries had built their Fascist regimes on propaganda and needed only to shift gears for the propaganda machines to prepare their people for each successive step of conquest and war. In *Mein Kampf* Hitler discussed the importance of propaganda, outlining the role it would play more than a decade later. *Mein Kampf* even foretold how he would attack: "the place of artillery preparation will be taken by propaganda, before the armies arrive. . . . Mental confusion, indecision, panic, these are the first weapons."

Collecting as much German propaganda to the German people as possible was a high priority, along with the British propaganda that motivated the population to fight against impossible odds. All of this propaganda had been discarded as soon as it was out of date or at the end of the war. There were no dealers offering it for sale—it was both rare and very inexpensive if you found it. The only places I could find it were British general flea markets. It was very labor-intensive, not just in going to towns all over England, but also poring through everything that people brought and had piled on tarps on the ground.

I think British people didn't want to throw out the information booklets and inspirational broadsides because they were relics of Britain's modern heroic age. There were so many small ephemera shows, and flea markets, all over England that I hired the son of a rare-book dealer friend to go every weekend and watch every country auction. His salary was significantly greater than the total I spent on what he found.

It was different in Germany. They wanted to forget what had happened to their country, and they saved almost nothing. American soldiers, however, took what they found as souvenirs, and these pieces would turn up in their estate sales in the United States.

There was a strong market in Third Reich artifacts, which had been brought back as souvenirs by most soldiers. These artifacts were offered for sale at general military shows, at estate sales, and by the few specialized dealers. From my earliest years three military dealers were particularly helpful: Hayes Outapalik, with American artifacts; and Bill

"The Russians are in Berlin."

Shea and Malcolm Fischer with Third Reich artifacts. Except for these dealers, everything was very literally "cash and carry," no matter how much and no matter how big. At military shows people acted as if they had never heard of a checking account, everyone said they had no idea how to write a receipt, and it was up to me to figure out how to get what I could not carry back to Boston. (Bill Shea's truck was invaluable!)

In 1983, during the Hitler diaries scandal, I met Wolf Hess, the son of Deputy Führer Rudolf Hess. Wolf Hess sold me the first important group of Third Reich artifacts I acquired, including a painting Hitler gave to his father and his father's gold Nazi Party badge. In the following years I acquired a number of other pieces from him. It was a series of acquisitions that troubled me. All my other Third Reich artifacts came from American soldiers, the spoils of war, and the money was a small recompense for what they had gone through. With Hess, the artifacts came directly from Hitler. They had been owned by his Deputy Führer, his son, and then me. It was a direct connection I found upsetting. I struggled to put my feelings aside; I needed to collect all sides of the European war, not just the good guys. Without the bad guys, there would not have been a war. I could never get over my emotional repugnance, but my intellectual pursuit of creating a collection that would be comprehensive was paramount.

The Hitler diaries made me well enough known that when I attended veterans' reunions, they wanted to talk to me. My interest in preserving the reality of what they had done was genuine and appreciated. I strongly viewed the war as a crime against humanity—no one should have had to go through what they did. I didn't treat them as heroes; I treated them as patriotic Americans who defended American freedom.

I made it well known that I wanted to preserve their reality for the future by collecting artifacts that would eventually be in a museum in their honor. Over a 25-year period I bought a huge number of artifacts from veterans, usually with detailed stories of how they used or acquired them.

In 1985 I was offered a document that was both horrifying and immensely important. It was Adolf Hitler's handwritten notes for his speech in the Reichstag, commemorating his 1933 election victory six years earlier:

In connection with the Jewish question . . . it is a shameful spectacle to see how the whole democratic world is oozing sympathy for the poor tormented Jewish people, but remains hard-hearted and obdurate when it comes to helping them. . . .

In the course of my life I have very often been a prophet. . . . During my struggle for power it was mostly the Jewish race that received my prophecies with laughter when I said that I would one day take over the leadership of the state; . . . and that I would then . . . bring the Jewish problem to a solution. Their laughter was uproarious. . . .

If the international Jewish financiers . . . [of] Europe should succeed in plunging the nations once more into a world war, . . . the results will . . . be the annihilation of the Jewish race in Europe!

The highly respected French dealer who offered these notes to me told me they came from Hitler's personal files, which was logical because the French army were the first to reach Hitler's house in Berchtesgaden. It was a cornerstone document and I had to buy it.

Two years later Shirley and I finally had a belated honeymoon in France, and when we went to the Normandy coast, I felt overwhelmed to actually be there. There were remains of landing craft and huge German bunkers and gun emplacements everywhere. The cliff top at Pointe du Hoc, where 225 American Rangers climbed up to destroy the German guns, had been left unchanged.

The Omaha Beach Museum was of particular interest because they had duplicate artifacts for sale, and I bought many pieces used in the D-Day invasion. Over the next ten years I made many trips to see the museum owner and was gradually able to acquire many iconic D-Day artifacts. At the time of the 50th anniversary of D-Day, he said he thought interest would trail off and he would not be able to keep the museum open without the income from visitors. Eventually I was able to acquire the museum collection.

A grappling hook fired to the top of the cliffs at Pointe du Hoc.

Shirley at a German bunker at Pointe du Hoc in Normandy.

We learned from Parisian friends there would be massive commemorations around June 14, 1990, the 50th anniversary of the fall of France. There would also be a large auction of French and German printed and manuscript documents concerning the invasion of France, the occupation, and the Resistance. It was the collection of a Frenchman who had started collecting during the war and eventually accumulated thousands of pieces. When we arrived in Paris, I was amazed. It looked like, and seemed like, a celebration, but my friends kept reminding me it was a commemoration. In the Place de la Concorde an enormous canvas radio was set up, continuously broadcasting Charles de Gaulle's radio speeches from London (50 years earlier he was under a French death sentence for treason). The city was festooned with flags, and there were fireworks at night.

Ken carrying out artifacts from the Omaha Beach Museum.

At the auction I kept buying lot after lot. This went on for three days, until I had bought nearly the entire auction. I was amazed the French government did not use its legal right to preempt the sale of this important national archive.

Thierry and Pierrette Bodin hired a large truck and rented space in a store near their office to hold everything until shipment. Shirley, Jason, and I processed the material for shipment until well after midnight. Whether France was celebrating or commemorating in June 1990, I would always be both celebrating and commemorating this auction.

With Jason at the Bodins' office, organizing the enormous propaganda collection.

September 15, 1990, was the 50th anniversary of the Battle of Britain. I wanted to be there, and Shirley and I experienced an unforgettable time. The night of September 15, 50 years after the Luftwaffe was defeated over Britain, lights all over London went out, World War II air-raid sirens wailed, and searchlights lit up the sky. They had not done this since the war, nor ever again, and everything about that amazing night is indelibly imprinted in my memory.

There had been a special reception for Battle of Britain pilots and their families the night before at the Royal Air Force Museum. I arranged

Leaving (on crutches) the Paris auction house, with Jason.

to get invited. Other than various members of the royal family, I was one of the few people not involved in the Battle of Britain. Earlier in the day we had stood in front of Buckingham Palace while a 100-mile-long armada of World War II planes flew over London at a low altitude.

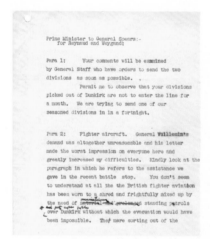

Churchill to the president of France, June 5, 1940: ". . . You don't seem to understand at all [that] the British fighter aviation has been worn to a shred . . . by the need of . . . prolonged standing patrols over Dunkirk without which the evacuation would have been impossible. . . . You have no right to ask us to deprive ourselves of the sole means of continuing the war by casting away in a single battle the already small forces upon which we rely as the sole sure hope of ultimate victory to us both."

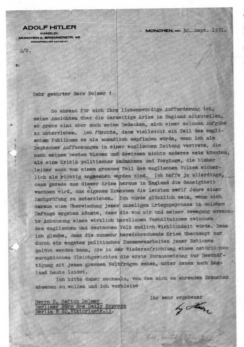

A letter written by Adolf Hitler in September 1931: "I hope . . . that out of this crisis a new readiness will grow up in Britain to submit the past twelve years to a reappraisal. I should be happy, if the unhappy war-psychosis could be overcome to permit the realization of the truly cordial relationship between the British and the German peoples so eagerly desired by myself and my movement. The crisis now breaking in on us can only be solved by the closest political collaboration of those nations who see in the re-establishment of a natural European balance of power the first precondition to dealing with those great world problems under which Britain too suffers today."

The document many consider the most important in my collection was offered to me in 1993 by Roy Davids. It was brought to Sotheby's for auction, but they, along with Christie's, had a policy of not offering Third Reich material. Adolf Hitler's draft of the Munich Agreement, which he and British prime minister Neville Chamberlain had fought over, contained Hitler's boldly written changes and the spidery, penciled translation notes in English of the British ambassador for Chamberlain. More than any other document, the Munich Agreement was considered the start of World War II. Hitler learned he could terrorize Chamberlain with his demands, and the British prime minister would not stand up to him. I couldn't argue with the price, but I couldn't afford it either. The owner agreed that I could pay him over three years.

Ben Swearingen, a Texas high-school teacher, had taught himself German and did extensive research into which American military units were most likely to have found important German artifacts. His research into the guards at Nuremberg, for example, tracked down wristwatches the condemned men gave to guards and the personal effects they left behind. These were not the kinds of artifacts I wanted, but he also located for me artifacts that were evocative of the nationalistic power of the Nazis. He contacted everyone he could, including Hitler's secretaries. He was my best source for important German artifacts all through the 1990s.

As World War II veterans reached their senior years and parted with what they had used or collected during the war, more artifacts moved into the market. By attending many military shows I also met collectors who started long before me and had put great effort into finding artifacts in their areas of specialization. Art Beltrone, for example, was interested in prisoners of war and spent several decades collecting everything related to the men and the camps. By the 1990s Art knew his collection was as good as it could ever be and, knowing my plans for a permanent museum, approached me to buy it. I later acquired several British prisoner-of-war collections and built a collection that is unequaled.

This was my golden age of collecting World War II material.

For several years I had in mind that I would build a museum west of Boston, not far from my home. The location would be away from the traffic congestion of Boston and easy to get to. In 1999 a 10,000-square-foot building, across the street from the major shopping mall west of Boston, came on the market. The building required extensive remodeling for my purpose, but the location and size were what I wanted.

To house my archives, I built a large, fireproof concrete room with a vault door. I worked out a detailed layout of exhibition galleries that would cover 25 different areas of the war. These exhibits would be designed chronologically to immerse the visitor in the complexities of the war.

I wanted the visitor experience to be overwhelming—World War II was overwhelming. I wanted to present the unexpected facets of courage that were demanded throughout World War II, from leaders to soldiers and from prisoners of war to people on the home front. I also wanted some displays to encourage visitors to handle the more durable artifacts. I wanted visitors to engage with their hands, their heads, and their hearts. Everything was original, including numerous photos of unheralded people in all areas.

A note from World War II historian Steve Ambrose after he climbed up into my attics.

The landing craft being unloaded after its trip from Valdez, Alaska.

Around this time the U.S. Supreme Court asked if I could create an exhibit, titled "The Supreme Court Goes to War." Most of the justices had served in the military, and some had their uniforms and a few pieces of equipment. They asked if I could incorporate my artifacts to illustrate the types of weapons and other artifacts the justices would have used. Most of the justices talked to me at length about what they had done and experienced. The exhibit, on display at the Supreme Court, was considered a great success and brought a sense of humanity to the justices.

Talking with Chief Justice William Rehnquist at the opening
of the exhibition "The Supreme Court Goes to War."

By then, sufficient time had passed, and more soldiers wanted to talk about what they had done, and the challenges and trauma they had faced. The Steven Spielberg / Tom Hanks movie *Saving Private Ryan*, based in part on Stephen Ambrose's books, marked a major change in World War II films. The movie showed the reality and terror of combat and was acclaimed by combat veterans. At the premiere, veterans said the only thing missing was the smell of cordite from explosives.

A different kind of challenge during the war was encountered by Dorothy and Prentiss Hill from Columbus, Ohio. Their extensive wartime correspondence was offered at an auction. The lengthy description said the Hills were a Black couple, and they recounted in great detail their passionate sexual encounters when she visited him at his Army base in Georgia. The description reflected a stereotyping I didn't like, but I theorized that people who were so explicit about sex would be equally explicit in describing their experiences in wartime. I had very little material in my collection from a Black soldier's point of view, so I bought the correspondence.

The letters gave exceptional insight into the lives of a Northern Black couple dealing with the segregated South as well as racism inside the military. Prentiss Hill told his wife, Dorothy, about getting promoted on the quality of his administrative work but having to be twice as good as White soldiers. He wrote extensively about the unfairness of the discrimination he felt, and the ways he adapted to get along.

Dorothy visited Prentiss as often as she could get to Georgia from Ohio. She was not used to the South's discrimination, and she fought back. When White women stepped in front of her in the grocery-store line, Dorothy stepped in front of them; when the clerk at the counter tried to cheat her by overstating the weight on the scale, she spoke up. Their letters to one another show that Prentiss constantly worried about Dorothy's safety. I edited their letters, more than a thousand pages, into a manuscript for potential publication. I

(From left) Dorothy Hill, myself, Prentiss Hill, and Danny Thomas at the Museum of World War II on the night of Thomas's riveting talk on surviving 28 days on Iwo Jima as a medic.

GALLANTLY STREAMING
The photo that inspired a nation

THE BURDEN OF HEROES

HE'S PLAYED SOME AND CREATED SOME. NOW THE DIRECTOR
EXAMINES WHO THEY REALLY ARE BY RICHARD SCHICKEL

Clint Eastwood's *Flags of Our Fathers* adapts
James Bradley and Ron Powers' book recounting the
story of the three survivors of the flag raising on Iwo Jima
during World War II. The event produced the most
famous photographic image of the war, and the men were
returned home to lead a war-bond tour, during which
they were heroically—and, in their view, erroneously—

The *Time* magazine cover story in which Clint Eastwood
talks about Danny Thomas's sacrifice.

shared the manuscript with two people I thought would be interested and helpful. One was Supreme Court Justice Clarence Thomas. He told me that Prentiss reminded him of his grandfather, who had raised him.

Henry Louis "Skip" Gates Jr., a Harvard professor, was also impressed with the correspondence. Both Thomas and Gates tried to get their university presses to publish the letters, but they never did. This literate and insightful description of the life of a Black couple during World War II remains unpublished.

Other opportunities to add to my collection were occurring at a rapid rate. I acquired a collection of clandestine radios that had been parachuted to the French and other resistance groups. Within several years I was able to form a collection of Enigma code machines, second only to the National Security Agency's collection.

Britain created propaganda that appeared to be German in origin to affect the morale of German soldiers and civilians. They also created forged currency, ration books and stamps, and even discharge papers

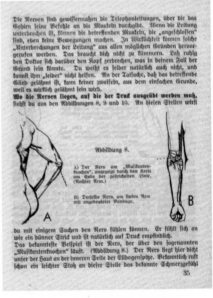

A manual for German soldiers
to fake medical problems.

from the Army. I had been able to find few examples of these, and when I had the opportunity to buy several collections, I never hesitated. The cleverness, insidiousness, and duplicity of British propaganda to Germany was enormously appealing to me. The Nazis had built the Third Reich partly by inflaming German nationalism, and I greatly admired the way the British used Germany's national psychology against them.

I was developing the museum to represent the all-encompassing nature of the world at war. I did not want it to be entertaining; education was the goal. I did not want to indulge some people's fascination with evil, but rather show how the Nazis' use of symbols, colors, designs, allegories, themes—of togetherness, inclusion, exclusion,

Britain created a wanted poster using a generic fake image, which caused a stampede to the police to collect the reward.

and mutual enemies—and banners (such as "For God and Fatherland") seduced a nation and empowered evil to even greater depths.

Many veterans who came to the museum wanted to tell me about their experiences, so I established a speaker's series every two weeks. These were informal talks, and with few exceptions they were intense and personal.

Most of the speakers were Americans, but we also had British civilians describing the bombings, a German soldier who had become a POW in Russia, French resistance members, an OSS agent who had operated behind Japanese lines, men who had climbed the cliffs at Pointe du Hoc on D-Day, and others who had landed on Omaha Beach. Several Marines who had been on Iwo Jima told of the horrors of the epic battle against the Japanese in early 1945. Richard Dinning, a B-17 captain who had flown 33 bombing missions over Germany, and Izzy Arbeiter, who survived concentration camps where his parents perished, were frequent speakers. Manny Abrams, a B-25 navigator, was also a frequent speaker.

It was amazing to have these men tell their stories in the midst of the collection that I had formed specifically to preserve their very personal World War II histories for the future.

Medal of Honor recipients at a luncheon in the museum.

Since I wrote an elaborately illustrated book, *World War II: Saving the Reality*, about my museum in 2009, and the Imperial War Museum in London described my collection as the most comprehensive in the world, filmmakers had approached me about a documentary. I rejected the overtures until Tim Gray, the founder of the World War II Foundation, proposed the right approach. Tim interviewed 40 veterans, each in the relevant exhibition area of the museum, and interspersed these interviews with a museum tour led by me.

A feature on the museum in *Architectural Digest*.

All the veterans featured in this film had served in combat, and all talked personally and candidly. With great emotion, Sammy Bernstein described the Iwo Jima battle, including hand-to-hand combat with his knife after he ran out of ammunition. Many veterans talked about survivor guilt: "Why was I saved, and others died?" Alba Thompson, one of two women interviewed,

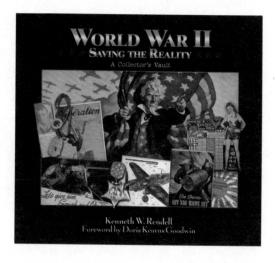

was on MacArthur's senior staff. Irmgard Schmid was a young woman in Germany, and she was interviewed against a background of Nazi banners. Her father was an army officer.

The documentary, *World War II: Saving the Reality*, builds chronologically towards the Allies' victory—and dramatically cuts away from the victory celebrations to show a military funeral as the actor Dan Aykroyd, the narrator, reads the most articulate letter about war that I've ever read. Dwight Eisenhower wrote to his wife, Mamie, on April 16, 1944:

> How I wish this cruel business of war could be completed quickly. . . . It is a terribly sad business to tot up the casualties each day—even in an air war—and to realize how many youngsters are gone forever. A man must develop a veneer of callousness that lets him consider such things dispassionately, but he can never escape a recognition of the fact that back home the news brings anguish and suffering to families all over the country. Mothers, fathers, brothers, sisters, wives and friends must have a difficult time preserving any comforting philosophy and retaining any belief in the eternal righteousness of things. War demands great toughness of fiber—not only in the soldier that must endure, but in the home that must sacrifice their best.

Aykroyd hosted a premiere and party at the House of Blues in Boston. The premiere was overwhelming. When the film ended, the audience was crying. It was a very emotional, and very meaningful, evening. Everyone was so thankful that their story was told.

The actor Tom Hanks, the star of *Saving Private Ryan*, appears in the documentary, speaking at the premiere of his television series about the Pacific War: "Ken has taken responsibility for being something of a personal repository for the actual Holy Grail documents of great repute. I recommend you pay attention to him and the amazing collection that cannot be seen anywhere else in the world."

He gave me the idea to write another book based on these documents alone. *Politics, War, and Personality: Fifty Iconic World War II Documents That Changed the World* was published in 2013. John Eisenhower wrote the foreword:

We are living today in a world in which our capacity to duplicate and create 'virtual reality' dominates our lives. That fact makes it doubly refreshing to participate in an area of activity in which authenticity is not only the norm; it is demanded. Nothing in Ken Rendell's Museum of World War II . . . is a copy; every item is authentic, original, and real.

Patton to the Sultan of Morocco, two days after landing in Casablanca: "Your Majesty must realize the painful sentiments which I entertain in contemplating the necessity of shedding the blood of my friends, but the stern necessity of war demands that if the French armed forces continue to demonstrate the hostility they have already shown, it is my military duty and purpose to attack by air, by sea, and by land, with the utmost violence known to modern war."

This book gives us a fleeting glimpse of the storehouse of historic items that are enshrined in that museum—the greatest collection of World War II items in the country.

For me *Politics, War, and Personality* has performed an interesting function, that of restoring perspective. . . . I personally recall a good many of the events covered by these documents when they happened. . . . I lived four years in the Philippines, always conscious of the Japanese menace. In the summer of 1938, my father and I, indulged in a long, sobering discussion of the notorious Munich Agreement. . . .

As time went on, however, my world began to focus on the European area. Circumstances made that inevitable. In 1942 my father became the Allied Commander for the invasion of North Africa, later Supreme Commander in Europe. I served in Germany during the last weeks of the war against Hitler.

Shirley and I had many ideas to develop the museum, but we could not afford to carry them out. It was all we could afford to run the museum as a private entity. Developing the museum as a public non-profit, and establishing it on a sustaining financial basis, would require very significant financing for a number of years. Ellen Michelson and Mike Michelson stepped forward and offered to donate the operating 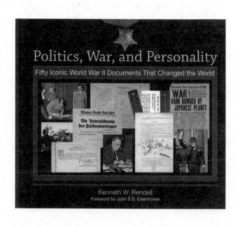 expenses for five years so that it could be established on whatever scale we could accomplish. Nothing would have happened without their tremendous financial and personal support. They had been longtime personal friends, as well as collectors, and shared our belief in the importance of preserving the reality of World War II.

Around this time the Grolier Club in New York City asked me if I could design and mount a large exhibition about World War II. The Grolier Club is America's oldest and largest society for manuscript and rare-book collectors. No member had ever, in the club's 130-year history, had more than two solo exhibitions. I would be the first member to have three. The public's dramatic increase in interest in World War II merited the decision, the director said. The layout would be similar to that of the museum, and I would design each section to immerse the visitor in the actual experiences of people during the war. I called the exhibition "The Power of Words and Images in a World at War."

New York Times critic Edward Rothstein wrote a review of the exhibition that he told me was as good as he ever wrote:

It is the ephemera that ends up reviving the past, jolting us into more vivid understanding, . . . and much of what we see in this exhibition does just that. Objects of everyday life during World War II—the posters, the signs, the leaflets, the newspapers, the letters—land on contemporary senses like sparks still smoldering. The Grolier show's displays consistently unite the familiar with the unexpected. So while we are acquainted by now with the "Degenerate Art" exhibition that Hitler staged (its guide is here), there is also an enameled sign created by the Nazi bureau overseeing cultural life. "Swing dancing forbidden."

So while the overall history is familiar, these artifacts give sharp, incisive glimpses of passions and experiences that can be missed in the larger currents of the war's history. But we also see the war itself unfolding, and in many instances are amazed that we are seeing these artifacts at all.

The exhibition manages to give a powerful compact survey, while suggesting how much of that epochal conflict yet remains beyond easy understanding.

One of twelve exhibition cases on World War II at the Grolier Club.

With Shirley at the World War II exhibition.

The exhibit at the Grolier Club brought more national publicity to our museum. In 2014 Shirley began writing quarterly newsletters to reach people who had visited or made contributions. Each newsletter described special exhibitions, new acquisitions, donations, speakers, and general news about the museum.

The depth and range of our collection enabled us to create comprehensive special exhibits on almost any aspect of World War II. In 2010, when the movie *The King's Speech* came out, the owner of the original manuscript offered it for sale, and the museum acquired it. The entire subject of the movie—Edward VIII's abdication, his pro-German sentiments, George VI's struggles—became an exhibit. We built another exhibit called "The Failed Artist," which included the contents of Hitler's artist's studio, along with paintings he had given to Rudolf Hess. We commemorated the 75th anniversary of the start of the war in "Hitler Attacks, Churchill Rises from the Ashes of Appeasement." In 2014 another Hollywood movie, *The Imitation Game*, about England's breaking of the Enigma code, resulted in a special exhibit of Enigma code machines.

The burden of fundraising was a necessary part of creating a self-sustaining nonprofit, and both Shirley and I went into it with a businesslike attitude of learning how it worked. Shirley took on the immense burden of applying for grants. You couldn't just write a normal business-like proposal—there were all kinds of bureaucratic rules to follow. Private philanthropies could be the most difficult if they were run not by the people providing the money but by people hired to determine who should be supported. We also found that as a newcomer in the Boston area, it was very difficult to even be considered. The great exception for us was the Shipley Foundation. Decisions were made by the founder, Richard Shipley, whom I met with personally and who provided very important grants to us. The CEO of MathWorks, Jack Little, was a frequent visitor and was very interested in the museum. We did joint events with MathWorks and they were financially very supportive.

A conversation with Roger Hertog, a prominent New York Jewish philanthropist, led to an important

exhibition at the New-York Historical Society. I mentioned to him that
I thought Holocaust museums did
not approach their subject sufficiently. The motto "never again" and
the exhibitions in general did not
address how the Holocaust actually
happened. I told him that educating
people in the history of how incre-
mental anti-Semitism led to the
Holocaust should be the focus. I
described to Roger the collection of
anti-Semitic artifacts that I had collected since the 1960s. They are all
quite rare. Neither Allied soldiers

THE POWER OF ANTI-SEMITISM;
THE MARCH TO THE HOLOCAUST
1919-1939

Wander si scht zeit!

An exhibition by The Museum of World War II
Boston

nor German citizens wanted them as souvenirs from the war, and there was
little, if any, market among collectors. I had bought everything I could find,
and they were in various exhibits throughout the museum because anti-Semitism was found everywhere. Anti-Semitism was a part of everyday life in all
countries.

Hertog lit up with enthusiasm for this idea for the New-York Historical
Society. He called the director, Louise Mirrer, and asked that the two of us
meet that morning. I described to Louise my concept of treating the incremen-
tal advance of anti-Semitism as an integral part of the Holocaust. She suggested
a special exhibit from April to August 2016. In conjunction with the exhibit I
wrote a 79-page catalog, *The Power of Anti-Semitism; the March to the Holocaust,
1919–1939*. This was the most difficult writing I have ever done. I was sub-
merged into the world of hate—irrational hate based on people's needs to blame
an identifiable group for their own failures in life. Every day for several months
I had to think about how these artifacts represented the worst elements of
Western society. At the end of every day I found it difficult to emerge from
that dark cave of hatred.

Louise Mirrer wrote the foreword to the exhibition catalog:

Anti-Semitism is among the most wrenching topics of twentieth century history. Most of us today associate the dogma and its correspond-
ing policies with Adolf Hitler's rise to power in Germany, beginning in
the early 1930s, but the extraordinary collection assembled by Kenneth
Rendell reveals a different timeline. A copy of the public announce-

ment of the Treaty of Versailles terms, owned and annotated by Hitler, gives evidence of virulent anti-Semitic sentiments and policies spanning the entire interwar period, with Hitler, in 1919, writing that the Treaty paved the way for a "Jewish dictate," and that the "Jews must therefore leave Germany." Other materials . . . including anti-Semitic books and signs warn that "Jews are not allowed" in restaurants or on park benches, and original anti-Semitic newspaper articles and cartoons similarly give evidence of a slow but steady indoctrination of citizens, both non-Jewish and Jewish, in Germany long before Hitler came to power.

This new—and path-breaking—understanding of the trajectory of anti-Semitism in Europe is without a doubt of tremendous historical significance. The materials in the Museum of World War II collection illustrate the ease with which propaganda can sink its roots in any society, and the dangers of underestimating its power.

The astonishing discoveries of the Museum of World War II collection underscore the old adage about the importance of history: how it is impossible to understand who we are today without knowing from where we came. This collection offers an incomparable opportunity to convey to young people why a significant part of our city's demographic came to be in New York; how this demographic, like so many immigrant groups today, sought not only economic opportunity but the much more basic right to live without fear or threat of violence because of their ethnicity or religious belief.

The public and media reaction to my exhibition was very gratifying.

In the following three years two large-format books were published by National Geographic Society based entirely on artifacts in the museum. The first, *The Secret History of World War II*, was 352 pages and the second, *National Geographic Atlas of World War II*, was 256 pages. I wrote the foreword to each. The public reaction was overwhelming.

The end of 2016 marked the end of our third year operating as a nonprofit, open to the public and hosting school groups five days a week. For school groups, the experience of the museum could be overwhelming. We developed an overall curriculum based on putting original artifacts directly in the hands of students. We followed with theme-based curricula, lesson plans, and teacher workshops. Teachers could earn college credit in our summer programs on how to teach about the human aspects of World War II using original materials.

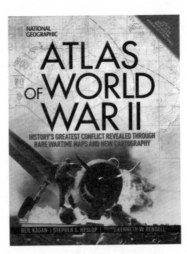

We raised funds for what we called our Urban Partnership, which allowed us to waive admissions and pay for buses to bring students from lower-economic areas to the museum. This amounted to 26 percent of all students and was particularly gratifying since some of these students had never been to a museum and were highly responsive to our way of teaching. One of the schools that came regularly was Somerville High School, from the area where I grew up. They eventually incorporated a museum visit into their curriculum planning.

We also formed a partnership with PBS Learning Media, which used our resources and our head of education, Sue Wilkins, to develop online materials for teachers to use throughout the United States. One of these offerings, *The Power of Propaganda*, won an award and continues to be available to teachers.

Our message to students was always that war was not a video game, and to help them realize what their lives would have been like if they had been living during World War II. Thanks to the power of original material, which they could hold in their hands, they got it.

Our fundraising for an expanded building had reached $16 million of our $30 million goal, which other nonprofits told me was phenomenal. I thought "phenomenal" would be to reach our goal. Fundraising was stalled. Then, one of our trustees, Jon D'Allessandro, contacted Federal Express founder Fred Smith, who invited me to lunch at FedEx headquarters in Memphis. Ahead of my meeting, I sent Smith our business plan, a market analysis, and our own propaganda about why the museum's future was important.

I knew that Smith had been instrumental in raising the money for the Marine Corps Museum in Virginia; he had served three tours of duty in Vietnam and credited his experiences in the Marines with the ideas that he later developed to start FedEx.

During our lunch, Smith questioned our assumption that the Boston area would be a viable location for a self-sustaining World War II museum. He didn't think the population of Boston, nor the level of tourism in the area, was enough to support our museum. Smith told me that if we decided to locate the museum in Washington, D.C., then he, as well as FedEx, would be interested in supporting it. He urged me to have a more comprehensive business analysis done. He thought what we had was unrealistically optimistic.

Our trustees agreed to commission a more in-depth study. It highlighted exactly what our problems were and concluded that Boston could not sustain another museum on the scale we were planning. Almost all of our fundraising had come from New York City, which has a far greater population, and the two major New York newspapers, the *New York Times* and the *Wall Street Journal*, regularly reviewed our exhibitions while the biggest Boston newspaper, the *Boston Globe*, would not even list them, let alone review them. The clear city that made sense for a museum of this importance and scale was Washington, D.C.

The Values. The Experiences. The Lessons.
They matter now more than ever.

THE INTERNATIONAL
MUSEUM OF WORLD WAR II

ADMINISTRATIVE OFFICE
46 Eliot Street, Natick MA 01760
508.653.1944 • email director@imww2.org

Our trustees—Army chief of staff General George Casey Jr.; Lieut. Col. Charlie Dean, an expert in robotic warfare; Jeff Farrell, who was in charge of visitor services; Doug Ginsburg, chief judge of the U.S. Appeals Court in Washington; Rick Godfrey, senior partner at Kirkland & Ellis; Doris Kearns Goodwin, Pulitzer Prize–winning historian; investment advisor Jim Joslin; foundation attorney Tom Jalkut; Boston businessman Jon D'Allessandro; Shirley McNerney; investment banker Mike Michelson; New York investment advisor Felipe Propper; Malcolm Rogers, retired director of Boston's Museum of Fine Arts; Norwegian shipping magnate Martin Schøyen; military dealer Bill Shea; and businessman Mike Young—agreed this new analysis had been very thorough and we needed to reconsider our future.

Ronald Lauder, the son of cosmetics entrepreneur Estée Lauder, came to see the anti-Semitism exhibition at the New-York Historical Society in 2016. I gave him a personal tour that was remarkable for both of us. Lauder read every letter and document, frequently in the original German, and knowledgeably discussed all the different elements that I had organized into the exhibit. At the conclusion of the tour, Lauder invited me to come to his office the next day to talk further.

When I sat across from him in his oversized leather lounge chair, he said he would cut to the bottom line. "I want to be a part of what you are doing in the future," he said bluntly. "What do you think of that?"

I told Lauder he was my kind of guy! This was the start of a fascinating and intense relationship. He was enthusiastic about the mission and importance of the museum and his desire to be supportive of it.

Many of our meetings, however, discussed his concern about the location of the future museum.

In 2017 he visited the museum and brought his two grandsons. He was overwhelmed and spent all day asking many intelligent questions, not only in the exhibit areas, but in the storage and archival sections as well. He was impressed with his grandsons' reactions, their observations and involvement in the exhibits.

After our marketing and business analysis report concluded that the museum was not sustainable in the Boston area, and that Washington, D.C., was the best location, Lauder said he agreed, and he offered to be financially responsible for the future of the museum.

Throughout 2017 and 2018 he and I met every two weeks to work on the exhibit designs and other areas of the building he was planning in Washington. Shirley and I traveled around the country and to Europe assessing museum exhibit designs and meeting with several designers. We concluded that Roger Mann in London had the sensitivity to execute what we wanted. Lauder concurred and took it upon himself to find a location in Washington to build the new building.

In the fall of 2018, after we had settled on the basic overall exhibit concept, Lauder said the problem of anti-Semitism in Europe was increasing at an alarming rate, and as president of the World Jewish Congress he had to concentrate on that into 2019.

While the outstanding success of our educational programs continued, with PBS Learning Media using our programs and making them available to virtually every teacher in America, our fundraising problems continued as well. It was clear we would not have operating funds beyond the end of the year, and it was necessary to permanently close the museum in Boston before we would have chosen to.

COVID-19 has played a role in delaying the process on plans for Washington, but Lauder has expressed his continued desire to build the museum there.

Chapter 22

The Western Pursuit of My American Dream

M y fascination with the American West has a simple origin. The Boston neighborhood where I grew up was a cramped, confining place of two- and three-family houses, tiny yards, and a suffocating Irish Catholic atmosphere. My grandparents, along with another family, lived upstairs. A single man lived in the attic. My father's mother lived with us on the first floor.

In the 1930s my father built a cabin on a peninsula that jutted into a small lake north of Boston. The cabin had no running water, no electricity, and an outhouse. We moved there each year from May to September, and until we got a propane stove when I was eight or nine years old, my mother cooked all our meals on a large wood stove. I loved every minute of my life on that lake.

My summers were Mark Twain–like adventures with kids who lived in other lakeside cabins. All the cabins were built on leased land that had been in the family of a brother and sister for several hundred years. The 170 acres were, to

My boyhood paradise. The cabin
is just visible in the trees.

Our cabin in winter.

My mother pumping water.

me, our own adventure land, where we could travel from the lake to the wetlands to dense forest. A single-lane dirt road, more of a trail, led two and a half miles from the paved road to where we parked. From there we walked a trail out the peninsula to our cabin.

This was during the late 1940s, when movies and radio and, eventually, television were full of stories about the West. My vision of the West was highly romanticized, but that romanticism didn't last long. One year I had to spend the entire summer in bed because of polio, during the epidemic in the early 1950s. Fortunately, it was the non-paralytic version. That summer I read constantly, and I learned enough history to realize that the West of Roy Rogers, Gene Autry, and Hopalong Cassidy was, except for the scenery, a fantasy world with no relation to reality.

It wasn't the fantasy that captured and held my attention. It was the beauty and openness of the landscape that captivated me. The dream of freedom and opportunity inspired me with a spirit that I thought was like the spirit of the first pioneers. While I never longed to be a cowboy, I did yearn to escape from my neighborhood to the wide, open spaces of the West, where a person could be whatever they could do.

In our community of 12 families on the lake, the person with the highest social ranking was Joey Fawcett. He was a professional fly fisherman. Early in the morning Joey was out fishing in his canoe, and he was back at it again later in the day. If you happened to be in a nearby boat, you would be astounded by the size of the fish that he regularly caught and released. Midday, he spent his time tying flies, which he sold through the mail. Joey had lived in Wyoming, always wore a cowboy hat and boots, and moved slowly because of a rumored injury sustained when he catapulted from a bronco in a rodeo. Joey hardly ever talked to anyone. He was a man of mystery, and myth. For me, Joey added to the mystique about the West.

My mother, father, and myself in our rowboat.

On our dock with my fishing pole and brother.

I was also influenced by my grandparents immigrating to the United States from Eastern Canada to find a better way of life. My paternal grandfather was a blacksmith, and my mother's father became a construction engineer. For them and others, America represented the pursuit of dreams. Henry David Thoreau's words, "Eastward I go only by force, but westward I go free," rang true for them and for me.

In the late 1950s, when I was still a teenager, I went to see a woman named Hester Browning in Brooklyn, to look at coins she had for sale. I was startled to see a large collection of Frederic Remington and Charles Russell Western bronze sculptures. Mrs. Browning said her husband collected these, along with some Western artifacts, and she was selling everything at the price he paid for them. The lowest price was $125, which I knew was a tiny fraction of their true value.

They might as well have cost $100,000, though, because I couldn't think about spending that much money on something for myself. There were three Indian knives I bought for $5 each. As I rode the subway back to Manhattan, I can still remember that I felt as if I had won the Irish Sweepstakes—which was the 1950s version of the lottery. Those handmade knives are the first Western artifacts that I ever collected. I treasure them to this day.

In the summer of 1961, when I was 18 years old, after my father's death, my family took a long summer trip across the northern part of the U.S., down the Pacific Coast, and back across the Southwest. We visited and camped at nearly all of the National Parks. I was finally seeing firsthand all the parts of the country that I dreamed about. Some places, like Yellowstone National Park, were amazing because of the natural wonders. But the exhilaration I felt came mostly from my sense of wide, open spaces and skies that went beyond the horizon, uninterrupted by buildings. The mountains beckoned me to climb them. The Grand Canyon was unfathomable—as it still is, as I found when I recently hiked down to the Colorado River and spent more than a week paddling down the river. I have spent 60 years visiting the West regularly, but that trip in 1961 established that there was a reality to my fantasies.

In 1962 a pioneering motion picture had a great influence on me. *How the West Was Won* was the first movie to be made in Cinerama with major actors. Cinerama used cameras in three positions to create a film, shown on three screens, that provided a sense of being surrounded by the action. Filming with actors proved difficult with the different camera angles, but from a landscape perspective it was spectacular. *How the West Was Won* traced three generations of an American family, from their early days as pioneers in Ohio through the end of the nineteenth century. Major hardships were chronicled, but the movie presented a romanticized view of how America was settled. At the end of the film was a segment connecting the pioneers to the development of the modern West. I loved it, and I was particularly taken with the musical lyrics:

> Away, away, come away with me where the grass grows wild and the winds blow free, awake, awake, come away with me and I'll build you a home in the meadow.

That was my West. My dream. My escape from my neighborhood. As I struggled in my new business, my fantasy of living in the wilderness became my outlet. I researched homesteading in Alaska, and in 1967, when I was 24 years old, I decided to see Alaska firsthand. I planned a four-month camping and driving trip, designed a canoe specifically for the Yukon River, and set out with Fairbanks as my expected farthest point.

In Northern British Columbia, 80 miles north of the beginning of the Alaska Highway, I was driving down a dirt road in search of a place to set up my tent, when I encountered a man named Morley Clark. He invited me to camp near his one-room cabin, and there I met his wife, Grace, and their young daughter, Carolyn. This was my first direct encounter with the "real" West—the untamed frontier that so intrigued me. The Clarks were self-sufficient. He was a subsistence hunter and fisherman. They grew their own food, raised horses, and, in the winter, Morley set a trap line and traveled by dog sled. They had no electricity or running water. Heat came from a wood stove where the day's main meal, some version of moose or caribou stew, was cooked.

I stayed with the Clarks for a month. It was as close as I could ever come to firsthand experience of the nineteenth-century American West.

Morley and Grace Clark's homestead cabin in Northern British Columbia.

280

I had to continue on; the trip could not be extended because winter comes early in the far north. The Alaska Highway was a nearly 2,000-mile unpaved road. I visited the center of the Klondike Gold Rush, Dawson City in the Yukon, but I wasn't prepared for the historical reality. Dawson City was almost unchanged from 1904, when it was abandoned as everyone rushed down the Yukon River to Nome and the new gold strike. Store windows displayed turn-of-the-century merchandise in a veritable ghost town— where I knew the ghosts because I had been reading their diaries. The records of the assay office and major mercantile store were strewn around the partially collapsed building—I couldn't leave them to the coming winter snows, and I filled my rooftop canoe with them.

I drove the short distance to Bonanza Creek, a few miles from the Yukon River. Prospectors' log cabins were everywhere, and I went into many. The windows would have been covered with animal skins, the floors were dirt, and the log roofs were covered with dirt and sprouted grass. The wood stoves provided heat. I found

The start of the Alaskan Highway: 2,000 unpaved miles to Fairbanks.

A general merchandise store ledger from the Gold Rush.

prospecting tools—shovels and pickaxes, and a rusted 22 caliber rifle—which became additions to my Western artifact collection.

There was no place to camp around Dawson City, so I stopped at the Royal Canadian Mounted Police office for advice. The officer told me the only flat area was on the other side of the Yukon, and the only way to get there was via a ferry. It was a scene out of Western movies. A ferry that could hold two cars was connected to a heavy rope across the Yukon to prevent it from being swept along in the river's current.

A week later I was camping on the Tanana River in Alaska when everything came together for me. My month-long experience on the Clarks' homestead, more than a month of camping while traveling, and nearly a week in the near-ghost town of Dawson City showed me that living in the wilderness far from civilization was not for me. I loved everything I was doing on the trip, but I also loved everything I was doing in business even more, and what I needed was a balance. I also realized how important people were to me, just like they were to my father. My father's liking for people led him to give them credit when he couldn't afford to, and it had ruined him. I came to the realization that my enjoying my interaction with people, and making people the center of my life, wouldn't lead me down the same path to ruin. My interest in history was the history of the people. My business was focused on what people wrote, my greatest personal pleasure was the people I did business with. I could also now see that my interest in the American West was in the people who explored it and who were motivated for a better life to emigrate and settle the West. What I was pursuing on this lengthy trip had been found, and while I was going to enjoy Alaska and Mount McKinley, I was now looking forward to returning to Boston.

An 1898 edition of the Yukon Midnight Sun.

I returned with the Dawson City archives stuffed into my canoe on the roof of my car for 6,000 miles. These were a very good archival record of the general merchandise store during the gold rush and the claims filed with the town. I put a one-page description in my next catalog, pricing the collection at $3,000—the cost

The Dawson City office of the *Yukon Midnight Sun* at the start of the Gold Rush.

of my Alaskan trip. I felt gratified when I received an order from the University of British Columbia, and I shipped it back to almost where it came from. I had paid for my life-changing adventure.

A few months later I saw an original book that really excited me: the expedition journal of Alexander Mackenzie, the first European to cross North America. I had canoed on Canada's Peace River, and this was Mackenzie's river route before he had to trek over land. The price was $300, more than I could afford. The dealer, Mike Ginsberg, was a good friend, and he sent the book to me with a note saying that I could pay for it in a year. This extraordinarily kind gesture brought me the first original book in my Western library.

A modern guidebook to the Oregon Trail—the great pathway from Independence, Missouri, to the Willamette Valley in Oregon—was published in the early 1970s, and I immediately started thinking about driving from Independence to the Wyoming/Idaho border. I would be meticulously following the wagon tracks through Kansas, Nebraska, and Wyoming.

The Oregon Trail was pioneered by fur traders and immigrants in the 1830s. In the 1840s the number of immigrants kept increasing until the news of gold in California set off a tidal wave in 1849. It was important to leave Independence in late spring to ensure that there would be good grass for forage near the trail. If you were too early there wouldn't be any grass, and if too late the earlier wagon trains would have used everything near the trail.

I set out with reprints of original Oregon Trail guidebooks and diaries. I stopped where the wagon trains stopped and walked to the springs that 1840s settlers visited for water. Every day I shared their vistas, the endless prairie

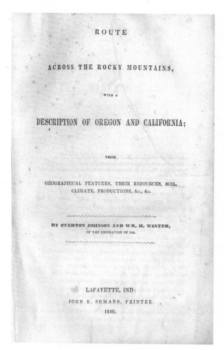

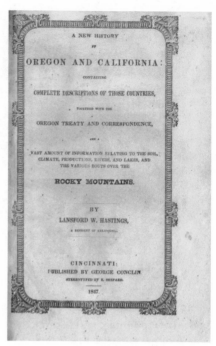

One of the first guide books to
the Overland Trail, 1846.

A guide book encouraging
settlement, 1847.

before huge mountains reaching to the sky. The landmarks they described were all there, just a little more eroded: Courthouse Rocks, Chimney Rock, Scott's Bluff, Independence Rock, Devil's Gate, Split Rock, South Pass.

My schedule was leisurely, but my experiences were intense. In later years I drove the Wyoming part with my wife, Shirley, and daughter, Julia, several more times, and 45 years after my first Oregon Trail adventure, I drove the complete trail to the Oregon coast with my son Jeffrey.

In 1976 I hit a milestone in terms of expanding my Western Americana library. I was able to afford three original guidebooks to the Oregon Trail. I read and reread these small volumes, which had advertisements from merchants in Independence offering equipment for the Western migration. The following year a Canadian bookseller offered me a handwritten letter of Alexander Mackenzie from the Rocky Mountains, and I made the rash decision to buy it. This letter was the most expensive historical letter I had ever bought for myself, but I knew it was likely to be a once-in-a-lifetime opportunity. More than forty-five years later that is still true.

I was beginning to see my growing collection was about the Western pursuit of the American Dream: the freedom to change your life from the bonds of your birth and upbringing and seizing the opportunity to be who you can be. My American Dream is about self-realization, the freedom to make my own destiny, independent of who my ancestors were. And I was seeing my American Dream in the history of the West. My collection—and the West itself—was not just about the fantastic open landscape; it was about a state of mind and hope for the future. And the knowledge that your initiative can take you there.

The essential nature of Americans to be optimistic is partly rooted in the perception that you could always go West. That perception was probably more important for many than the reality. A worker at a slaughterhouse in Chicago at the turn of the century knew that he could go to Oklahoma and claim 160 acres as a homestead. Thirty years later that same worker could then claim a homestead in Alaska. Most people would never become homesteaders, but they knew they *could*.

The hope that a better life awaits your initiative, your perseverance, your cleverness, and your hard work is my definition of the American Dream.

Original manuscripts and contemporary books about the American West had been collected by several wealthy people who shared my own sense of the importance of the West in American culture. Prices were not a consideration for them, and their collections are at the heart of historical research. The Beinecke family created a library in their name at Yale University, one of the premier Western history collections. The Beineckes and other collectors didn't leave much in private hands. Fortunately, my interest focused on the activities of everyday life, not just prominent names in Western lore.

In 1978 the Americana collection of Phil Sang came up for auction. I was interested in many of the historical letters and documents for inventory—actually, the entire auction. One lot, however, was of paramount importance to me. It was a manuscript page of Washington Irving, handwritten in 1831:

One of the most striking characteristics of an American is his self-dependence. Born to no fortune he knows, from his earliest years, that he has nothing but his own mental and bodily exertions to rely on in the great struggle of existence. This self dependence produces a remarkable quickness and versatility of talent. He turns his mother wit, as the Indian does his knife, to all purposes, and is seldom at a loss. At his first outset in life the world lies before him, like the wilderness of his own country, a trackless waste, through which he must cut his own path; but what would be a region of doubt and despondency to another mind appears to him a land of promise, a region of glorious enterprize tinted with golden hope.

Irving's definition of the American spirit was what my Western collection was all about. I went to the auction at Parke-Bernet with great anticipation—and great anxiety. I didn't think a Washington Irving manuscript would attract the attention of Malcolm Forbes, but if Forbes happened to read what Irving wrote, he would buy the manuscript and use it as an editorial in his magazine.

When the Irving manuscript came up for sale, I watched Forbes talking with his son, paying no attention to it. To my great relief, no one else paid much attention either. I was able to buy the manuscript at a very reasonable price, less than $1,000.

Washington Irving.

In that sale at Parke-Bernet (later sold to Sotheby's), I ended up spending hundreds of thousands of dollars for business inventory, yet the Irving manuscript, which means so much to me personally, is the only item I remember. When the Grolier Club asked members to propose one piece to be part of an exhibition entitled "The Grolier Club Collects," I submitted this Washington Irving as the piece that most represented my collection.

In the summer of 1998 my friend Steve Ambrose was doing research for his next book on the building of the transcontinental railroad. I arranged for us to ride in a diesel locomotive from Sacramento to Reno, on the railroad's original route. My friend Mike Michelson knew the CEO of Union Pacific and arranged this special trip. It was amazing in every way.

Going up the Sierra Mountains, we both took turns driving the locomotive, which appeared a simple matter of keeping to a set speed determined by signs along the track. The complication was that this was a freight train, 3,400 feet long, and the track had endless curves which to greater and lesser degrees were slowing down or increasing the speed because of the sideways pressure on the train's wheels. Coming down on the eastern side, the real Union Pacific engineer took over.

For a long time, Steve and I had been planning a Lewis and Clark trip across Montana by canoe on the Missouri River, hiking, and horseback, concluding with a very challenging horseback trip on the Lolo Trail into Idaho. Steve's history of the Lewis and Clark expedition, *Undaunted Courage*, was then number one on the *New York Times* bestseller list. Several close friends had asked me to approach Steve about organizing this trip and being our guide, in exchange for financial donations to help finish the D-Day Museum building in New Orleans. Steve told me that 14 people was the ideal number, and two weeks was needed. It would be

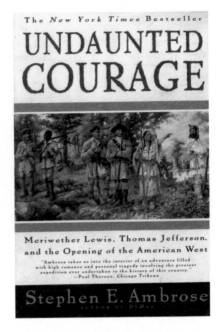

The New York Times Bestseller

UNDAUNTED
COURAGE

Meriwether Lewis, Thomas Jefferson,
and the Opening of the American West

"Ambrose takes us into the interior of an adventure filled
with high romance and personal tragedy involving the greatest
expedition ever undertaken in the history of this country."
—Paul Theroux, *Chicago Tribune*

Stephen E. Ambrose
AUTHOR OF *D-Day*

rugged, with many long days of canoe paddling and challenging horseback riding in the mountains.

I very carefully considered who I would invite. Two weeks of being together, with many tiring days, would be challenging.

Our final "Corps of Discovery," as we called the group, included my wife, a filmmaker, a financier, a farmer, the founders of Intuit, a ski resort owner, a writer, the director of a D.C. think tank, a presidential speechwriter, and a Pulitzer Prize–winning historian. It was a socially cohesive group. Steve brought along an entourage of Lewis and Clark historians, and he had experts join us at different points of the trip to tell us about the flora, the animals, the Indians, and other aspects of the Louis and Clark expedition. Everyone had read Steve's book, and most had read it multiple times. I felt like I was putting together the ultimate dinner party that was going to last two weeks—and it would be around the campfire.

It could not have been a more enjoyable group. At our first campsite on the Missouri River, Steve talked about the friendship of the members of the Lewis and Clark expedition, an appropriate subject as our group was forming new friendships. At many points over the next two weeks Steve would read from Meriwether Lewis's journal when we were at the same point as the legendary explorer was.

Our "Corps of Discovery": Dick Goodwin, Hugh Ambrose, Mike Michelson,
Shirley Rendell, Chris DeMuth, Steve Ambrose, Alice and Dick Bass,
Doris Kearns Goodwin, Scott Cook, Rives Neblett, Ken, Dayton Duncan,
Signe Ostby, Ellen Michelson, Rick Dehinel, and Will Fuhrman.

Steve's experts talked about the different aspects of Lewis and Clark's expedition. A particularly memorable talk was about the rifles they carried. It was critically important they kill a grizzly bear with their one and only shot. With a reproduction of the rifle they carried, the accuracy was demonstrated by hitting a target across the Missouri River. The expert then showed the different elements of reloading, and how long it took even when someone was practiced. Dayton Duncan, Ken Burns's screenwriting partner, was on the whole trip with us and spoke frequently, particularly about the plight of the Indians.

One of the people on our trip was Dick Bass, who had been the first person to climb the Seven Summits (the highest mountain peaks on each of the continents) and the oldest person to have climbed Mount Everest. Dick was a wonderful coach and guide as our members climbed to the summit of Lewis and Clark Pass. Dick, even though he was still suffering from broken ribs that he had sustained in an accident a few days before our trip began, reached the summit quickly. When several of our

The White Cliffs on the Missouri River.

group didn't arrive in due time, he hiked back down to the bottom and guided them up, using the method of breathing that had gotten him to the top of Mount Everest. Dick's gesture was extraordinarily kind and indicative of the camaraderie throughout our shared two-week adventure.

Shirley & Dick are victorious!

Dick Bass, the first conqueror of the Seven Summits and the oldest person to climb Mt. Everest, coached Shirley to the summit of Lewis and Clark Pass.

My next adventure with Steve Ambrose was when the Union Pacific Railroad was sending its two prized steam engines from Council Bluffs, Iowa, to Sacramento and we were invited on the trip. The owner of the railroad in 1900, E.H. Harriman, had had a private railroad car built. Steve and Moira, his wife, stayed in Harriman's bedroom and I had an adjoining compartment. It was a seven-day trip—I rode in the steam locomotive every day and became increasingly aware that I was seeing the same prairies and mountains as those immigrants who traveled West to new lives.

There were few fences, far apart, and long stretches between towns. The land was undisturbed, and hundreds of thousands of people had

Edward Harriman's private railroad car.

The dining room in the Harriman car.

looked through the train windows in astonishment at the size of the country and the distance of the horizon. I had collected and read dozens of their letters and had read the railroad's booklets offering lands for sale. I felt intimately connected with their spirit. My life was always about being motivated to take on intelligent challenges, to take calculated risks, and to rely on my ingenuity and hard work to succeed. We had much in common.

By the end of the week I was determined to write a book using the words of these pioneers' letters, diaries, and journals to tell their own story. I would use the texts of printed guidebooks, instruction manuals for new farmers, and maps that helped them decide where to settle, as well as illustrate artifacts they had used—all from my growing collection.

This turned into a 358-page book with 625 illustrations. Published by the University of Oklahoma Press in 2004, *The Western Pursuit of the American Dream* contained 22 chapters, from early exploration to the California Gold Rush to the West of the twentieth century.

One of my favorite letters in the book was written by Davy Crockett in 1827, when he was the freshman congressman from Tennessee. Crockett had attracted

The steam locomotive on our trip.

In the cab of the steam locomotive.

attention in Washington for his backwoods appearance and rough-and-tumble manner. Rumors were circulating that he had behaved badly in front of President John Quincy Adams. Defending his behavior, Crockett wrote:

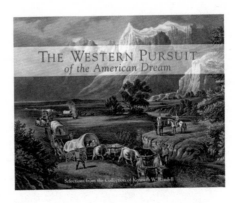

THE WESTERN PURSUIT
of the American Dream

Selections from the Collection of Kenneth W. Rendell

> I have enemies who would take much pleasure in magnifying the plain rusticity of my manners into the most unparalleled grossness and indelicacy. I have never enjoyed the advantages which many have abused. . . . I have never so far prostituted the humble advantages I do enjoy.

Another early acquisition was written by Sam Houston, who took an interest in Texas as early as 1822, when he applied for a grant of land. In the spring of 1829 Houston resigned the governorship of Tennessee after an acrimonious and very public estrangement from his wife, and he then settled in the Arkansas Territory as a trader with the Cherokees. From Wigwam Neosho in 1831, he wrote an intimate letter to a friend in New York about his frontier activities:

> I am done with goods, but not with good things I trust. In the next month I hope to sell out, close my concern and migrate to some other theater—say Natchez, and resume my profession, and to do whatever else I may as an honest and honorable man. . . . This will disappoint my enemies and gratify my friends! Furthermore mercantile business is not adapted to my cast or disposition! Nor if it were possible for me to enjoy all the luxuries of life, could I endure indolence as a past time—I must be active, or I would sink into the horrible gulph of dissipation and debauchery!

In 1833 Sam Houston settled in Nacogdoches, Texas, where his popularity quickly elevated him to leadership in the growing rebellion against Mexican rule.

Of all the letters contained in *The Western Pursuit of the American Dream*, my favorite will always be the first Western letters that I acquired for my collection. Their detailed description of an 1849 wagon trip to California via the Oregon Trail gave me a window into that same wagon trail that I would follow several times in later decades.

The first was written from Independence, Missouri, on March 13, 1849, by D.B. Crist to his cousin:

> Independence is within twelve miles of the Indian Teritory, is a business place on account of the Emigration to California and Origon. Mules cost sixty to Eighty Dollars, oxen sell from fourty to sixty Dollars pr. yoke, waggons from eighty to one hundred. Every thing is high price. . . . Plenty of Indians here. They are a miserable looking set of Beings; I pity them in my soul. They ware no clothing except what we call leggings and a Blanket now and then.

A year later he continued:

> I . . . am in the promised land of gold. After four months and four Days travel we reached a Land inhabited by Whites. . . . I suffered most every thing but Death. Thousands have left their Bones on the plains and Rockey Mountains. Many Died from hardships which were greater than they could endure. It is reported that there is over two thousand souls Died during this journey last summer. . . .
>
> We had much trouble with the Indians. They would steal our Cattle and murder our men. . . . They are a cowardly and treacherous Nation; they will not attack the whites unless they have every advantage of them.
>
> [We] was in the Buffalo country. . . . I discovered five Indians all mounted on their ponys. I immediately put my spurs to my horse and steared my course for the train. They followed me until I got in sight of my Company. I injured my horse so I was obliged to travel the remainder of the road afoot. This Chase took place in the South Fork of Platt River about six hundred miles from the stateson. . . . This was the Sioux Tribe. There ware some of the whites killed by the Indians, but far more Indians were killed by the whites, as most of those wild Tribes have no other weapon than Bow and arrow and Lance.
>
> Now as I am in California I have found nothing but a Wild Mountainous Country Inhabited by Indians, Grizzely Bars, Woolfs, Deers and gold Diggers, but we are numerous and all well armed. Gold is fully as plenty as the reports. Still some have but Little success in their undertaking. Hundreds of miners leave for home with barely anoughp to pay their way home while hundreds is making from two to Eight thousand Dollars a year and a few as high as twenty and thirty thousand

a year. It depends upon luck to strike a rich place and second it takes hard Laibour to Digit. Many of the men that came here are not used to hard laibour such as Clerks Doctor and Lawyers. The[y] thought all they had to do was to pick up the gold.

In May 2005 my Western book became the outline for a major exhibition at the National Heritage Museum. It included 150 artifacts and then opened in New York City at the Grolier Club with the announcement, "The American West has made dreamers of Americans."

The *New York Times* review, titled "They Went West: Explorers, Traders, Miners, Thieves," was lengthy and gratifying: "With the 200th anniversary of the Lewis and Clark expedition coming up next year, the time is ripe for an advance briefing about the opening of the great American West that the expedition helped make possible. . . . [The exhibition] succeeds in giving a sense of the struggle to tame the gorgeous wilderness that stretched beyond the tidy civilizations of the East. . . . It is worth spending time with."

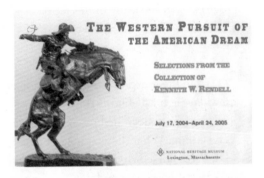

THE WESTERN PURSUIT OF
THE AMERICAN DREAM

SELECTIONS FROM THE
COLLECTION OF
KENNETH W. RENDELL

July 17, 2004–April 24, 2005

NATIONAL HERITAGE MUSEUM
Lexington, Massachusetts

My exhibition of the American West at the National Heritage Museum.

I always regretted not being able to acquire one letter in particular, "the one that got away." In 1981 a letter handwritten by Jesse James was auctioned and sold at $11,000. I was the underbidder, and it had been a financial stretch for me to bid $10,000. It was bought by a dealer promoting historical letters in expensive shopping malls. He priced it at $1.5 million.

Thirty-eight years later it came up for sale in a New York auction. I don't know its history over those years, but I do know I was finally able to add it to my collection at 10 percent of the asking price of nearly four decades earlier.

I don't see outlaws as romantic—they were robbing hard-working people who were making a life for themselves—but the irony of this letter was priceless. Jesse James wrote in 1875:

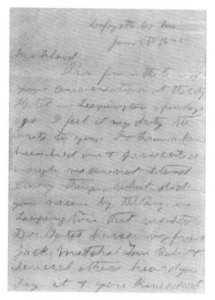

Jesse James.

. . . from the tone of your conversation at the city hotel in Lexington a few days ago I feel it my duty to write to you. I and Frank [his outlaw brother] have been lied on and persecuted enough. We cannot stand everything. What did you mean by telling in Lexington that we stole Dr. Yates horse. My friends Zach Mitchell, Tom Bull and several others heard you say it and you need not deny it and if you don't go to my mother and explain why you said what you did we will hold you responsible and you will be brought to grief. . . . it is impossible for such men as you to slander us without us hearing of it. . . . Do you suppose If we were thieves we would steal a horse from one that has been so kind to mother as Dr. Yates has. Not far from it and they are no men in Missouri who scorned horse thieves more than we do and if we were free men we would do all in our power to put it down. . . . If you value your life you had better retract your slander.

In 2011 the publisher of my first World War II book, *Saving the Reality*, came to me with the idea for a second book about the American West. It would include new pieces in my collection and there would be more emphasis on the Indians. My Indian artifacts focused on their mystical and magical beliefs, expressed in artifacts that were used in ceremonies and religious rites. I have always been fascinated with the belief systems that people all over the world have created to try to understand fundamental human concerns, especially

I visited Morley Clark 37 years after I stayed with him on
his homestead in Northern British Columbia.

mortality. I titled the book *The Great American West: Pursuing the American Dream.*

My longtime friend Alan Simpson, a native of Cody, Wyoming, who was Senate minority leader in Washington, wrote the foreword:

> . . . Ken Rendell's concept of history is to open windows into the lives and times of people and see them as they were, along with the events in their period of history as they experienced them. His goal is to make available the thoughts and feelings of the people who were actually there so that today we can have some sense of their experiences. We can never experience their anxieties, but their original letters and diaries bring us as close as possible to them and their lives.
>
> In this book, the pioneers of every generation, pursuing their many different American dreams, are personally experienced in their own words—writing not retrospectively but in their present about their hopes and realizations. Their words haven't been distilled by historians, and their experiences haven't been copied from one book to another, so the reader isn't separated from them. . . . From the earliest explorers writing about their hopes of riches to . . . Jesse James writing about buying a farm and retiring, this book illustrates in its unique way the intimacy of the daily life and dreams of those who . . . have defined America. Ken Rendell's collection is their story, and this book puts their letters in the reader's hands, their lives in the reader's mind, and their dreams in the reader's heart.

In my preface I wrote:

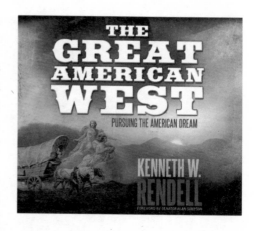

The American Dream . . . is about entrepreneurship in all senses—being responsible for one's self and making the most of your abilities and opportunities.

The Western pursuit of the American Dream manifested itself in many ways beginning with the first settlers seeking religious freedom—the Pilgrims and the Quakers—alongside those seeking economic opportunities—the colonists who founded Jamestown in Virginia, and the Spanish in Florida and elsewhere. The pursuit of new economic opportunities drove Western expansion from the Appalachians to the Pacific. New towns on the frontier provided opportunities for everyone, from blacksmiths to merchants to clergymen. The American Dream could be pursued in places where the past was forgotten, previous failures didn't count, and frontiersmen had to prove themselves using individual skills that frequently blended Indian ways with those of the settled areas, which were becoming more distant to the east.

As the rocky soil of New England wore out, . . . the lands of the Ohio and Mississippi river valleys beckoned. As these farmlands in turn produced less, the rich soil of the Willamette Valley in Oregon and . . . areas of California drew settlers. . . .

The American Dream of the Mormons was . . . to pursue their religious beliefs, and their journey to the Valley of the Great Salt Lake is one of the great Western epics.

Gold wasn't just an American dream—but where to find it and how to get there was. Thousands of people went to California in 1849 and the early 1850s and a great many found a new dream—to go back home to their families.

The American Dream was fundamentally about hope: the hope that a better life awaits your initiative, your perseverance, your cleverness, your hard work.

Chapter 23

Balancing Life

I have always viewed my business life like a very fast-moving train that travels constantly into new areas. I realize that I could never keep up this pace without balancing my adventurous and normally hectic business life with my great experiences in nature. From my earliest years nature has been a refuge and a source of mental wellness.

Hiking in the White Mountains in New Hampshire, particularly, has been a time of clearing my mind and thinking of new ways to consider challenges. Biking up the Haleakalā volcano, 10,023 feet from sea level, on Maui requires intense effort not only physically but mentally, but I still keep my notebook handy to write down ideas.

My activities in nature have provided the relaxation for my brain that has enabled me to operate aggressively in the world of business challenges. It has always been important to me to have the feeling that I am working with nature, not conquering it. Nothing I have done has involved motorized sports—except once I took a car-racing course and was terrible at it. I was afraid to drive fast. Later I skied in downhill races at the same speed that had made me uncomfortable in a car. The sense of flowing with nature is at the heart of the sports that give me the greatest pleasure.

Another tenet of my life is to challenge myself continually. In my 30s I took up ski racing and was very serious about it. I raced against myself, not against other racers. I was constantly trying to improve my ability and my performance. Ability is more physical; performance is more mental. I could be satisfied about a race even if I didn't end up in the top five.

By the time I decided to retire from ski racing in my mid-40s, I was placing second in slalom races (including in a World Cup Masters race in Aspen) and consistently third in giant slalom. Even though I was placing well, I felt stagnant in terms of improving my techniques, and I doubted I could get any better. It was time to start something new.

I went back to extreme helicopter skiing, and then in my 60s I focused on snowboarding. I ride the contours of the mountain—I'm not interested in speed or jumping. I told instructors I wanted to dance on a snowboard—to snowboard the way Fred Astaire would have (none of my young instructors had any idea who he was). I feel fortunate to have the financial ability, from my decades of business, to be able to afford learning new skills from the best instructors. Today, at age 80, I love the feeling of floating down the mountain on a snowboard. I also love windsurfing the big waves and wind in Hawai'i, where Shirley and I own a second home. Working with the wind and the waves in the warm water of a paradise setting is, for me, tremendously relaxing.

Competing in the Silver Skates Race in Boston Garden at 13 years old.

Winning the Eastern Slalom Championship.

Aspen World Cup Masters Downhill.

Covered in snow from making turns under deep snow while helicopter skiing.

With longtime heli-ski partners Mike Young, Dave Gorsuch, and Jack Binion.

Hiking in New Hampshire with Jason in his perch on top
of my pack. Jeffrey was still shorter than me.

Shirley reaching the highest point she had hiked to,
while Jason waited atop the summit.

Myself, Shirley, Jason, and Jeffrey with the Tetons behind us.

Jason rappelling in the Tetons.

The first time I made it to the top of Haleakalā on Maui, 10,023 feet from sea level, on my bike.

Julia sitting in Winston Churchill's chair in the Cabinet War Rooms.

Julia and I in the White House Rose Garden. From the Oval Office she could see President Bush's dogs playing and was invited to go outside and play with them.

An emotional challenge as great as any sport: Jeffrey and I
return to where Jason and I had climbed in the Tetons.

Wagon ruts in the Oregon Trail.

Windsurfing at our beach in Maui.

A thrilling experience, standing twenty feet from the wing tip with Top Gun instructors on the aircraft carrier *Lincoln* during flight ops in the Pacific.

Chapter 24

What I am Proud of

I can't remember a time when I wasn't striving to do better, when I wasn't setting new goals, or when I was accepting things the way they were. Neighborhood kids dug holes in their tiny yards—I did at three or four years old, but I told my mother I was going to dig down to China, and I meant it. I built a clubhouse under our back porch, but my friends and I were soon too tall to use it. When I was seven or eight years old, I spent a summer clearing bushes near our cabin because I wanted to have a lawn like one I had seen. It was back-breaking work, but I had a fierce determination.

I have no idea why I have always had these ambitions, but I have been very fortunate because I do. I didn't choose to have them—I seem to have been born with them, and for that reason I don't see any reason for being proud of them.

I am proud of how many different endeavors I have made successful. This memoir has detailed many challenges where my analysis of factual issues as well as understanding my own psychological involvement and that of others, combined with fortitude and thinking out of the box, have led to success.

As I was writing some of these chapters, I at times marveled at the self-confidence and the nerve I had tackling these challenges at a young age. I had the confidence that I was well prepared, that whatever challenge I was taking on was well thought out. The first time I appeared in court, I knew I was going against the major appraiser in the field and one of the best law firms in America, but I also knew I had carefully and analytically prepared my case. But I certainly was very anxious until I was finished with cross-examination. I think the confidence I had in setting up a network of dealers in Europe, particularly using self-taught French, came from establishing a network of New York coin dealers when I was 12 years old.

I am proud that in all the ventures I took on, I never lost sight of who I was and the limits of my knowledge and talents. This was especially true in situations where everyone else felt obliged, or confident, giving opinions about issues they knew nothing about.

I am proud that my attitude in business has been that every situation should be a win-win: I make a good sale and the collector acquires something that enhances their life. I've always viewed business as identifying what I can do to improve delivering an experience. I wanted to succeed by being better.

But what I am really proud of is my personal life.

I was very proud of my mother. She was a normal housewife of her time. She didn't work outside the home, her education was in art school, she was a Cub Scouts den mother, she had to balance having her domineering mother upstairs and her mother-in-law living, very literally, with us. Everything changed with the drugstore; she had to work there full-time, dealing with people she previously had never related to. After our family finances collapsed and my father died, she became a nurse and worked two jobs for us to survive.

I am also very proud of all the things I learned from my father before his downfall. He was completely unprepared for the social and business challenges of the drugstore, but he previously was a very good salesman and gave me many good insights into people and salesmanship. He always encouraged me, and he thought I could do very well in life. He told me he chose my name because he thought it would look good on an office door or on a building. I wish he could have lived, as my mother did, to see how far his nurturing and hopes took me.

I am very proud of the way I took care of my two sons when my disastrous first marriage came apart. I had always taken the time to do things with them, and they always knew how important they were to me. When the court gave me sole custody (at the court's urging) I made a home for them in the basement apartment I had (along with their collection of reptiles and snakes). It was a dramatic change to become a full-time father while I was trying to rebuild my business and my finances, but I am very proud that I devoted myself to making a new life for them.

I am very proud that Shirley chose to marry me. I was looking for a permanent relationship and briefly dated a large number of interesting and successful women, but from the instant I met her, I knew I had found the person I wanted as a life partner. That I was the person she wanted was the most important event in my life. She was the first, and last, woman my sons met.

I am proud of the loyalty I have had to people. For decades I continued to do business with people I originally started with. My staff would tell me that we could get better prices from bigger printers and suppliers, but I knew that withdrawing my business would hurt them. I have also been loyal to employees who have had medical problems, particularly when AIDS first ravaged New York.

I am proud of how we survived losing our son. The first thing I said when Shirley called me with the news was that we were going to keep our marriage together.

I am proud of my 50-plus-year relationship with my son Jeffrey. We have been united through many traumas and many shared adventures together. I am proud that we have not grown apart as he has grown up.

I am very proud that Jeffrey developed his own identity as a screenwriter and was not caught up in the reflected glory so many sons are. When I have been asked if I am related to him I am thrilled. Our annual trips together throughout the West are a highlight of my life.

I am proud of my role as my daughter Julia's father. I rose to the challenge of a new baby when I was 51 and have been spectacularly rewarded with an extraordinary relationship. Despite our multi-generational age difference, we have a very close relationship and constantly learn from each other.

I am also very proud that our daughter Julia wanted an identity of her own and is pursuing a career in the cultural worlds of her generation.

I am proud of starting the Spark Foundation to help students who are doing very well in school, but don't feel they have a place outside of their social and/ or economic world.

After the death of our son, I relied on alcohol to suppress the despair, and to be able to turn on "the show" at business dinners. It became a too regular crutch: I felt dependent on it to act how people expected me to. I abruptly stopped in my mid-60s and it was one of the best decisions I have made. I stopped being in social situations I don't want to be in, and I know that my thinking is how I really see things.

In the final assessment, I have been very fortunate in life, and most fortunate that I was able to survive the deaths of my father and my son. I should probably be most proud that I am a survivor.

Acknowledgments

For the past forty years my wife and partner has been my most important confidant. For decades, she has urged me to write my business memoirs and her advice, always honestly presented, has been instrumental in encouraging me to delve into my history.

Doris Kearns Goodwin finally convinced me with her enthusiasm, which coincided with the Covid lockdown. Doris read several versions and wrote the very appreciated foreword.

Susan Farrington, my longtime executive assistant, typed many different drafts as I worked my way down to the present length. I think she has spent the Covid years endlessly working through the details of seventy years.

Two research assistants were instrumental in my being able to develop the business to the extent I did. Pat Bozeman came in 1971 when my office was still in the basement of the house I grew up in. She was tall enough to have to duck under the heating pipes. During her 12 years we issued the most comprehensive catalogs ever published of the ancient, medieval, and Renaissance worlds as well as numerous others. She left in 1983 to become Director of Special Collections at the University of Houston. Rosalie Fawcett, Mei Ying, followed Pat as the business expanded to include galleries and formation of large and comprehensive collections. Rosalie was instrumental in all areas. After ten years she joined her partner in creating and managing the Jupiter Symphony in New York.

Abby Walters of Creative Artists Association and Dennis Tucker of Whitman Publishing have been enthusiastic supporters of this project from the beginning.

I especially appreciate those who took the time to read the manuscript and write the comments on the jacket. Many others are mentioned throughout the book.

As a general statement, I am very appreciative of the life I have had so far; the rough times have been rough, but the good experiences and opportunities have been wonderful, and I am very thankful.

Image Credits

Illustrations in *Safeguarding History* are from the author's collection and archives, unless otherwise noted. On page 17, the photographs of an English farthing are courtesy of Collectors Universe. On page 20, the Rittenhouse Society newsletter is courtesy of the Newman Numismatic Portal. For newspaper, book, and magazine covers and excerpts illustrated under editorial fair use, copyright is owned by their respective copyright holders.

Index

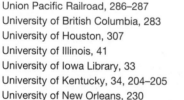